New Horizons in Research on Sustainable Organisations

Emerging Ideas, Approaches and Tools for Practitioners and Researchers

New Horizons
in Research on
Sustainable Organisations
Emerging Ideas, Approaches and Tools
for Practitioners and Researchers

Edited by Mark Starik and Sanjay Sharma with Carolyn Egri and Rick Bunch

Greenleaf
PUBLISHING
2 0 0 5

The editorial team dedicates this volume to
Margery, Pramodita, Smita, Gary, and Amy.

© 2005 Greenleaf Publishing Ltd

Published by Greenleaf Publishing Limited
Aizlewood's Mill
Nursery Street
Sheffield S3 8GG
UK
www.greenleaf-publishing.com

Printed on paper made from at least 75% post-consumer waste
using TCF and ECF bleaching.
Printed in Great Britain by William Clowes Ltd, Beccles, Suffolk.
Cover by LaliAbril.com.

British Library Cataloguing in Publication Data:
   A catalogue record for this book is available from the British Library.

ISBN 1 874719 77 2

Contents

Introduction
EMERGING IDEAS, APPROACHES AND TOOLS FOR PRACTITIONERS AND RESEARCHERS

Mark Starik and Sanjay Sharma
Lead Co-Editors

Carolyn Egri and Rick Bunch
Guest Co-Editors

Welcome to our academic–practitioner sustainability collaboration! Sustainable organisations, in theory and practice, are at once wondrous and tortuous phenomena. Like the horizon itself, businesses, governments and non-profit organisations that embody our societal ideals of holistic quality and longevity, or sustainability, can appear simultaneously idyllic and just beyond our reach. This dreamy, mirage-like trait of this volume's theme has several origins.

First, as academics and practitioners in the sustainability field, we—the editors and readers of this volume—all likely have our own perspectives (Starik and Rands 1995) on what a sustainable organisation is or might be, but seldom do we take the opportunity to share our respective sustainability visions, let alone the multiple ways to achieve them. This volume provides at least some of us that opportunity.

Second, even if we did agree on what a sustainable organisation is, the sustainability or holistic quality-oriented long time-frame aspect probably precludes us from judging just when a sustainable organisation achieves 'sustainableness'. Hopefully, this volume advances us in the direction of consensus on what conditions constitute an organisation approaching sustainability.

Third, given that both nature and human organisations change over time, the interaction of the two could find organisations periodically moving into and out of 'sustainableness'. Again, this volume provides some evidence that these interactive changes occur and need to be addressed.

These are just a few of the challenges that academics and practitioners encounter as the field of sustainable organisations evolves in our collective consciousness. How can we help one another, if not realise, then at least advance, a bit closer to a common understanding of the sustainable organisation ideal?

This volume was proposed as one pathway for researchers and practitioners in the general area of organisations and the natural environment to address issues of common interest. Hopefully, our authors and our readers can both integrate and develop the concept and practice of sustainable organisations, so that when we 'awaken' from our 'dream', we at least find ourselves in a better world for our efforts. After working on sustainability-related projects involving other academics, both research- and practitioner-oriented graduate students, consultants, managers and activists, the lead co-editors of this volume saw the need to encourage information exchanges among these networks of sustainability stakeholders.

Several of these entities have their own conferences, their own publications and their own networks, but these information venues do not often intersect. For instance, while the Academy of Management Organisations and the Natural Environment (ONE) interest group membership includes more than 5% non-academics, far fewer either submit papers for presentation at the annual meetings or attend the meetings themselves. Much the same can be said for another group of sustainability academics and practitioners, the Greening of Industry Network (GIN). Alternatively, academics comprise a non-negligible part of the membership of the (American) National Association of Environmental Professionals (NAEP), but its journal, *Environmental Practice*, includes very few articles written by academics. These situations exist even though all three organisations are actively involved in promoting sustainable development and, occasionally, express interest in working with representatives of the 'other profession'.

The quest of the lead co-editors of this volume for sustainability integration across professions verified that these gaps in our sustainability networks need attention, so we decided to collaborate on a project that included inviting two guest co-editors (one academic and one practitioner) to present both academic and practitioner contributions on sustainable organisations. Happily, we are able to offer the perspectives of a diverse set of authors with a different mix of academic and practitioner orientations, approaches and information. We hope that this blend of backgrounds and products will interest both sustainability practitioners and academics, as well as those who identify with both audiences. And we hope this interest is broadened and deepened through and beyond this volume to advance both the concept and the practice of organisational sustainability.

In acting on this hope, we are aware that, even if the two groups share an interest in sustainability, academics and practitioners have their differences. In this, and other fields, academics and practitioners often differ in their ends (knowledge generation via publications versus effective allocation of resources), their language (evidence versus benchmarking) and their contexts (reflection versus solution orientations) (Alberta Heritage Foundation for Medical Research 2004). How members of the two groups conduct research has been identified as another source of differences, with academics often employing a smooth-flow, few-step and curiosity-driven process, and practitioners exhibiting a multi-looping, multi-step and problem-driven research approach (Martin 2004). Similarly, academic and practitioner journals exhibit some obvious differences in purpose, subjects, appearance, audience and, of course, authors. In this regard the two groups also have exhibited differences in where to publish and when to publish in the research process (Rynes *et al.* 2001). However, other efforts to integrate academic and practitioner perspectives and approaches have been attempted in other management-related fields, including co-sponsored special volumes in the marketing area (Marketing Science

Institute 2004), co-sponsored student projects in product development (Ford and Paynting 1995) and co-development of accounting curricula (Wu and Tong 2004). Most recently, a series of essays written by both practitioners and academics was featured in a special section of the *Academy of Management Executive* on the topic of corporate governance, which some observers associate with social sustainability. We thought the sustainable organisations topic was an appropriate one to attempt to follow in these footsteps since sustainability has both theoretical and practical aspects.

Regarding publications in particular, a not uncommon approach for integrating academic and practitioner perspectives is to produce and market 'theory and practice' collections. A search of one major university US metropolitan library consortium identified more than 8,000 such volumes, with more than 175 of these relating to 'environmental' topics. An example of the former group is a collection of article chapters on international relations with separate sections for academic perspectives, practitioner perspectives and 'practical dilemmas of the two worlds' (Hill and Beshoff 1994: 137). An example of the latter is a 1,500-plus page tome on 'human and ecological risk assessment' which consists of 32 chapters with explicitly identified 'theory' chapters, on the one hand, and 'case study' chapters on the other (Paustenbach 2002).

Beyond this volume, a main source of academic contributions on sustainability to a practitioner-oriented management publication are the handful of articles that have appeared in the last few years in the *Academy of Management Executive*. Since 1998, this journal, which targets a readership of organisation executives, has included articles on the 'greening' of the bottom line (Forte and Lamont 1998), The Natural Step (Bradbury and Clair 1999), sustainable development (Bansal and Roth 2000), global environmental programmes (Christmann and Taylor 2002), private-sector and non-governmental organisation (NGO) partnerships in the sustainability domain (Rondinelli and London 2003) and engaging so-called 'fringe' stakeholders to build sustainable business models (Hart and Sharma 2004). Other mainstream management practitioner-oriented journals that have published articles on sustainable organisations include the *Harvard Business Review* (Porter and van der Linde 1995; Prahalad and Liberthal 1998; Walley and Whitehead 1994), *California Management Review* (Howard *et al.* 2000; Delmas and Terlaak 2001; Toffel 2003) and *Sloan Management Review* (Hart and Milstein 1999). Three other journals of note have varied in their proportions of academic-oriented versus practitioner-oriented content: *Business Strategy and the Environment* (mostly academic); *Greener Management International* (academic/practitioner mix); and *Corporate Environmental Strategy* (mostly practitioner).

We are honoured to follow these pathfinders in an attempt to integrate academic and practitioner work on the topic of sustainable organisations.

Multi-level sustainable organisation considerations and content

The chapters in this volume are presented in three subsets, generally proceeding from the most 'macro' to the most 'micro' in terms of perspective and applicability. However, this arbitrary division belies the integration from macro through meso (or mid-range) to micro levels that is apparent in these studies. Macro approaches typically include wider geographic scopes, greater numbers and diversity of stakeholders and more complex explanatory factors than do micro approaches. Each chapter adopts one or more particular sustainability world-views and then grounds these and the other chapter elements within actual organisations. Therefore, rather than a one-dimensional continuum, the reader is advised to envision a circle in which the macro view both feeds back and feeds forward to the micro view.

To begin with the most macro-level perspective, Robert Boutilier in his chapter entitled 'Views of sustainable development: a typology of stakeholders' conflicting perspectives', identifies that societal value types and development processes that lead stakeholders in different societies to consider sustainable development differently. Using a Papua New Guinea organisation case study in which he was involved, Boutilier illustrates interesting relationships, both collaborative and conflictive, among several categories of sustainability-oriented group types. These types include commons harvesters, green parties and deep ecologists, among others. Sustainable organisation proponents, especially those involved with multinational corporations (MNCs) that operate in difference cultures, should both heed and take heart in this analysis. This chapter reminds readers not only of the complexity of consensus on sustainability but also of the opportunities to ally ourselves with others toward overall societal and ecological improvement.

Roger Ballantine, in 'The next environmentalism: creating a new political dynamic for progress in the US', develops the argument that American environmental politics is greatly in need of transformation. Specifically, the current interest-group gridlocked approach needs to transform into a 'new environmentalism' in which organisations and individuals build a broad, diverse coalition in the political 'middle ground' to forge more effective environmental policies. Drawing on his experience as the director of the Office of Environmental Initiatives in the Clinton administration, Ballantine highlights several sources of this movement, including economic, health and spirituality motivations, and several necessary strategies, such as drawing on multiple political bases and using 'both carrots and swords'. This chapter reinforces the complexity and opportunity theme of sustainability in the preceding chapter, but applies it in a political rather than a sociological context.

Deborah Gallagher's chapter, entitled 'Building environmental management systems focused on sustainability', fleshes out three general types of environmental management systems (EMSs) that vary according to which groups were involved in their design and the particular sustainability focus that was adopted. Gallagher studied 41 US manufacturing facilities in several industries and found that their EMSs could be classified as 'middle roader', 'efficiency expert' or 'visionary' based primarily on two factors. She found that EMSs differed by the involvement of different sustainability stakeholders, such as environmental, health and safety staff and external groups, and on different programme goals, such as pollution prevention and product stewardship. Researchers studying and practitioners designing EMSs may want to focus on programme stakeholders and goals if they are targeting particular EMS profiles. This chapter is the third of three that takes the most macro perspective on sustainable organisations, crossing multiple industries, sectors or societies.

From a middle-range (meso) perspective, 'The relationship between environmental sustainability, environmental violations and financial performance' by Peter and Sarah Stanwick attempts to connect corporate environmental commitments with both firm US Environmental Protection Agency (EPA) violations and net income-to-sales ratios. They sampled 61 US chemical industry firms that were Responsible Care programme members and found evidence that firms with online comprehensive sustainability reports were more likely to be ranked as better financial performers and less likely to be ranked as EPA violators than were industry firms that did not have such reports. This is one of a number of studies that have identified a positive link between sustainability and other organisational outcomes, thereby providing additional weight to the intuition of many sustainability academics and practitioners.

Also from a meso perspective, Chris Durney, Glenn Eugster and John Wilson combine their significant experience consulting with and working for the US federal government to illustrate how federal involvement in social and environmental sustainability issues has moved, and will continue to move, toward the recognition of these issues and their associated communities as complex adaptive systems. Such systems are, according to the authors, 'a richly connected web of independent, interacting, and intelligent agents, each of which is operating according to their local knowledge and conditions'. Focusing on the South Florida Everglades and Delmarva (Mid-Atlantic American states) Peninsula federal projects, these authors derive several tactics, including what they term 'sustained nudging' (or continuous light pressure) and 'incremental co-evolution' (of different stakeholders). They also identify a number of conditions under which federal environmental and social issues projects could best be managed as complex adaptive systems. Well beyond the quick-fix bumper-sticker approach to social and environmental problem-solving, the authors encourage multi-stakeholder efforts at developing mutual, deep understandings of multiple societal and physical interacting factors.

Finally in this meso category, Melissa Schilling and her colleagues offer the case of the 'Honda Insight: development and launch of a hybrid electric vehicle' which has implications for the worldwide automobile market. The authors provide an in-depth description of several of Honda's (and its competitors') product introduction strategies that reflect the company's proactive investments, forgoing of partnerships and alternative marketing approaches. This case study illustrates that industry leaders adopt different sustainability strategies to set themselves apart, even when much of their respective industries are implementing nearly polar opposite plans. Together, these three meso chapters identify the implications of industry associations, value networks and supply chains for sustainable organisations.

The last set of chapters focus on sustainability micro models for individual organisations. By providing brief case studies of one or two companies, each chapter brings readers full circle with models that are applicable to organisations in all sectors in many world cultures. Lise Langeland, in 'Cultivating the sustainable corporation', uses Whole Foods Market, a US health food supermarket chain, to illustrate her four-part change model of sustainability intention, envisioning, implementation and investment realisation. She argues that each of these sustainability process steps is necessary to achieve both overall organisational sustainability (ethical, social and environmental) and financial goals, and that neglecting any of the four steps imperils that performance. Her study follows a long stream of research that recommends well-known change management approaches as sustainability prescriptions.

Andrew Griffiths, Dexter Dunphy and Suzanne Benn also suggest a sustainability development model in 'Corporate sustainability: integrating human and ecological sustainability approaches'. They assert that sustainability-focused organisations first need to build capabilities for human (social) sustainability before focusing on ecological sustainability. Using examples from the sustainability-related experiences of Fuji Xerox and Scandic Hotels, they make the case that sustainability change can be either incremental or transformative, and that human sustainability approaches that enhance teamwork, continuous learning and related systems have led, and can lead to, environmental innovations necessary for ecological sustainability. This research identifies the importance of sequencing sustainability change factors and of perceiving sustainability as an evolutionary process that can unfold at different rates in different organisations.

Finally, in her chapter entitled 'Business ecology: the future of green business?' Amy Townsend provides several models that identify important components and principles of business ecology which go beyond 'greening' to achieve both organisational and ecological health and renewal. Employing the experiences of two organisations—the Regenesis Group and the Land Institute—she contends that the physical sites and scales of organisations are key sustainability concerns and that, rather than trying to integrate environmental concerns into organisational processes, businesses (and others) should focus on integrating their organisations sustainably into their respective natural environments. This study reminds readers that all human organisations are subsets of the much larger and intricate natural environment and that all organisations have numerous local impacts and resource needs. Collectively, these last three chapters illustrate that individual organisations can yield lessons that can be applied well beyond their individual situations.

Future and further sustainable organisations research (and practice)

Thankfully, the field of sustainable organisations, including its research and practice, appears to be growing. To the extent that sustainability research and practice actually result in societal movements toward sustainability, this growth also appears to be desirable. Increases in both sustainability membership organisations (and often in their memberships), such as the previously mentioned ONE interest group in the Academy of Management, the Greening of Industry Network and Net Impact (an international group of sustainability-oriented business students and alumni), are signs that sustainability research and practice continue to expand in interest and activity. Publication outlets and presentation venues for sustainability-related researchers and practitioners also appear to be increasing, as demonstrated by this and similar volumes and by topic-related conferences, forums, workshops and other gatherings.

Given this expansion of the sustainability field, academics and practitioners often have no trouble generating research and/or practice ideas that are ripe for further development. However, from the experience of the co-editors, we assert that we can all use some assistance in focusing on potential future projects. Therefore, in this section, we suggest several topics in the research and practice of sustainability that appear to deserve future attention, exploration and execution.

Drawing from the first set of chapters at the more macro (societal/sector) level (Boutilier, Ballantine and Gallagher), the obvious question for further investigation is: How can these studies' findings be used by sustainability-oriented industries, organisations and individuals?. Can, and should, entities that are undergoing modernisation, postmodernisation and neotribalisation attempt to maintain, speed up, slow down or reverse these processes, and what would be the implications of their efforts and results for the advancement of sustainability? In the Boutilier environmental movements/societal value typology, how do (or how should) businesses that have operations in all three societal types treat stakeholders who are associated with more than two environmental movements? What are the implications for businesses with increasingly global supply chains that source and market in societies with different sustainability values and stages of sustainability development? Should such organisations follow universal pathways to sustainability or should they develop different strategies for different contexts? Indeed, is a sustainable organisation more feasible and relevant at the local, regional or global levels? Whichever the sustainability path, organisations cannot set out on it without a deep empathy and understanding of how various stakeholders view sustainability in different contexts (Hart and Sharma 2004).

Ballantine's suggestion that conservationists and environmentalists (in any sector) need to work together already occurs in the US to a certain extent (for example, the broad consensus supporting national parks). But how can this sustainability policy co-operation be broadened and deepened, and how can the collaboration of potential adversaries be applied outside the US (or at sub-federal levels)? Further, how can NGOs and NGO coalitions constructively engage corporations to achieve their sustainability objectives (Rondinelli and London 2003)? Can national government agencies such as the EPA and state, provincial or local governments play a more effective role in fostering such engagement and partnerships?

Gallagher's three types of EMSs generate a number of questions about EMS types. For each type (and perhaps hybrids of them), what is the role of both sustainability values and information sharing among departments and subsidiaries within a single organisation (perhaps across national borders)? Do these EMS types, values and information exchanges vary within and among industries, alliances, value chains or regions? Do different units or divisions of an organisation follow different EMSs in different countries (developed and developing), different industries (for example, extractive mining and renewable forestry) or different regulatory jurisdictions? Should an organisation develop a global strategy that seeks similar objectives and pathways to sustainability in all industries and jurisdictions within which it operates?

Clearly, these more macro-level studies will likely help maintain the organisations' and the natural environment field's focus on the many stakeholders of sustainable organisations. In addition, they reinforce the field's need to continue to internationalise and to connect sustainability to public policy.

The second set of chapters, which all project a multi-organisational perspective (the Stanwicks, Durney *et al.* and Schilling *et al.*), prompt questions about the applicability of their findings to industries and sectors not examined, and to the breadth of the sustainability concepts they studied. For instance, would the Stanwicks' results on the connection between sustainability reporting and financial performance be found in other industries, countries and time-frames? While they used environmental violations as a measure of environmental sustainability, other more proactive environmental outcomes, including social sustainability effects and outcomes, could be researched.

The complex adaptive system idea that Durney *et al.* apply to two cases of US federal government involvement may also be relevant in other contexts. These include not only other governments (at various levels) around the world but also businesses and non-profit organisations in situations where entities from two or all three of these sectors are engaged in multi-organisational sustainability problem-solving. While this study did include both social and environmental sustainability features, its regional scope is just one of the many geographic and demographic perspectives that researchers can adopt. Further, their time-frame of several years is another variable that future researchers may want to vary.

The Honda case study by Schilling *et al.* focused primarily on one car manufacturer and its hybrid technology (a set of technologies that is available throughout that worldwide industry), and provided information on one main competitor and other Honda stakeholders. One mystery that future researchers may want to unravel is why so few of Honda's competitors and its industry association have followed a similar sustainability strategy. More generally, what prevents organisations in the same industry from following sustainability leaders in any industry (using any particular technology)?

The last set of 'micro-focused' but 'macro-applied' chapters (Langeland, Griffiths *et al.* and Townsend) generate questions relating to the theme of organisational barriers to sustainability. These are more internally focused studies than either of the other two sets of contributions, but could be applicable to many other organisations in many other industries and sectors on the planet. Langeland's sustainability cultivation process moves from sustainability formulation through implementation to evaluation. Thus, researchers might ask how to initiate, maintain and progress through each stage most effectively and efficiently, while ensuring that the concepts, practices and other organisational sustainability 'batons' are passed from person to person and from one stage to the next. Would organisational characteristics such as size, industry, region, organisation age and structure be involved in this sustainability cultivation process? And, if sustainability is prevented from being cultivated because of one factor, can it be 're-cultivated' by another?

Griffiths and colleagues' sustainability phase model evokes similar questions. Like the preceding chapter, their overall approach of asset-integrating human and ecological sustainability leads to the conclusion that 'sustainability management' is roughly equivalent to 'sound holistic management'. If this is the case, can the decades-long research and practice of good management be interpreted with a sustainability perspective? And, if their supposition that human sustainability capacity needs to be developed *before* ecological sustainability capacity is generally accepted, how much of the former, over how long a time period, involving how many employees and organisational units, appears to be necessary before ecological sustainability can be realised?

Finally, Townsend's business ecology perspective identifies five important organisational sustainability characteristics. These include interactions among, as well as ranges and quality differences within, missions, employees, operations, facilities and products. While comprehensive, her listing of a dozen sustainable organisational characteristics is likely to be quite daunting to many of the best-intentioned organisations. So, if societies themselves are to become sustainable, researchers may want to tackle the real-world challenge of how the very broad and deep concept of 'the sustainable organisation' can be grasped and operationalised into everyday practice for the millions of organisations that apparently need to do so.

Conclusion: some roads suggested but not yet travelled

This volume addresses a number of intriguing and important sustainable-organisation phenomena, such as multiple sustainable development perspectives, changing environmental politics, EMS variations, voluntary environmental programme performance, complex adaptive systems and environmental technology development. Additionally, several models were suggested, such as cultivation, capabilities and business ecology frameworks. We suggest that some of the questions in our initial call for papers on the topic of sustainable organisations, that were not addressed by submitters to this volume, may still be relevant and salient to both academic and practitioner sustainability researchers. These include: What are the appropriate sustainability criteria for organisational objectives in different industries, cultures and life-cycle stages? What are the key factors in sustainability strategy implementation actions and how can these be enhanced for greater sustainability success? And what have been the lessons learned from sustainability-related strategic alliances, networks and information systems?

Focusing on the academic–practitioner nexus, the several questions in the initial call for papers that we believe still deserve attention are: How can sustainability-oriented practitioners and academic researchers develop more effective dialogues and other communication vehicles for themselves and their respective stakeholders? How can sustainability ethics be better integrated into both sustainability practice and academic research? What can be learned about sustainability practice and research that may be shared, not only among organisations but also among societal sectors and cultures?

Finally, we encourage researchers to review previous sets of future research recommendations to translate the many suggestions for further study into opportunities for academic–practitioner research connections. Some areas in which this integration perspective might be adopted, especially by academics, include a focus on advancing environmental technologies, on 'greening' academic and other educational organisations, and on working on the environmental problems of disadvantaged communities, whether domestic or international. Each of these areas has significant potential for investigating, analysing and recommending practical environmental solutions (Starik 2002). Other suggestions for advancing this field can be found in Sharma 2002.

We invite both academic and practitioner researchers to address any or all of these questions in their respective venues, and we look forward to interacting with both networks to help advance both our organisations and our societies toward the sustainability ideal.

References

Alberta Heritage Foundation for Medical Research (2004) 'How the RHAs and PHAs View Research', www.ahfmr.ab.ca, accessed 14 February 2004.

Bansal, P., and K. Roth (2000) 'Why Companies Go Green: A Model of Ecological Responsiveness', *Academy of Management Journal* 43.4 (August 2000): 717-48.

Bradbury, H., and J.A. Clair (1999) 'Promoting Sustainable Organizations with Sweden's Natural Step', *Academy of Management Executive* 13.4: 63-74.

Christmann, P., and G. Taylor (2002) 'Globalization and the Environment: Strategies for International Voluntary Environmental Interactions', *Academy of Management Executive* 16.3: 121-35.

Delmas, M., and A. Terlaak (2001) 'A Framework for Analyzing Environmental Voluntary Agreements', *California Management Review* 43.3: 44-63.

Ford, D.N., and R. Paynting, (1995) 'Linking Academic Theory and Industry Practice through Interactive Student Projects: A Case Study of System Dynamics and Product Development', *Center for Quality of Management Journal* 4.2: 23-41.

Forte, M., and B.T. Lamont (1998) 'The Bottom Line Effects of Greening', *Academy of Management Executive* 12.1: 89-90.

Hart, S.L., and M.B. Milstein (1999) 'Global Sustainability and the Creative Destruction of Industries', *Sloan Management Review* 41.1: 23-33.

—— and S. Sharma (2004) 'Engaging Fringe Stakeholders for Competitive Imagination', *Academy of Management Executive*, February 2004: 7-18.

Hill, C., and P. Beshoff (eds.) (1994) *Two Worlds of International Relations: Academics, Practitioners and the Trade in Ideas* (New York: Routledge).

Howard, J., J. Nash and J. Ehrenfeld (2000) 'Standard Or Smokescreen? Implementation of a Voluntary Environmental Code', *California Management Review* 42.2: 63-82.

Marketing Science Institute (2003) 'MSI Competition: JMR Special Issue Practitioner–Academic Collaborative Research', www.msi.org/msi, accessed 14 February 2004.

Martin, J.R. (2004) 'The Academic and Practitioner Research Models Compared', adapted from V.R. Boehm, 'Research in the "Real World": A Conceptual Model', *Personnel Psychology* 33 (1980): 495-504, www.maaw.info, accessed 14 February 2004.

Paustenbach, D.J. (ed.) (2002) *Human and Ecological Risk Assessment: Theory and Practice* (New York: John Wiley).

Porter, M.E., and C. van der Linde (1995) 'Green and Competitive', *Harvard Business Review* 73.5 (September/October 1995): 120-34.

Prahalad, C.K., and K. Lieberthal (1998) 'The End of Corporate Imperialism', *Harvard Business Review* 76.4: 68-79.

Rondinelli, D.A., and T. London (2003) 'How Corporations and Environmental Groups Co-operate: Assessing Cross-sector Alliances and Collaborations', *Academy of Management Executive* 17.1: 61-75.

Rynes, S.L., J.M. Bartunek and R.L. Daft (2001) 'Across the Great Divide: Knowledge Creation and Transfer between Practitioners and Academics', *Academy of Management Journal* 44.2 (April 2001): 340-55.

Sharma, S. (2002) 'Research in Corporate Sustainability: What Really Matters?', in S. Sharma and M. Starik (eds.), *Research in Corporate Sustainability: The Evolving Theory and Practice of Organizations in the Natural Environment* (Cheltenham, UK: Edward Elgar): 1-30.

Starik, M. (2003) 'Childhood's End? Sustaining and Developing the Evolving Field of Organizations and the Natural Environment', in S. Sharma and M. Starik (eds.), *Research in Corporate Sustainability: The Evolving Theory and Practice of Organizations in the Natural Environment* (Cheltenham, UK: Edward Elgar): 319-37.

—— and G. Rands (1995) 'Weaving an Integrated Web: Multilevel and Multisystem Perspectives of Ecologically Sustainable Organizations', *Academy of Management Review* 20.4 (October 1995): 908-35.

Toffel, M.W. (2003) 'The Growing Strategic Importance of End-of-life Product Management', *California Management Review* 45.3: 102-29.

Walley, N., and B. Whitehead (1994) 'It's Not Easy Being Green', *Harvard Business Review,* May/June 1994: 46-52.

Wu, T., and Y. Tong (2004) 'Issues and Challenges of Accounting Education in China: Practitioner and Academic Perceptions', *The Journal of the American Academy of Business, Cambridge* 4.1–2: 208-17.

1
Views of sustainable development
A TYPOLOGY OF STAKEHOLDERS' CONFLICTING PERSPECTIVES

Robert Boutilier
Simon Fraser University, Canada

One of the frustrations of a stakeholder-oriented approach to managing for sustainable development is that stakeholders disagree with one another about what sustainable development means. Workers in Chilean copper mines want to sustain the development of their communities with mining-related jobs while eco-activists in the UK want to reduce global mining in order to preserve finite resources for future generations. Both groups can claim that the principles of sustainable development justify their positions. What can a stakeholder-oriented company do when its stakeholders cannot agree?

The concept of sustainable development acquired an international profile in business and policy circles with the publication of the report of the World Commission on Environment and Development (WCED 1987), also known as the Brundtland Commission report. At the most abstract conceptual level, the principles enunciated by the WCED can be summarised and simplified as portraying sustainable development as whatever contributes to the balanced endurance of a set of three relationships. The first relationship is between humankind and the environment. The second is between the present generation and future generations. The third is among present generations in different parts of the world or different global social classes (for example, the rich and the poor). The second and third principles specify that the humankind–environment relationship must be sustainable for all and for the future.

Since the Brundtland Commission report, the concept of sustainable development has been appropriated by many different movements. Each one highlights a new application of the principles and promotes a course of action to achieve sustainable development. For companies, the interpretations and expectations surrounding the term 'sustainable development' become more numerous each year. A multitude of corporate social and environmental performance monitoring and rating systems have been developed to spell out the concept in concrete, action-based detail (IISD 2003; Leipziger 2003). These systems, however, tend to reflect only some of the interpretations and actions that stakeholders advocate in the name of sustainable development. They often neglect the perspectives of stakeholders in developing countries who want equal access to the freedom and material prosperity that they see Westerners, including Western environmentalists and eco-tourists, enjoying.

The requirement that sustainable development applies equally for the benefit of the world's 'have-nots' as well as 'haves' places a particularly heavy responsibility on today's international businesses. As national economies have become enmeshed in a global economy, corporations have begun to struggle with the meaning and implications of sustainable development for their operations in the rest of the world. In the developed countries of the North, sustainable development includes a strong focus on consumer issues (Cowe and Williams 2000). In the developing countries of the South, producer issues are more predominant. In the global minerals sector, for example, the developed Northern countries are concentrated among those with the highest per capita levels of mineral consumption. Less developed Southern countries and former Soviet bloc countries are concentrated among those with the highest per capita production (MMSD 2002: 45-48). Because of the diverse socioeconomic locales in which they operate, internationally active corporations must understand sustainability issues at the humankind–environment interface from the multiple perspectives of different societies at different levels of economic development.

Internationally active corporations have stakeholders around the world. Those stakeholders live in diverse socioeconomic and political conditions. This contributes to diversity in stakeholders' interests in their respective relationships with the natural environment. Consequently, when dealing with these diverse interests, international corporations often encounter conflicts, paradoxes and dilemmas. Stakeholders from societies at different levels of development often urge the company to take diametrically opposed courses of action on matters that at least some of the stakeholders portray as sustainable development issues. When stakeholders disagree with one another about how the human–environment interface should be managed, corporations need a framework that translates the concept of sustainable development across the all-too-often narrow and partial perspectives held both by their own managers and by diverse stakeholders in subsistence, industrialising and post-industrial economies. This chapter presents a typology of sustainable development perspectives and shows how they can either conflict with, or align with, one another. Distinct versions of the ideal interface between humans and the natural environment are outlined and then used to unravel the misapprehensions and misgivings that companies encounter when trying to apply the concept of sustainable development.

Modernisation and postmodernisation

The typology proposed here is based on two well-accepted propositions and on one that is new. The first proposition is that different perceptions of sustainability reflect differing views of the human relationship with nature. The second is that at the root of the differing views of the human–environment relationship are differences in socioeconomic, sociopolitical and ecological contexts. The new proposition is that these contexts are best described by Inglehart's (1997) tripartite typology of societies and social values. After briefly describing Inglehart's three groupings (traditional, modern, postmodern), I map Castells's (1997) typology of environmental movements and their associated views onto the Inglehart typology of societies.

In the process, I propose three extensions. First, I add a type of environmental group neglected by Castells. Second, I create a link between Inglehart's two endpoints, thereby defining a new process in societal evolution that I call 'neotribalisation'. Third, I use both Inglehart's empirical findings and Castells's theoretical analysis to construct six distinct views of sustainable development, each corresponding with either a type of society, or a type of transition between two types of societies (i.e. modernisation, postmodernisation and neotribalisation). These six views are illustrated with an example from a developing-country mining project. Finally, I show how this typology can help companies anticipate how the views of various stakeholders will be congruent or contradictory with respect to what constitutes sustainable development.

Before discussing Inglehart's typology of societies, it should be noted that one of them, the modern society, is a longstanding field of study (Giddens 1991; Harrison 1988). Since the time of Marx (1965), Durkheim (1893/1984), and Weber (1958, 1983), theorists have speculated about the values that produce, and are produced by, the macro-societal process of modernisation. Despite this, the distinction between modern and postmodern views of sustainability remains unclear. Ecological modernisation theory (EMT) (Mol and Sonnenfeld 2000; Mol and Spaargaren 2000) supposedly derives its name from the application of modern themes to environmental issues, but actually contains a mix of modern and postmodern themes. Mol and Sonnenfeld (2000) identified the major themes of EMT. First, science and technology are seen as helpful in solving environmental problems. Second, market dynamics are deemed to have a role to play in restructuring society in a more sustainable way. Third, private and civic-sector arrangements are seen as increasingly important in creating effective *de facto* regulations relative to the legislation of nation-states. Fourth, environmental social movements are observed to play an increasingly participative role in social change, as opposed to a role giving voice to calls for the complete restructuring of society. Fifth, EMT eschews the complete neglect of either environmental or economic interests in favour of intergenerational solidarity in dealing with the interaction of the two.

Despite its name and its respect for rationality, EMT should not be mistaken for a perspective that assumes or celebrates modern phenomena such as Weberian bureaucracies or Fordist principles of industrial production. Mol and Spaargaren (2000: 26) distinguish EMT from 'green postmodernity' while acknowledging that EMT has been elaborated since its inception in the 1980s to accommodate postmodern and other critiques. Indeed, Mol and Sonnenfeld's third and fourth themes accord with postmodern themes of deconstructed authority and participative social constructionism. Moreover, Cohen (2000: 78) cites Jänicke (1985) and Simonis (1988) as authors who view the use of science and technology to solve environmental problems as a third stage of social organisation that arises after modernity. Pre-modern societal organisation is portrayed as agriculturally based. Modern society is seen as organised around industrial production. Finally, in ecological modernity, science and technology correct the problems of the transitional modern period. Because it has these diverse elements, EMT seems to inhabit the contested terrain between the modern and the postmodern.

EMT's perspective on sustainability invokes dimensions that differentiate modernity from postmodernity. This is likely to be a reflection of broader debates in Western societies. Mol and Spaargaren (2000) acknowledge that EMT was developed on an empirical base limited to Western European countries. They call for more international studies in order to broaden its applicability because it is not yet clear how applicable EMT concepts would be in subsistence developing-world contexts. Internationally active corporations need a perspective that is based on broader, global data.

The World Values Survey (WVS) provides one of the most global perspectives on values and attitudes available to date. Inglehart used WVS data to confirm empirically the existence of three categories of societal values, namely, the traditional, the modern and the postmodern. The WVS is a multinational project being conducted by researchers around the world. The data that Inglehart reported on in 1997 came from the 1981–84 and 1990–91 waves of WVS data collection. It sampled over 55,000 respondents in 43 countries representing 70% of the world's population. Inglehart described the differences among three economic and political systems on three dimensions: authority; economy; and values. Societies dominated by traditional values combine the steady-state economics of subsistence agriculture with an all-pervasive tribal and religious authority. They hold religious and communal values. Societies dominated by modern values combine a dynamic industrial economy with the authority of a rational–legal nation-state. Their values highlight achievement motivation and the disciplined drive for material success. Societies with a high proportion of people subscribing to postmodern values combine the post-industrial economics of information- and service-based work with the authority of participatory democracy, global governance networks and autonomous ethical decision-making. They value tolerance, self-expression, trust and individual rights. Inglehart did not find any societies that were dominated by postmodern values, but the Scandinavian countries came closest. Even though a society might be dominated by one set of values, other value orientations co-exist within it. For the sake of convenience, I will refer to these three categories as 'types of societies' with the understanding that the categorisation is based on the relative preponderance of the designated value set.

The movement from traditional to modern values is part of the process of modernisation. The movement from modern values to postmodern values is called postmodernisation (Harvey 1990; Jameson 1991; McGowan 1991). Postmodernisation occurs when societies cross a certain threshold of affluence such that scarcity of life's necessities no longer dominates daily decision-making (Inglehart 1997,

2000). Inglehart estimates this threshold to be approximately at the level of afflu-ence experienced in countries such as Taiwan and Ireland in the early 1990s. In terms of politics, postmodern societies move away from deference to authority (Nevitte 1996) and the politics of class-based economic interests towards decen-tralised, participatory governance and identity politics (Melucci 1985, 1989). Qual-ity-of-life issues take precedence over survival issues, as evidenced by the rise of social movements such as gay rights, feminism and environmentalism.

Traditional societies undoubtedly appeared first. Modern societies were layered on top of traditional foundations as urban centres began to form trade networks. Postmodern perspectives emerged with the increasing internationalisation of trade (Eisenstadt 2000). However, they continue to contain traditional and modern ele-ments. Thus, postmodern societies contain the most diverse populations in terms of their perspectives and values. They include some people who adhere to traditional values, some who adhere to modern values and some who hold postmodern values.

The progression from traditional to modern to postmodern is one that has been observed only in the history of Western societies. We do not know if other societies will necessarily follow the same progression. Inglehart and Baker (2000) present evidence to suggest that the progression is apparent in some non-Western societies as well, even though cultural distinctiveness persists. For example, the set of mod-ern values have consistently different profiles in Protestant, Roman Catholic, Orthodox, Confucian or communist societies. Likewise, the set of postmodern val-ues each bear a different emphasis in Protestant postmodern society compared with a Catholic postmodern society. Egri (1997) reviewed the perspectives that Western, Eastern and shamanistic religious traditions adopt regarding the humankind–environment interface. Like Inglehart and Baker, she found both diversity and similarities among these traditions. However, Eisenstadt (2000) argues that there is a distinct stage of societal evolution called postmodernity that supersedes mod-ernity. Instead, he views the postmodernity of Western society as just one of many diverse 'modernities'. Either way, the WVS data empirically show the cluster of values and views that Inglehart identifies as postmodern to be distinct and perva-sive in the West. Giving it a separate identity for analytical purposes helps sort out the various versions of sustainable development that companies with at least some presence in the West are likely to encounter.

As with any notion of developmental progression, the idea that societies develop from traditional to modern to postmodern raises several questions. Are these irreversible stages or is regression possible? Can societies become permanently arrested at a stage or can they skip a stage? Without evidence and analyses that go beyond the scope of this chapter, we can only speculate. The sequence of stages seems quite contingent on numerous factors. In terms of regression, climate induced the Polynesians, who settled New Zealand's cold Chatham Islands, to give up agriculture and return to hunting and gathering (Diamond 1997: 60). In terms of becoming arrested, several stone-age societies were discovered in the 20th century in Papua New Guinea (Connolly and Anderson 1987) and the Amazon (Moran 1993), which suggests that modernisation is not inevitable, given sufficient isolation. In terms of skipping stages, relevant evidence might be found in cases of transitions from subsistence to consumer prosperity in a single generation, as has happened in societies such as Nauru, several oil-rich Arab states and a few mineral-rich indigenous communities in Alaska and Canada's far north. Studies of the values of community members across several generations are needed to yield a thorough description of the developmental sequence.

Views of the human–environment relationship

While Inglehart and his colleagues have provided a typology of values and attitudes that encompasses both developed and developing societies, no one has yet matched it with a comparably global typology of views on sustainability. Several scholars have developed typologies of the views found in Western societies, but none of them appears to capture the perspectives of those living in subsistence circumstances. Gale and Cordray (1994) proposed nine distinct views of sustainability reflecting answers to the question: 'What should be sustained?'. Dobson (1996) focused specifically on views of *environmental* sustainability. His four classifications reflected views ranging from a technology-oriented emphasis on human welfare to an ecocentric emphasis on humankind's obligations to nature. Dunlap *et al.* (2000) updated Dunlap and Van Liere's (1978) new environmental paradigm (NEP) scale with data from residents of Washington state. Although they began with five conceptually distinct facets of views on the environment and humankind's relationship with nature, a principal components analysis indicated that the concepts all belonged to one primary dimension. That dimension ranged from a low to high belief in the possibility of a global ecological crisis and humankind's dependence on the delicate balance of nature. Cohen (2000) embellished EMT with a typology of environmental epistemological orientations. Cohen's two-by-two matrix contrasted weak versus strong ecological consciousness orthogonally with an epistemological commitment dimension that ranged from rational scientism to numinous aestheticism. Cohen showed how the resultant four quadrants describe varieties of views found in the developed world. Satterfield (2001) coded projective-style, open-ended responses to stories and pictures in order to assess the environmental values of readers of a university newspaper in Oregon. She developed 25 coding categories but found that 2 were used much more frequently than the others. The 'ecological sustainability' category emphasised ecosystem health from a resource management perspective. The 'rights/equity' category emphasised the rights of nature versus the rights of humankind. All of these typologies offer insights into the range of views held by people in the US and Western Europe. None, however, was deliberately designed to include the views of those with a subsistence relationship to nature. Indeed, even within the US, Dunlap *et al.* (2000) found that high scores on the NEP scale were positively and significantly correlated with growing up in an urban area and were negatively correlated with being employed in primary industries.

Castells (1997: 112) took a more overtly political approach to his typology of views on the environment in the developed world, classifying social movement organisations. Because these organisations are often stakeholders of internationally active corporations this approach appears to have the most immediate relevance for companies. Most of the interpretations of the sustainable development concept embedded in the various typologies reviewed above are evident in the cognitive frames (Gamson 1997; Snow and Benford 1992) advanced by new social movements that take a postmodern approach to environmentalism (Buechler 1997; Castells 1997). For example, these movements assume development is not only easy to achieve but difficult to restrain. They view the natural environment as needing protection, not as something from which we need to protect ourselves. However, subscribing unswervingly to the postmodern presuppositions underlying so much of the current analysis of the sustainable development concept leaves one ill equipped to enter into a dialogue about the human–environment relationship with stakeholders from traditional and modern societies. In order to help advance mutual understanding in such dialogues, Table 1.1 shows a proposed list of dimensions, developed by the author, on which traditional, modern and postmodern views of the human–environment relationship can be compared and contrasted. The list is neither exhaustive nor definitive. It simply attempts to highlight some similarities and differences among the views. After the hypothesised sustainability views for each type of society are described, the typology is applied to a case involving a subsistence society. Then the typology is elaborated using Castells's categories of social movements.

Dimensions		Tradi-tional	Modern	Post-modern
Traditional views distinctive				
1	Local environment needed for subsistence	Yes	No	No
2	Low priority on non-local natural resources	Yes	No	No
Modern views distinctive				
3	Nature is infinitely renewable	No	Yes	No
4	Trade makes local environment dispensable	No	Yes	No
Postmodern views distinctive				
5	Humans have global impacts	No	No	Yes
6	Humans could permanently destroy nature	No	No	Yes

TABLE 1.1 Dimensions of difference among the traditional, modern and postmodern views of the human–environment relationship

The traditional view of the human–environment interface emphasises the local environment. The first dimension in Table 1.1 highlights the fact that traditional societies depend on their local environments for survival. Over-harvesting or polluting that environment would have negative consequences fairly quickly. Therefore, such societies must continually seek a sustainable balance between human needs and the natural environment. The second dimension addresses the freedom from subsistence dependence on the immediate natural environment that comes with modernisation. Trade in resources from distant natural environments allows for population concentrations in urban areas that are far beyond the carrying capacities of the natural environment in those locales. Traditional societies have very limited access to resources from non-local environments and therefore do not tend to develop views that take account of distant environments. The third statement implies the distinctly modern perspective that local environments can be endlessly harvested and polluted without danger because nature always renews itself. It follows that there need be no limits on economic growth. By contrast, traditional and postmodern perspectives emphasise balance instead of growth. The fourth dimension proposes that both traditional and postmodern views endorse the need for ecological stewardship while modern societies operate on assumptions of unlimited growth. Because they trade over long distances, modern societies can spread their environmental risks across the natural environments inhabited by themselves and all their trading partners. Local environmental stewardship becomes less of a life-and-death matter compared with traditional societies.

Postmodernism takes environmental stewardship to the global level. In these societies, trade has created so much specialisation and interdependence that the sustainability of the whole trading system becomes a widespread concern. As illustrated by the fifth statement, the global trading system's relationship with the global natural environment comes to the fore with concern for issues such as the hole in the ozone layer and climate change. The last statement emphasises the postmodern fear of ecological collapse as a result of human activity overpowering the global ecosystem.

In traditional societies, the subsistence economy necessitates local stewardship of the environment. The integration of economic and environmental activity is necessary for human survival. The same is true in the postmodern view, except at a global rather than a local level. Only in the modern view is there an apparent conflict between economic development and environmental stewardship. As Castells (1997) points out, this rift in modern societies has typically correlated with class divisions. The wealthy take an interest in environmental conservation, and may appropriate large preserves for their own enjoyment. The poor live by the factory gate and hope that, under the right sociopolitical conditions, their own personal prosperity can be advanced by industrial growth.

Case study from Papua New Guinea

A specific case may help illustrate the misunderstandings that can appear when traditional, modern and postmodern views collide. All three views were held by different actors on the remote Melanesian island of Misima in south-east Papua New Guinea. A globally active mining company, Placer Dome Inc. (PDI), was closing its exhausted gold mine on the island. The management of PDI and Misima Mines Limited (MML), a subsidiary, wanted to leave behind a sustainable economy. PDI asked this author to conduct a study of the network of relationships among the local stakeholders, including MML. As of writing, this five-year longitudinal project is still under way. However, the aspects of the case presented here were obtained from three other sources. First, I reviewed background material consisting of two documents prepared by the company (Hood 2000; MML 2000), two studies of Misima conducted by anthropologists (Macintyre and Gerritsen 1986; Byford 2000), an anthropological survey of the history and development of social change in Melanesia (Sillitoe 2000) and a study of Misima by a geographer who specialises in mining in the South Pacific Islands (Jackson 2001). Second, over a period of three years from 2000 to 2002, I conducted a series of context-setting interviews with 13 MML employees who dealt with stakeholders on Misima. A written summary of the events presented here was submitted for comment and verification to five of those employees. The employee interviews were supplemented by conversations with two Papua New Guinea-based representatives of Conservation International, two of the anthropologists who conducted the aforementioned studies of Misiman society and three representatives of Australian aid agencies. Third, I co-facilitated a workshop with the leaders of 11 organisations that considered themselves stakeholders in the mine closure. The workshop was designed to articulate the community's sustainability goals for the post-closure period.

The MML mine began operating in 1989. Planning for closure began in 1999. Before MML arrived, Misimans mostly lived off the land. Slash-and-burn gardening supplied the primary food source, supplemented by raising pigs for mortuary feasts and by fishing. Land was, and still is, communally held by clans and allotted for gardening along matrilineal lines. Land is not bought or sold. By the 1980s, the coconut and cocoa plantations that flourished in the 1970s had gone bankrupt and the remaining cash returns from these crops fell so low that some people returned to making their own clothing (e.g. grass skirts) out of local plants. The economy was sustainable because disease, infant mortality and maternal death during childbirth kept the population from growing beyond the carrying capacity of the land.

With the mine came improvements in healthcare and an influx of people. During the 1990s, MML tried to diversify the local economy with projects and initiatives in forestry, boat building and commercial fishing. None of these was successful in the Western sense, partly because Melanesians generally believe that excess wealth (i.e. profits) should be immediately shared among concentric circles of relatives, clan members, neighbours and acquaintances. To 'retain earnings' for reinvestment is to risk ostracisation. With few alternative income sources, the impending closure of the mine meant a return to subsistence gardening. Unfortunately, the larger population required more food from the same land area. This demand had already shortened the fallow periods from the optimal 14 or more years to as few as three years. The shorter fallow periods completely exhausted the soil because Misimans did not use any fertilisers or nitrifying fallow crops. As more land was ruined, the shortage of gardening land became more acute. The traditionalist response was to reactivate claims on land at the fringe of each clan's territory. This caused rising tensions and acrimonious disputes among clans and villages.

Most of the locals who worked for the mine held traditional subsistence views. One of them spearheaded a company-sponsored agricultural research and training centre to show Misimans how to use nitrifiers so that shorter fallow periods would not destroy their land's productive capacity. Unfortunately, the company had neither the people nor the expertise required to promote the adoption of these new gardening techniques. The company tried to get outside non-governmental organisations (NGOs) to help, but none was interested, mostly because there were so many other communities with worse problems and more urgent needs.

Meanwhile, a few locals with a more modern view took a different approach. They wanted to start an export trade based on marine life harvesting from the nearby coral reefs. Misima belongs to the Louisiade archipelago, a chain of islands in Milne Bay province that includes a pristine coral reef with more marine diversity than the Great Barrier Reef. Modern locals realised that there was an international market for various exotic marine fauna and flora such as sea cucumbers, coral and live reef fish for aquariums. They hoped to replace at least part of the disappearing mining wages with income from the export of sea products. Since there were not many of these modernists, they felt that their activities would have little detrimental impact on a large reef that stretches for hundreds of kilometres. If they had been successful, of course, their numbers would have swelled with newcomers wanting the same opportunity. However, postmodernists from the developed world had different plans for the reef.

Conservation International managed to have the Louisiade reef declared part of a marine conservation area. That meant strict restrictions on harvesting. This was great news for postmodern environmentalists in the cities of the developed world. Unfortunately, it closed off one option for averting the impending food and cash shortages on Misima. At that point, it appeared to be a tragic conflict among worldviews, with the postmodernists saving the planet by keeping third-world villagers from enjoying the benefits of the West's material prosperity. What was needed was a way to understand the sustainability aspirations of all three viewpoints.

Fortunately, key players in the mining company, Conservation International, and the Papua New Guinea government were able to see sustainability from multiple perspectives. A deal was arranged in which some of the reef conservation money was allocated to Misima's agricultural research and training centre. The rationale was that, if the locals had terrestrial food sources they would be less motivated to harvest the reef. Therefore, helping to ensure an adequate food supply for Misimans could be justified because it helped preserve the marine ecosystem. This satisfied both the traditionals and the postmoderns. The would-be moderns, however, still wanted cash incomes. For them, there was the promise of a diving tourism industry. Also, the agricultural research and training centre had a separate programme to promote cash export crops such as coconut oil, vanilla and nutmeg.

If any one of the three views of the human–environment relationship had prevailed, the outcome could have been tragic. More sustainable plans were devised by taking account of all the perspectives at once. One might object that the modernist perspective could have been ignored without tragedy. However, the reform of agricultural practices was a prime example of modernisation. Without that option, the population would have had to decrease, one way or another. Tragedy would have then taken the form of more malnutrition. Moreover, modern healthcare and medical facilities directly and indirectly brought by the mine reduced the number of tragedies arising from inadequate to non-existent healthcare. Neither traditionalism nor postmodernism would have given Misimans these benefits.

Typology of views of sustainable development

As the Misima case shows, the three views of the human–environment relationship can collide even in very remote parts of the world today. If the hypothesis is correct that the three views of the human–environment interface are correlated with the three types of societies, then one would expect the proportions of the human–environment views to vary from place to place. This would follow from Inglehart's findings that postmodern values are less common in modern societies but flourish in the developed world. Manuel Castells (1997: 112) classified the environmental movements of the developed world into the five categories. Although Castells himself never tried to match his five types with traditional, modern or postmodern political and economic systems, there appear to be some fairly obvious links. Figure 1.1 shows how they could be matched by linking some of the movements with the societal systems and some with the transition processes from one system to another (i.e. modernisation, postmodernisation, neotribalisation). In the remainder of this chapter, I clarify the meaning of the transition processes, add a sixth category of movement (responsible commons harvesters) and suggest how sustainable development is interpreted within the cognitive frames of these six movements.

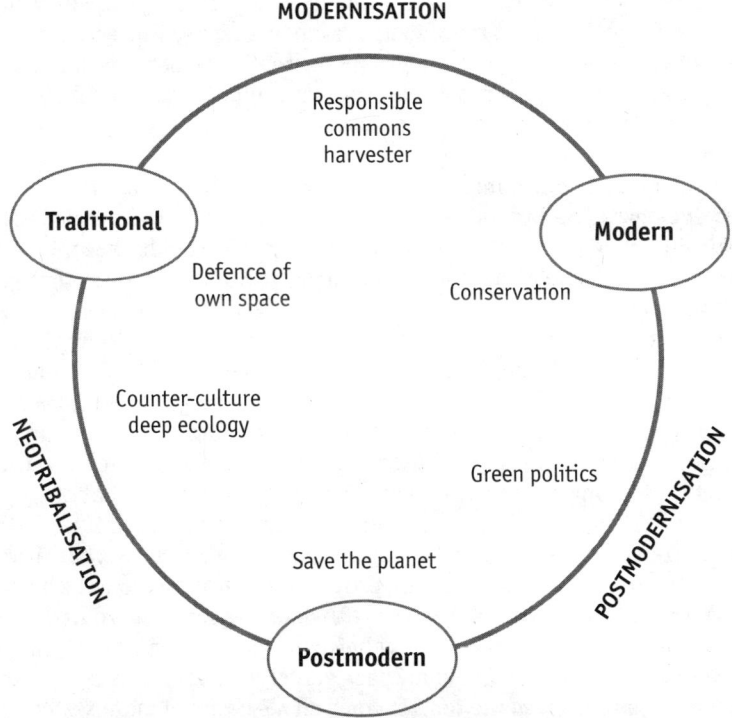

FIGURE 1.1 Types of environmental movements mapped against societal value types

Two of the arcs in Figure 1.1 represent the processes of modernisation and post-modernisation. The third arc, neotribalisation, is a relatively new concept. I use it to refer to the thrust towards constituting communities on the basis of collective identities rooted in postmodern critiques of modernism. Antonio (2000) describes several reactions to the homogenisation of identities caused by modernism's globalisation. Some of these are reassertions of ethnic identities in newly emerged nation-states, particularly those of the former Soviet Union. He calls this reactionary tribalism or 'retribalisation'. Rata (2000, 2003) uses the term 'neotribal capitalism' to refer to aspects of how the Maori in New Zealand have responded to global capitalism and threats to their culture. The reactions I wish to refer to as 'neotribal' do not manifest themselves as nation-states and are not necessarily based on ethnic identities or indigenous cultures. By 'neotribalisation' I wish to refer to community formation that may arise from new social movements (e.g. deep ecology, gay rights, eco-feminism), from geographically centred communitarian movements or from virtual communities. Not all expressions of neotribalism concern themselves with sustainable development. Those that do, however, not only recognise the impotence of the modern nation-state but also place little faith in efforts to create international governance structures to control the excesses of global capitalism (Mander 2001). Instead, neotribalists opt for a more anarchist, locally autonomous model. The affinity group mode of governance (Gamson 1992) is a good example of neotribalism in action. Affinity groups are close-knit cells of 10–20 people that work for a movement's cause in a very self-directed, autonomous fashion. They are joined to other groups in the movement by loose networks. Norberg-Hodge (2001) also provides several examples of communities striving for independence from the global economy and greater local self-sufficiency and interdependence.

The neotribal view of humankind's relationship with the natural environment stands between the traditional and the postmodern. It advocates applying the local stewardship ethic of subsistence societies (e.g. limited harvesting of natural resources) to the whole planet through local action more than through international organising. It applies the implications of global phenomena and perspectives (e.g. global warming, ozone depletion) to local stewardship practices, but tends to place the sustainability of the local community above global concerns. Egri (1997) describes several threads of contemporary, ecological and spiritual philosophy that revisit and renew traditional views of the humankind–nature relationship. Insofar as neotribalism represents a return to elements of the traditional society, it is an example of a spiral-form change process (Eisenhardt 2000).

Five of the six types of environmental movements named inside the circle in Figure 1.1 are attributed to Castells and one is original. These six are discussed in the order that they appear in Figure 1.1, proceeding clockwise from the one matched with the traditional type of society. The type of environmental group that seems to be most congruent with traditional values and views is one that Castells called 'defence-of-own-space' (i.e. not in my back yard). Members of these types of movements view themselves as the local community. These ubiquitous groups oppose pollution (e.g. noise, toxins) and other economic externalities (e.g. traffic, eyesores) in their vicinity. Their goal is to preserve or enhance the quality of life and health in their local area. The kinds of disputes that this type of environmental movement engages in often raise questions of 'environmental justice'. These include concerns about corporations taking advantage of lower environmental standards in poorer countries and municipal governments locating green spaces in wealthy neighbourhoods while relegating waste disposal sites, for example, to poorer neighbourhoods.

In the Misima case, the traditional locals' environmental concerns were very much of the defence-of-own-space type. The landowning clans imposed environmental conditions on the company before agreeing to the mine. They insisted that their water supply and ocean-front fishing areas would not be polluted. At the same time, they favoured alterations to the natural landscape. They were promised that, after the mine was closed, their mountain would be flattened into terraces and reforested with natural vegetation. The clan elders liked the flatter mountain idea because it made more land available for arable farming. However, they preferred the planting of certain 'useful' trees rather than those that nature alone would yield. Pristine wilderness was clearly not their goal. They needed an unpolluted environment but, because it was going to have to 'sustain' them, they also preferred certain alterations.

Proceeding clockwise in Figure 1.1, one view of the human–environment relationship that corresponds to modernisation, but functions best in the least industrialised, most agrarian geographic locations, I dub the 'responsible commons harvester' view. On the road to modernisation, commons resources (e.g. wild game, fish, whales) come under increasing harvesting pressure. This leads to the familiar 'tragedy of the commons' (Hardin 1968). Groups have emerged at various times and places to manage such common resources. For example, groups such as rod and gun clubs and Ducks Unlimited try to preserve the natural environment and promote adherence to fishing and hunting regulations in attempts to preserve wild populations of game for future harvesting. Members of these groups would include many rural residents who see themselves as 'outdoorsmen', and many members of rural and remote North American Indian communities. Some hunt and fish to provide food for their families, thereby freeing up cash for alternative uses.

Responsible commons harvesting bears similarities to both traditional subsistence defence-of-own-space approaches and conservationism. Although a vital part of traditional subsistence economies, hunting and fishing are not optional activities. Game preservation is part of conservation, but it is not done with harvesting as the goal. In terms of sustainable development, the responsible commons harvester might be mostly concerned with wildlife habitat preservation in agricultural areas. The goal would not be wilderness but rather mixed-use rural land that accommodates plenty of wildlife. In this view, it would be irresponsible to over-harvest or destroy habitat. Over-harvesting would include trophy hunting and taking more than can be consumed by oneself and one's dependents.

The next type of environmental movement Castells identified is 'conservation of nature'. Its adversary is uncontrolled development and its goal is wilderness preservation. Members view themselves as nature lovers. In this category, Castells places American groups such as the Sierra Club, the National Parks and Conservation Association, and the National Wildlife Federation. We might speculate that, from this environmental perspective, sustainable development consists of creating a legal boundary on the landscape with development on one side and wilderness on the other. Conservation International's campaign to have Misima's reefs declared conservation areas would exemplify a version of this approach to sustainable development.

Castells' next type contains groups that mix modern and postmodern views together. We have already examined how EMT mixes modern and postmodern themes, but Castells does not mention EMT, probably because it is not associated with a social movement. Nonetheless, EMT does represent a view of sustainability that is congruent with the actions of green entrepreneurs and the green economy in general. Castells, however, focused on more politically oriented movements. He placed the German Green Party (*Die Grünen*), and environmental parties and caucuses elsewhere, into this category. He noted that their collective identities as groups of concerned citizens are rooted in nation-state politics. They oppose the political establishment and attempt to offer a counter-power for a variety of marginalised groups and movements. *Die Grünen* is thus an anti-party party. Although its goals are postmodern, its means to those goals are modern. The goals include giving voice to marginalised identities and communities, but the means depend on the modern rational–legalistic institutions of government. Sustainable development from this perspective is likely to be anti-development in flavour, with the legalistic understanding that the other parties and their capitalist friends will look after the pro-development advocacy.

The fifth type on Figure 1.1 is one that Castells called 'save-the-planet'. He noted that this includes Greenpeace, the largest environmental group in the world. Groups such as the Earthday Network and the Environmental Investigation Agency would also qualify. Save-the-planet groups project an eco-campaigner identity and take a distinctly internationalist perspective. The opponent is unfettered global development and the goal is the sustainability of the global ecosystem. Such groups gravitate towards issues of planetary significance such as nuclear weapons, global warming, rainforests and oceans, biodiversity and toxic chemicals. They see development as something that has its own momentum and one that adversely affects the environmental policies of relatively weaker governments and international institutions. Their view of sustainable development is like that of *Die Grünen* in that they do not advocate for development, but rather for limits and restrictions on development, thereby making development more sustainable. They differ from *Die Grünen* in their thoroughgoing internationalism. Single-country issues are only of interest to save-the-planet environmentalists if there is a connection with the global ecosystem.

The sixth type is 'counter-culture, deep ecology'. It includes members of Earth First!, the Earth Liberation Front, animal rightists and some eco-feminists. Their goal is an 'ecotopia' beyond the overthrow of industrialism, technocracy and patriarchalism. The worldwide social change agenda gives these groups an affinity with save-the-planet groups, but their activism tends more towards covert civil disobedience and eco-sabotage (Foreman and Haywood 1993) than the save-the-planet campaigns that veer towards creating opportunities for interviews, photo-opportunities and soundbites. At the same time, their strong anarchist proclivities bear similarities to the localism of defence-of-own-space environmentalism, particularly as the latter is manifested in self-sufficient subsistence communities. Deep-ecology environmentalists are probably the most philosophical type. Their view of sustainable development is rooted in a fundamental change in humanity. To deep ecologists, sustainable development means a decrease in humankind's impact on nature through less consumption and a deliberate diminution of the human population worldwide. That might be achieved, for example, by reducing the use of healthcare services so that natural causes keep the human population at a more sustainable level, not unlike pre-mine Misima but without the male dominance exhibited by the latter.

Dealing with conflicts

Conflicts can occur between any pair of environmental types but the most intractable ones are likely to be between those diametrically opposed in Figure 1.1. For example, when commons harvesters sell their harvest for cash instead of substituting the harvest for cash in their family food budget, they incur the wrath of those with save-the-planet views.

Conflicts between defence-of-own-space environmentalists and green politics environmentalists generally involve disputes between national and local levels of government. For example, the green caucus in a national legislature might support the building of a rapid train line to reduce automobile use, thereby reducing the country's greenhouse gas emissions. But the neighbourhoods on the proposed new train route might strenuously object on grounds of noise pollution, loss of wildlife habitat and loss of agricultural land.

Conflicts between counter-culture deep ecologists and conservation environmentalists would generally involve issues related to humankind's dominion over nature. High-profile examples would include the treatment of domestic and captive wild animals, the use of animals in research, the consumption of animal products and the ethics of eco-tourism. While conservationists might encourage eco-tourism, some deep ecologists would oppose it as an infringement on the rights of wild creatures to be left undisturbed.

Alliances and coalitions among environmentalists with adjacent views are not uncommon. For example, even though their proposed solutions differ, deep ecologists, save-the-planet activists and political greens all seem to draw on a common pool of anti-modern sentiment and anti-globalisation alienation. Likewise, responsible commons harvesters, conservationists and EMT adherents are less likely to view economic growth as too risky to tolerate.

Corporations can easily find themselves in conflict with any of these six environmental perspectives, no matter where they operate. Corporations have historically operated from a modernist set of values, emphasising growth, jobs and increasing consumption. Even in predominantly modernist societies, however, there are perspectives on sustainable development that would limit corporate freedom. Furthermore, even companies committed to sustainable development, however they define it, can encounter quite vexing conflicts when their stakeholders hold diverging views of sustainable development.

Executives sometimes complain that a stakeholder approach to corporate governance places them in too many 'damned if you do, damned if your don't' dilemmas by virtue of being caught between the conflicting demands of different stakeholders. One of the several possible approaches to resolving such dilemmas is to grasp what underlies those inter-stakeholder disputes. Swanson (1999) has provided a detailed description of how companies can become attuned to stakeholders' values and perceptions. This involves integrating an understanding of stakeholders' perspectives into the executive's orientation towards social policy, the company's formal and informal organisational decision-making processes, and its external affairs management. The typology presented here provides a framework for the development of a comprehensive attunement to stakeholder perspectives on sustainable development.

Having a framework that encompasses the diverse guises in which sustainable development advocacy manifests itself makes companies better prepared to facilitate dialogues among conflicting stakeholders. If nothing else, the typology presented here can at least help companies anticipate the different kinds of sustainability issues that might arise from their actions. By looking at what each of the perspectives on sustainable development share in common, it might even help find grounds for agreement among diverse environmental stakeholders.

In terms of future research, the immediate need is for a further refinement of the concepts and categories. Then, an empirical test of the matching hypothesised in Figure 1.1 would be in order. This would require measures of traditionalism, modernity and postmodernity which Inglehart (1997) and colleagues (Inglehart and Abramson 1999) have already begun to develop. It would also require measures of the perspectives on sustainable development hypothesised to be associated with societal value types. Sampling would require *bone fide* members of the various categories of environmental groups. The research agenda could then be extended to transform these measures into practical management tools that would help companies become attuned to stakeholder perspectives, anticipate inter-stakeholder conflicts and facilitate mutual understanding in multi-stakeholder dialogues.

Finally, at the executive level, corporations with operations that span traditional, modern or postmodern societies can use the typology presented here to make sense of the demands and opportunities they might encounter when participating in the various global governance initiatives that are emerging today. Whether it be the Global Compact (Kell 2003; Waddock 2003), the Global Reporting Initiative (Holland and Gibbon 2001) or any of the many other multi-sectoral initiatives related to corporate citizenship (Leipziger 2003; Waddell 2000), fundamentally different views of sustainability often underlie the diverse proposals and critiques executives will encounter. This typology of these views can shorten executives' learning phase when starting to engage in such processes. Also, compared to civil society and government, the private sector has often gained more broad experience in traditional, modern and postmodern societies. This typology may help executives communicate their resultant multiple perspectives more effectively to those with narrower views, thereby helping to advance an autopoietic system (Schütz 2000) of global sustainability.

References

Antonio, R.J. (2000) 'After Postmodernism: Reactionary Tribalism', *American Journal of Sociology* 106.2: 40-87.

Buechler, S.M. (1997) 'New Social Movement Theories', in S.M. Buechler and F.K. Cylke Jr (eds.), *Social Movements: Perspectives and Issues* (Mountain View, CA: Mayfield Publishing): 295-319.

Byford, J. (2000) *One Day Rich: Community Perceptions of the Impact of the Placer Dome Gold Mine, Misima Island, Papua New Guinea* (Report to Community Aid Abroad, September 2000).

Castells, M. (1997) *The Information Age: Economy, Society and Culture.* II. *The Power of Identity* (Oxford, UK: Blackwell).

Cohen, M.J. (2000) 'Ecological Modernisation, Environmental Knowledge and National Character: A Preliminary Analysis of the Netherlands', *Environmental Politics* 9.1: 77-106.

Connolly, B., and R. Anderson (1987) *First Contact* (New York/Harmondsworth, UK: Viking Penguin).

Cowe, R., and S. Williams (2000) *Who Are the Ethical Consumers?* (London: The Co-operative Bank).

Diamond, J. (1997) *Guns, Germs and Steel: The Fates of Human Societies* (New York: Norton).

Dobson, A. (1996) 'Environmental Sustainabilities: An Analysis and Typology', *Environmental Politics* 5.3: 401.

Dunlap, R.E., and K.D. Van Liere (1978) 'The Environmental Paradigm: A Proposed Measuring Instrument and Preliminary Results', *Journal of Environmental Education* 9: 10-19.

——, ——, A.G. Mertig and R.E. Jones (2000) 'Measuring Endorsement of the New Ecological Paradigm: A Revised NEP Scale', *Journal of Social Issues* 56.3: 425-42.

Durkheim, E. (1893/1984) *The Division of Labor in Society* (trans. W.D. Halls; New York: The Free Press).

Egri, C.P. (1997) 'Spiritual Connections with the Natural Environment', *Organization and Environment* 10.4: 407-31.

Eisenhardt, K.M. (2000) 'Paradox, Spirals, Ambivalence: The New Language of Change and Pluralism', *Academy of Management Review* 25.4: 703-705.

Eisenstadt, S.N. (2000) 'Multiple Modernities', *Daedalus* 29.1: 1-29.

Foreman, D., and B. Haywood (1993) *ECODEFENSE: A Field Guide to Monkeywrenching* (Chico, CA: Abbzug Press).

Gale, R.P., and S.M. Cordray (1994) 'Making Sense of Sustainability: Nine Answers to What Should Be Sustained?', *Rural Sociology* 59.2: 311-32.

Gamson, W.A. (1992) 'The Social Psychology of Collective Action', in A.D. Morris and C. McClurg Mueller (eds.), *Frontiers in Social Movement Theory* (New Haven, CT: Yale University Press): 53-76.

—— (1997) 'Constructing Social Protest', in S.M. Buechler and F.K. Cylke Jr (eds.), *Social Movements: Perspectives and Issues* (Mountain View, CA: Mayfield Publishing): 228-44.

Giddens, A. (1991) *Modernity and Self-identity: Self and Society in the Late Modern Age* (Cambridge, UK : Polity Press).

Hardin, G. (1968) 'The Tragedy of the Commons', *Science* 162: 1,243-48.

Harrison, D. (1998) *The Sociology of Modernization and Development* (Boston, MA: Unwin Hyman).

Harvey, D. (1990) *The Condition of Postmodernity: An Inquiry Into the Origins of Cultural Change* (Cambridge, MA: Basil Blackwell).

Holland, L., and J. Gibbon (2001) 'Processes in Social and Ethical Accountability: External Reporting Mechanisms', in J. Andriof and M. McIntosh (eds.), *Perspectives on Corporate Citizenship* (Sheffield, UK: Greenleaf Publishing): 278-95.

Hood, A. (2000) *From Community Relations to Community Development: A Brief Review of Mine Closure and Sustainability Planning at Misima Mines Limited* (Vancouver, BC: Placer Dome Inc.).

IISD (International Institute for Sustainable Development) (2003) 'Compendium of Sustainable Development Indicator Initiatives', www.iisd.org/measure/compendium, accessed 4 April 2003.

Inglehart, R. (1997) *Modernization and Postmodernization: Cultural, Economic, and Political Change in 43 Societies* (Princeton, NJ: Princeton University Press).

—— (2000) 'Globalization and Postmodern Values', *The Washington Quarterly* 23.1: 215-28.

—— and P. Abramson (1999) 'Measuring Postmaterialism', *American Political Science Review*, September 1999: 665-77.

—— and W.E. Baker (2000) 'Modernization, Cultural Change and the Persistence of Traditional Values', *American Sociological Review* 65.1: 19-55.

Jackson, R.T. (2001) *Kekeisi Kekeisi: A Long Term Economic Development Plan for the Misima Gold Mine's Impact Area* (Manila, Philippines: Richard T. Jackson Consultancy Services): 1-186.

Jameson, F. (1991) *Postmodernism: Or, the Cultural Logic of Late Capitalism* (Durham, NC: Duke University Press).

Jänicke, M. (1985) *Preventive Environmental Policy as Ecological Modernization and Structural Policy* (Berlin: Springer).

Kell, G. (2003) 'The Global Compact: Origins, Operations, Progress, Challenges', *Journal of Corporate Citizenship* 11 (Autumn 2003): 35-49.

Leipziger, D. (2003) *The Corporate Responsibility Code Book* (Sheffield, UK: Greenleaf Publishing).

Macintyre, M., and R. Gerritsen (1986) *Social Impact Study of Proposed Mining Project on Misima Island* (Port Moresby, Papua New Guinea: Institute for Applied Social and Economic Research).

Mander, J. (2001) 'Facing the Rising Tide', in E. Goldsmith and J. Mander (eds.), *The Case against the Global Economy and for a Turn Towards Localization* (London: Earthscan Publications): 1-19.

Marx, K. (1965) *Pre-Capitalist Economic Formations* (trans. Jack Cohen; ed. E.J. Hobsbawm; New York: International Publishers).

McGowan, J. (1991) *Postmodernism and its Critics* (Ithaca, NY: Cornell University Press).

Melucci, A. (1985) 'The Symbolic Challenge of Contemporary Movements', *Social Research* 52.4: 789-816.

—— (1989) *Nomads of the Present: Social Movements and Individual Needs in Contemporary Society* (Philadelphia, PA: Temple University Press).

MMSD (Mining Minerals and Sustainable Development Project) (2002) *Breaking New Ground: Mining, Minerals, and Sustainable Development. The Report of the MMSD Project* (London: Earthscan Publications).

MML (Misima Mines Limited) (2000) *Sustainability Plan: Year 2000 Consultation Document* (Misima Island, Papua New Guinea: MML).

Moran, E.F. (1993) *Through Amazonian Eyes: The Human Ecology of Amazonian Populations* (Iowa City, IA: University of Iowa Press).

Mol, A.P.J., and D.A. Sonnenfeld (2000) 'Ecological Modernization around the World: An Introduction', *Environmental Politics* 9.1: 3-14.

—— and G. Spaargaren (2000) 'Ecological Modernization Theory in Debate: A Review', *Environmental Politics* 9.1: 17-49.

Nevitte, N. (1996) *The Decline of Deference: Canadian Value Change in Cross-National Perspective* (Peterborough, Ontario: Broadview Press).

Norberg-Hodge, H. (2001) 'Shifting Direction: From Global Dependence to Local Interdependence', in E. Goldsmith and J. Mander (eds.), *The Case against the Global Economy and for a Turn towards Localization* (London: Earthscan Publications): 393-406.

Rata, E. (2000) *A Political Economy of Neotribal Capitalism* (Lanham, MD: Lexington Books).

—— (2003) 'Late Capitalism and Ethnic Revivalism: A "New Middle Age"?', *Anthropological Theory* 3.1: 43-64.

Satterfield, T. (2001) 'In Search of Value Literacy: Suggestions for the Elicitation of Environmental Values', *Environmental Values* 10.3: 331-59.

Schütz, J. (2000) 'Sustainability, Systems and Meaning', *Environmental Values* 9.3: 373-82.

Sillitoe, P. (2000) *Social Change in Melanesia: Development and History* (New York/Cambridge, UK: Cambridge University Press).

Simonis, U.E. (1988) *Beyond Growth: Elements of Sustainable Development* (Berlin: Edition Sigma).

Snow, D.A., and R.D. Benford (1997) 'Master Frames and Cycles of Protest', in S.M. Buechler and
F.K. Cylke Jr (eds.), *Social Movements: Perspectives and Issues* (Mountain View, CA: Mayfield
Publishing): 456-72.

Swanson, D.L. (1999) 'Toward an Integrative Theory of Business and Society: A Research Strategy
for Corporate Social Performance', *Academy of Management Review* 24: 506-21.

Waddell, S. (2000) 'New Institutions for the Practice of Corporate Citizenship: An Intersectoral,
Developmental and Historical Perspective', *Business and Society Review* 105.1: 107.

Waddock, S.A. (2003) 'Learning from Experience: The United Nations Global Compact Learning
Forum 2002', *Journal of Corporate Citizenship* 11 (Autumn 2003): 51-67.

Weber, M. (1958) *The Protestant Ethic and the Spirit of Capitalism* (trans. Talcott Parsons; New York:
Scribner).

—— (1983) *Max Weber on Capitalism, Bureaucracy and Religion: A Selection of Texts* (trans. Stanislav
Andreski; London: Allen & Unwin).

WCED (World Commission on Environment and Development) (1987) *Our Common Future* (Oxford,
UK: Oxford University Press).

2

The next environmentalism
CREATING A NEW POLITICAL
DYNAMIC FOR PROGRESS IN THE US

Roger S. Ballentine
Senior Fellow, Progressive Policy Institute, USA

Relations between the President and the Congress were uneasy, to say the least. The President's conservative opponents on Capitol Hill—particularly those from western states—opposed him on ideological as well as personal grounds; some thought him unfit for office. These tensions came to the fore in the debate over federal land policy in the west. The westerners chafed against what they saw as an already too great federal role in their land—much of which was owned by the federal government. These fights spilled over into the appropriations process, whereby prominent western representatives sought to slash the budgets of key federal land agencies and added legislative language to key spending bills that would have placed restrictions on executive power over land use issues.

At the same time, the White House was under pressure from environmental advocates not to back down. But with his opponents in control of the Congress the President's options seemed limited. He did, however, have a few tools in his toolbox—including the Preservation of America's Antiquities Act of 1906. The Antiquities Act gave the President unilateral authority to foreclose development and other harmful activities on federal lands. Knowing full well that there would be a political outcry from the west, and in the face of potentially negative electoral consequences for his party, the President nonetheless set aside huge tracts of federal land throughout the region. This was the state of environmental politics in 1907.

History has now validated the political courage shown by Republican President Theodore Roosevelt a century ago as being in the best interests of his and future generations. President Roosevelt's designations allow Americans to enjoy a natural heritage that includes places such as the Grand Canyon—which some at the time thought would make a perfectly nice lake. Almost a century later, and facing virtually identical circumstances, President Bill Clinton, a Democrat, would demonstrate the very same type of political courage in using the Antiquities Act to protect vast tracts of land. History is likely to render a similar verdict.

These actions by Teddy Roosevelt and Bill Clinton could simply be viewed as examples of far-sighted leadership in the face of strong opposition. On the other hand, the fact that these issues remain so politically controversial today—just as they were a century ago—suggests that the American political system has done a very good job in making what should be relatively easy decisions hard.

Getting to the third rail

The compelling moral obligation to provide economic security to our senior citizens, as well as being assured return on one's life-long contributions to the system, make social security among the most sacrosanct of American political issues; attacking social security is like touching the third rail of the subway line—it will kill you. Social security is so pervasive in its political popularity in the US that it really has become more than just bi-partisan—it is truly non-partisan. One might come up with a number of reasons for this cross-party popularity. Social security benefits a vulnerable segment of the population, addresses economic interests, fills a moral obligation to take care of older people and it works. There is no overt and hard-working anti-social security lobby that rounds out the typical bi-polar model of interest-group politics. The political debates about social security are only around the edges—virtually everyone is 'for it'. In the case of social security, real-world values and priorities manifest themselves as top political priorities.

But the connection between real-world values and political priorities is not always rational or proportional. Environmental issues suffer from great disparity between their importance in the real world and their priority in American politics. One could make a compelling argument that environmental and natural resource conservation issues are, quite simply, the most important issues that we as a society face today. Anyone who has ever been ill knows the powerful truth behind the notion that little else matters if one is not healthy. The air, water and natural ecological balance upon which life depends is the 'health' of the world. Without it, not much else matters.

Yet as policy-makers go about their political election-cycle to election-cycle life they tend to focus less on long-term foundational issues than they do on the issues of current public focus. Issues that require long-term evaluation, and which yield benefits over long periods, often fail to gain priority in the short political attention spans of politicians and policy-makers. Environmental issues are consistently shown to be important in public opinion surveys, but rarely are they among the top two or three things on the minds of voters—despite their real-world relevance.

The failure of the pervasive relevance of environmental issues to be matched by political priority is as much as anything else a failure of interest-group politics. Only a fundamental shift from the old-style political tug of war over these issues can make the environment a truly unifying political issue.

Beware 'wooden nickels':
anti-environmentalism couched as 'reform'

There have been, of course, numerous claims to 'new' approaches to these issues. A recent example is the 'new environmentalism' of the incumbent Bush administration. Spearheaded by Secretary of Interior Gale Norton, the tenets of this so-called 'new' approach are to minimise procedural costs and delays of regulation, create a larger role for the private sector in carrying out environmental policy, and devolve federal authority and responsibility to states and localities. While there is considerable merit to these concepts, many critics believe that the administration's actions reflect a policy that is less about finding new ways to achieve environmental goals than it is about simply easing the impact of environmental policies on the private sector.

Pushed strongly in light of severe forest fires in the American west in 2001 and 2002, the administration's Healthy Forests initiative is billed as 'a good, commonsense piece of legislation that will make our forests more healthy, that will protect old-growth stands, that will make it more likely endangered species will exist, that will protect our communities, that will make it easier for people to enjoy living on the edges of our national forests'.[1] Yet the administration's plan also seems designed to address the long-held major frustrations and policy goals of the timber industry by limiting the procedural tools available to logging opponents and allowing increased access to timber in national forests—including the harvesting of older, fire-resistant (and more commercially valuable) timber far from the forests' interface with communities.

Similarly, the administration's Clear Skies initiative is promoted as an effort to 'aggressively reduce air pollution from electricity generators and improve air quality throughout the country' by setting new limits on sulphur dioxide, nitrogen oxides and mercury.[2] While these limits appear new and stronger than the status quo, they are part of a package of clean air rules that respond directly to top industry concerns, forestalling other pending proposals that call for tougher limits for these pollutants *and* for new restrictions on greenhouse gas emissions, and rolling back regulations that require anti-pollution upgrades to older power plants otherwise exempted from clean air regulations (Ballentine and Mazurek 2002).

The Bush administration clearly seems to believe that environmental values and economic priorities are necessarily in conflict, and that one must choose sides in a political fight between business and the environment.

A 'next environmentalism', on the other hand, might similarly pursue creative new approaches, a greater role for the private sector, and minimisation of conflict and costs. But it must, first and foremost, be based on the premise that environmental and conservation issues deserve the utmost primacy in our political decision-making.[3]

1   President George W. Bush, 21 August 2003, Redmond, OR.
2   *Clear Skies Fact Sheet*, www.whitehouse.org, accessed 14 February 2002.
3   The terms 'environmentalism' and 'conservation', and 'environmentalist' and 'conservationist', are used together here and sometimes interchangeably. As explained in detail later in this chapter, however, the terms have distressingly dissimilar connotations in the current politic. Bridg-

This chapter seeks to outline a new approach that will better vindicate that prem-ise by building a new 'middle-out' political imperative that utilises tools based on inclusiveness, ethics, responsibility, economic value, private-sector action, flexibil-ity and democratic principles.

The primacy of conservation and environmental well-being

There are numerous justifications for the political primacy of issues impacting the conservation of natural resources and a clean and healthy environment.

Economic well-being

A clean and conserved environment is a prerequisite to economic well-being. An atmosphere that moderates temperature, an ozone layer that protects from the sun's rays, insects that pollinate crops, water and air that cool industrial processes and disperse waste, and natural resources that allow workers to produce, are all fundamental to economic activity. Because of the historical abundance of this 'natural capital', it was once the case that economic wealth was curtailed only by the limits of 'human capital'. But in a paradigm shift, limits to wealth are now being caused by limits to natural capital (e.g. the amount of fish caught was once limited by the number of boats seeking them; it is now limited by the depletion of the stocks themselves) (Hawken *et al.* 1999: 3-6). Because of this bygone abundance, eco-nomic and political systems have often taken the supply of natural capital for granted—thus the market has historically 'priced' indispensable and irreplaceable natural inputs such as oxygen produced by plants at US$0. But 'price' and 'value' are not the same thing; a healthy environment is simply invaluable to economic activity.

Physical well-being

It is also increasingly clear that environmental health affects human health. In many ways, the modern environmental movement in the US gained broad following after public health incidents such as the release of toxins at Love Canal in New York during the 1960s. But the link between the environment and public health is not limited to isolated (and usually unlawful) occurrences.

It is now firmly established, for example, that air pollution (from legal vehicle and power plant emissions) exacerbates and may even cause childhood asthma, heart disease and respiratory illness (Willhelm and Ritz 2003; Natural Resources Defense Council 1999; Levy *et al.* 2002; Clear the Air/Physicians for Social Respon-sibility 2002; Clean Air Task Force 2000). One study found that exposure to air

ing that divide is one of the keys to improving the political primacy of all the issues associated with these terms.

pollution doubles the chance of a child growing up in Los Angeles developing cancer later in life (National Environmental Trust 2002), and another study found that exposing children to particle soot can harm their lungs as much as smoking (University of Southern California Keck School of Medicine and the National Institute of Environmental Health Sciences 2001). Further, the predicted temperature and humidity increases of global warming models track the increasing range of infectious diseases such as West Nile Virus (Shen 1995). And, while no one has completely explained the widespread growth of Lyme Disease over the second half of the 20th century, some scientists suggest that a key factor may be human interference with the ecology of the Passenger pigeon. These formerly ubiquitous birds, travelling in flocks of millions, were wiped off the face of the Earth by habitat destruction and over-hunting. Passenger pigeons loved to eat mast acorns and, with populations in the billions, they ate quite a few of them. Other connoisseurs of these nuts are mice whose population increases in eastern deciduous forests have been linked to Lyme Disease. Take away a few billion acorn-eating birds and it's great news for acorn-eating mice (Heal 2000: 109).[4]

While being at the top of the food chain certainly has it advantages, humans are dependent on many pieces of an increasingly fragile and always complex foundation of environmental health. As E.O. Wilson has famously said about microbes: 'We need them, but they don't need us' (Wilson 1992).

Religion and faith

Environmental and conservation issues are also increasingly being adopted as priorities by religious communities. While certainly some interpretations of the world's major monotheistic religions hold that the natural world was given to 'Man' by 'God' for our 'use', strong conservation ethics and respect for nature permeate sacred text. In the scripture, a Jewish prayer quotes God: 'This is a beautiful world I have given you. Take care of it; do not ruin it.' The archetypal prophet of the Old Testament warned: 'Woe unto them that join house to house, that lay field to field, till there is no place that they may be placed alone in the midst of the Earth.' (Isaiah 5:8). Similarly, fundamental concepts of Islam teach that the natural world has been given to the living in trust and that we have sacred responsibilities of stewardship (Gardner 2002: 14).

An ecumenical array of clergy and religious persons has long been present in the debates over the environment, and that trend is broadening in the US. The National

---

4   This also recalls an anecdotal lesson of the dangers of interfering in the natural balance and the clumsy attempts we have made at repairs. Amory Lovins gave a speech at the US Environmental Protection Agency a few years ago entitled 'How to Not Parachute More Cats'. After a significant malaria outbreak in Borneo in the 1950s, the World Health Organisation (WHO) came up with a solution—spray DDT everywhere to kill the mosquitoes. Soon thereafter, the roofs of the homes of the local Dayak people began to collapse. It turned out that the DDT also killed a species of wasp that preyed on thatch-eating caterpillars. DDT also entered the food chain; geckoes ate the poisoned insects and the local cats ate the geckoes. Soon the cats died and the local rats flourished, bringing with them increased threats of typhus and plague. Again, the WHO had a solution. With the help of the British Royal Air Force, they parachuted 14,000 live cats into Borneo (Wolbarst 2001).

Council of Churches has joined with the Sierra Club in running public media campaigns aimed at influencing issues such as oil drilling in the Arctic. The Inter-faith Center for Corporate Responsibility (ICCR) represents nearly 300 Protestant, Catholic and Jewish institutions and seeks to promote corporate environmental stewardship through the strength of its institutional investments. The interfaith National Religious Partnership for the Environment seeks to position environ-mental protection fundamentally as a religious challenge. The Vice President of the World Jewish Congress has stated that: 'It is our Jewish responsibility to put the defence of the whole of nature at the very centre of our concerns' (Gardner 2002: 31). Evangelicals have formed the Evangelical Environmental Network which has aggressively entered the policy-making arena in Washington with well-funded lobbying campaigns aimed at issues such as preservation of the Endangered Species Act (Gardner 2002: 27).

Perhaps what is most important about these efforts is that they are decreasingly seen as extracurricular: for the people of faith involved, environmentalism is central both to their faith and to their religious duty. Increasingly, environmental and conservation issues could become a core tenet of the political ideology (and theology) of the religious right, left and middle. And as they do, the political rele-vance of the religious voter in environmental policy disputes will only increase.

Spirituality

As president, Theodore Roosevelt held an historic White House conference on con-servation in 1907 attended by 45 state and territorial governors, the President's Cabinet, all nine Justices of the Supreme Court, numerous Members of Congress, and a wide array of scientists, professionals, activists, academics and trades people. In addition to reflecting Roosevelt's oft-stated tenet that conservation is 'a national duty', the gathering's core theme was that the use and development of the 'natural endowment' must be subject to both human and spiritual constraints (Morris 2001: 516).

Many persons who might not label themselves 'religious' certainly consider themselves 'spiritual', and the spiritual value of the natural world outside of any organised religion also has a long and strong tradition. Indigenous cultures past and present have had both cultural and spiritual connection to the fecundity of the natural world. When Aldo Leopold (1949) wrote: 'There are some people who can live without wild things and some who cannot', he most certainly was referring to the latter's need for 'spiritual' completeness. To Ralph Waldo Emerson (1836), nature was almost a spiritual aphrodisiac: 'In the presence of nature a wild delight runs through the man, in spite of real sorrows.' The spiritual importance of the natural world to Emerson, Leopold, Muir and Abbey is not felt so differently by millions of hunters, anglers, gardeners, hikers, climbers and bird watchers. The natural world is an essential part of who they are.

Moral responsibility

But the importance and primacy of conservation and environmental issues comes as much from an obligation to others as from fulfilment of one's own needs. In the keynote address of the White House conference on conservation, President Roosevelt reminded the attendees that all they would discuss was within 'the great fundamental questions of morality' (Morris 2001: 516). The moral obligation to following generations has long been a major theme of environmental thinking and of the conservation community especially.

The first director of the Forest Service, Gifford Pinchot, was keenly aware of the intergenerational equity of preserving our natural world (Millar 2001: 153-54):

> The central thing for which conservation stands is to make this country the best possible place to live in both for us and our descendants . . . conservation of natural resources is the key to the future . . . and the key to the safety and prosperity of the American people, and all people of the world, for all time to come.

As Edmund Morris recounts, Pinchot's boss, Theodore Roosevelt, consistently exhibited a similar view, believing that 'government can both serve [current generations] and conserve, and that future generations had as much right to natural resources as contemporaries' (Morris 2001: 223). Certainly, his preservation of the Grand Canyon bears out such thinking. Speaking at a spot near the then threatened natural wonder, Roosevelt said (Morris 2001: 226):

> Leave it as it is. You cannot improve upon it. The ages have been at work on it and man can only mar it. Keep it for your children, your children's children, and for all who come after you.

Stewardship on behalf of future generations has always been a core tenet of the conservation movement. Now, as even more fundamental questions of the state of the world's endangered species, threatened ecosystems and changing climate present themselves, the moral obligations that the present generation feels toward its children and its children's children may become more relevant than ever to the politics of the environment.

Cultural, family and traditional American values

Despite the fact that terms such as 'family values' or 'American values' have become loaded (and perhaps diminished) phrases in the American political lexicon, to large portions of the population they retain core political resonance. Thus, for example, agricultural subsidies gain political support in part because of the resonance of the need to support 'family farmers', conjuring sympathetic images of 'American gothic' even in those far removed from actual farms or farmers.

While images and values of America's natural heritage, frontier romanticism and rural traditions certainly are of importance, even to the city dweller, the natural world is simply a central component of life to many Americans. Just as it is an iconic American rite of passage for a father in The Bronx to take his son to a Yankees' baseball game, in the Northeast Kingdom of Vermont or in West Texas, it is no less central to family, tradition, community and American values for a father to take his son or daughter bird hunting.

The family vacation to the beach, the Boy Scout or Girl Scout Jamboree at the state park, or summer camp at the lake, all depend fundamentally on environmental health. Across class and urban–suburban–rural divides, environmental values are part of family and traditional American values.

The broken politics of the environment today

Given the many and demographically cross-cutting reasons that environmental and conservation issues are important to so many people, a well-functioning representative democracy should efficiently translate such widespread core values into a message to policy-makers that they act against those values at their extreme peril.

The reality in the US today, however, is that a strong 'pro-environment' record is not seen as a political necessity by the majority of elected officials. Notwithstanding timely and localised issues, such as water contamination or a mill closing, relatively few elections are decided over environmental issues.

This lack of electoral urgency has contributed to the difficulty of making significant policy-making progress on environmental and conservation issues. Watershed achievements in the 1970s and '80s such as the Clean Water Act and the Clean Air Act are increasingly distant memories. Those proactive, bipartisan achievements were once the main focus of environmental and conservation advocates. Today, on the other hand, the legislative battles have become mostly defensive.

Environmental advocates have been able to gather enough support to defeat or delay some of the most egregious and/or charismatic challenges such as drilling off the beaches of Florida and California or the opening of the Alaska National Wildlife Refuge to oil exploration. Indeed, these are the types of issues that have helped environmental organisations raise money and that have had the most success breaking into the higher tiers of electoral messaging. But being forced onto the defensive on these big issues has extracted a price. First, because there is only so much political oxygen for the environmental movement and its supporters to consume, pulling out all stops to hold off Alaska drilling leaves less political capital to fight a myriad of lower-profile but nevertheless environmentally significant initiatives. The evidence for this effect in recent years includes slashed federal environmental budgets, the introduction of snowmobiles in Yellowstone National Park, derailed efforts to save the Florida Everglades, dolphins dying again in the nets of tuna fleets and global warming demoted to a mere research issue.

Second, of course, a defensive orientation makes assembling a sustained political majority to pass strong proactive measures all but impossible. For example, even with overwhelming evidence of climate change and a geopolitical dynamic that in stark terms demonstrates the relationship between oil consumption and national security, the environmental community has repeatedly failed to enact legislation to meaningfully increase US automobile fuel economy standards. The fact is that environmental advocates are increasingly on the defensive and decreasingly victorious.

What's gone wrong: the failings of traditional interest-group politics

If there are social, economic and moral superiorities to positions of environmental and conservation primacy, then it is all the more perplexing why environmental advocates are not winning more often. Certainly, well-meaning and hard-working environmentalists and conservationists have scored many important political victories that have bettered the world. And there will always be powerful interests aligned against environmental progress and priorities. But it shouldn't be this hard.

Born of crisis—schooled in regulation

The modern American environmental movement and many of its greatest environmental achievements were born out of crises. It is true that American waterways are cleaner than they were 30 years ago. But it is also true that it took highly publicised events such as the Cuyahoga River catching on fire to really bring the issue into political focus. Similarly, the chemicals used for pest control are less lethal than those in use in decades past. But it is also true that it took the foundation-rattling work of Rachel Carson (1962) and the near extinction of the bald eagle to drive a course-changing political consensus.

In many ways, the problems with today's political dynamic are a result of what was for many years a necessary and very successful policy response to these environmental challenges. Employing 'command and control' mechanisms, the federal and state governments addressed environmental threats through banning or limiting the use of certain substances and through company-level regulation aimed at requiring certain practices and forbidding or limiting others. To enforce these prescriptions and proscriptions, the government became investigator and prosecutor.

In part because it focused on the worst practices and most glaring problems, the command-and-control approach to environmental policy yielded great gains for the environment. It was also a boon to attorneys and private-sector compliance officers, as regulatory compliance and liability avoidance became bottom-line concerns for many businesses. Not surprisingly, the result was the development of a largely adversarial dynamic between those seeking environmental improvement (government regulators and environmental advocates) and the private sector. And, because it then saw environmentalism as a threat to the bottom line, company managers became very effective at convincing workers that they were equally, or at least derivatively, threatened by environmental controls.

Environment versus business

Thus, even for businesses that fully complied with all regulatory mandates, environmental 'values' were calculable only as costs to be minimised; there were few positive or profit incentives for environmentally preferable practices. One can then see how a political dynamic developed over these issues that pitted those who were for environmental values against those who sought to lower costs on business (and all the economic benefits to owners and workers that presumably go with that).

Today's oft-repeated mantra among modern environmentalists that there is no need to choose between the environment and the economy struggles against the command-and-control legacy which did, in fact, exact such trade-offs.

This is not say that there isn't great merit to the argument that compliance costs and non-compliance penalties incurred by businesses under a command-and-control regime are really just proxies for the uninternalised costs of pollution and other environmental externalities—one could argue that businesses were not really being burdened with 'added' costs; they were getting more accurate pricing information. Government-imposed compliance costs (such as waste-water treatment or exhaust gas treatment) and non-compliance penalties might be a bit of a rough proxy for these costs, but the basic point is sound: without regulation businesses were often getting something valuable for free (clean river water or clean air, for example). On the other hand, from a political perspective, this argument was useless; the politically relevant point was that businesses were being forced to pay for something they had not paid for before.

Demonisation, polarisation and partisanship

Consistent with a larger trend in American politics toward political polarisation and simplistic negative messaging, the adversarial history of environmental issues has created a political dynamic of a battle between the 'best' on the left and the 'worst' on the right. Each side paints the other in the most extreme light and seeks to add support along the political spectrum inward from their base on the right and left extremes. Yet, while this largely combative 'outside-in' approach is conducive to the dynamics of interest-group politics and modern political campaigns, it is alienating to the elected officials and critical electorate in the political middle.

The other result of such a dynamic is that it makes these issues more partisan than, ideally, they should be. With their diminishing intrinsic national relevance, political parties increasingly need differentiating ('wedge') issues. Thus, issues that might otherwise be best addressed by resolving marginal differences through measured dialogue and creative engagement become most effective to partisans when expressed in exaggerated (and often distorted) extremes. Therefore, one hears that Democrats care more about sucker fish than family farmers and that Republicans think children should have more arsenic in their diet.

In part because of electoral exaggeration and over-simplification, and in part because they have each earned it, the Republicans wear the anti-environmental label and the Democrats have the overwhelming support of environmentalists (with some geography-driven exceptions—the Democratic governor of Alaska wanted to drill in the Alaska National Wildlife Refuge and some north-eastern Republicans are among the most reliable environmental votes in Congress). But, particularly when it comes to national leadership, the two parties have indeed staked out clearly different places in the last 25 years. As manifested most clearly in the presidencies of Ronald Reagan and George W. Bush, the national Republican Party has often decided that more marginal political gain is to be had by subjugating environmentalists' concerns to what it sees as competing priorities. Democrats have felt more compelled to side with the most politically activist environmentalists when faced with competing requests from other interests.

But, while a partisan approach can be effective in winning some elections, it presents a problem for policy-making. Politically, the US is evenly split, so, if an issue is made partisan, it locks in roughly 50% support and 50% opposition. Due in part to parliamentary rules that make narrow majorities often inadequate, this can be a very effective model for an interest group looking primarily to prevent things from happening (e.g. the plaintiff's bar has been effectively used by the Democrats to block national tort reform legislation and the firearms lobby has successfully invested in the Republicans to block federal gun control). But a partisan strategy, even one with some exceptions, is not a good model for achieving proactive and enduring policy achievement, notwithstanding the fleeting years when one or the other party is firmly in control of the government.

The paradox of the grass roots and institutionalisation of advocacy

Another obstacle to proactive policy achievement for environmental and conservation issues is the nature of grass-roots advocacy. The grass-roots constituents of any interest group tend to be the most ideological. This is not surprising, since grass-roots support is often developed by disseminating the strongest and most ideologically infused messages. But, while grass-roots mobilisation gives leverage to advocates in Washington, it also ties their hands. Once the would-be deal-makers have used the grass-roots strength to push initially for the strongest and often overly optimistic starting position (standard negotiating strategy), it is difficult to fall back to an otherwise attractive resolution of a dispute that would serve the cause of the environment lest they lose credibility with (or incur the wrath of) the grass roots.

The competition among environmental groups for the same grass-roots and donor support can also prevent the strategic compromises that would best serve the environment. Industry trade associations are notorious for being poor negotiators because often one or two intransigent corporate members can hold back the association from taking any forward-leaning positions that might result in a deal: this is known as the 'lowest common denominator' phenomenon. Environmental groups, on the other hand, are sometimes susceptible to a 'highest common denominator' dynamic, as one group is reluctant to move off the 'moral high-ground' and risk the ire of the grass roots and competition of colleague groups.[5]

Further, partisan aims and the need to meet organisational fundraising goals can lead advocates to prefer failure over the resolution of an issue that may be less than ideal, but might still represent real progress. Advocacy groups do their best fundraising when their issues are unresolved and under threat. Sometimes this approach can end up being the best for the environment in the long run as more sympathetic office holders get elected; but often it is not. And, given that many environmental problems are irreversible (such as species extinction or cutting an old-growth forest), this is a risky and high-stakes approach.

---

5   Liberals like to call themselves 'progressives', and indeed many are. But the true meaning of 'progressive' is one who seeks and achieves progress. An all-or-nothing, perfect-to-the-exclusion-of-the-good approach to policy-making may have many virtues and labels, but 'progressive' is not one of them.

Byway bubbas and beltway elites

Political consensus building is more difficult when interest-group leaders are geographically and culturally disconnected from the people and communities affected by their actions. The US environmental community arguably suffers from this phenomenon more than most interest groups. First, when compared to other progressive interest groups (such as labour, for example) the leadership of the environmental community is disproportionately made up of white, urban elites. This may not provide the best basis for truly identifying with the many stakeholders in environmental politics who are from rural communities, the lower–middle class or who hunt, fish, farm, build cars, build houses, drive trucks or otherwise live and work in a very interconnected way with the environment. Many in this segment of the population do have an innate concern about environmental issues, but they also often face fundamental concerns about job security, paying for their children's education or ensuring their parents' welfare in old age. This cultural disconnect can make it more difficult for national environmental leaders to marshal this large and politically powerful segment of the population behind environmental priorities.

The political split among 'environmentalists' and 'conservationists' is a related obstacle to elevating environmental issues to political primacy.[6] Many hunters and anglers, while proud to call themselves 'conservationists' are just as strongly loath to call themselves 'environmentalists'. And, as one edge of the environmental movement tends to overlap with another edge of the animal rights movement, it is not surprising that there are tensions with the hunting and angling communities. The environmentalists, in turn, often refer to field sports enthusiasts derisively as 'the hook and bullet' crowd and suspect them of lacking true commitment beyond ensuring that there are animals to shoot and fish to catch.

This split is not new. John Muir (the founder of the Sierra Club) and Gifford Pinchot (first director of the US Forest Service) argued famously over whether lands should be managed for the 'public good' or whether strict preservation was the only true 'conservation'. Nor will all substantive and philosophical differences ever be completely eliminated, as there will always be principled disputes over issues such as the appropriate degree of management of lands and ecosystems. These substantive differences in philosophy, however, are minuscule when compared to the interests these two communities share: clean water, clean air, open space, and healthy ecosystems. Unfortunately, these would-be allies have largely been unable to exploit their common ground and form effective coalitions, largely because of differing political allegiances.

The leadership and funders of the environmental community have, overall, much closer ties to liberal, urban Democrats. Culturally and politically, the 'hook and bullet' community has found much more in common with rural, conservative and often Republican policy-makers. These allegiances are not always in the best interests of conservation. While some hunters and anglers may be more comfortable working with a Member of Congress who talks like them, they are not getting much for that commonality when that Member turns around and votes for

---

6   Again, the terms have been used somewhat interchangeably here even though there can be distinct substantive distinctions. For example, the amount of arsenic deemed acceptable in drinking water is an environmental issue, but it might not be considered a conservation issue.

decreases in conservation budgets, for easing of development limitations in important habitats or otherwise sides with those promoting measures that negatively affect fish and wildlife.

A major cause of these partisan alignments is the politics of guns. In pursuit of partisan gain, the gun lobby and its champions in Congress have stoked paranoia and fear among hunters and driven them across the political divide away from moderates and Democrats. Some Democrats, similarly, have sought political gain in demonising guns and gun owners in sometimes quite broad terms. The result is a culture of mistrust and political oversimplification that leads many conservationists who are also gun owners to support politicians who do not otherwise support a conservation agenda. On the other side, by dismissing and alienating hunters, the environmental community has both failed to appreciate the undeniable contributions hunters have made to the environment and greatly marginalised its own political influence.

The next environmentalism: minimising conflict and maximising progress

In his second term, President Bill Clinton repeatedly articulated a vision of environmental policy that at the time was somewhat radical: that the old 'big idea' (as he liked to call it) that the environment and the economy are in conflict was no longer true. He believed that advances in knowledge, technology and experience meant that we really could have both, and that true progress would only be achieved on contentious environmental issues such as climate change if we abandoned the old 'big idea' and adopted a new one. But President Clinton was not describing a new political reality as much as he was articulating a vision of environmentalism that was within reach but not yet at hand. He believed in a new approach to the politics of the environment where values that have been seen as being in conflict in fact become reinforcing, and where collaboration and progress would replace conflict and gridlock.

The next political dynamic for achieving consensus and progress for environmental and conservation issues should be based on four foundational notions:

1. The protection and conservation of the environment is a policy priority of the highest order.

2. It is the role and responsibility of democratic government to establish strong and enforceable goals and policies to vindicate those priorities.

3. Meeting environmental mandates should be as inexpensive, simple and attractive as possible; but non-compliance should be costly.

4. Political consensus should come from a broad and diverse coalition grounded in the political middle.

1. Invoke and build on all bases of political primacy

All of the bases for the political primacy of environmental and conservation issues discussed above should be understood and invoked in support of political progress:

- **Responsibility and patriotism**. Leaving behind a clean and healthy environment is a basic responsibility we owe to our children and to future generations.

- **Religious, ethical and spiritual values**. Stewardship of God's creation, a 'land ethic' and spiritual importance of natural places support strong action to protect and conserve.

- **Recreational, cultural and family values**. A clean and healthy environment is central to the lives and families of the millions who hunt, fish, hike, bike, bird-watch or otherwise enjoy the outdoors.

- **Human health**. Human health is directly tied to clean air, clean water and safe and nutritious food.

- **Direct and indirect economic well-being.** Countless industries and jobs depend directly on conservation and environmental protection (tourism, agriculture, outdoor recreation products, firearms, etc.); virtually all others depend in some fundamental way on healthy and abundant 'natural capital'.

2. Set strong and achievable government standards

Because of these diverse and powerful justifications, setting strong national priorities and standards for conservation and environmental protection is a legitimate and high-priority role for government. When setting 'tough' standards and goals, policy-makers should be guided by several principles:

- **Seek achievability and durability**. The writer Arthur C. Clarke once observed that people tend to overestimate what can be done in the short term and underestimate what can be done in the long term. Proponents of strong environmental protection sometimes ask for too much too fast, while opponents forecast dire consequences of even moderate steps. Environmental policy objectives should be realistic and achievable while furthering true public values and discounting the incumbents that portend economic ruin. They should seek *progress* through achievable, sustainable and enduring policies that further environmental and conservation values. These values are not well served if standards cannot be met or cannot get set in the first place.

- **Welcome and invoke cost–benefit analysis**. Famously, or apocryphally, in the mid-1980s, the then Office of Management and Budget director, David Stockman, was said to have used cost–benefit analysis to kill a proposed acid rain programme. In a decisive briefing for President Reagan, Stockman followed a detailed and impassioned presentation in support of the programme by Environmental Protection Agency (EPA) director William Ruckelshaus with a simple chart that showed the total cost of the programme, the number of fish predicted to be saved and the resulting price per fish. Stockman won the argument and the proposal was killed. The current Bush administration's Office of Management and Budget has promised a renewed rigour in subjecting government proposals to cost–benefit analysis.

Environmental advocates often find themselves on the defensive end of arguments about costs and benefits. In part this is because, historically, economic and cost–benefit analyses either excluded or discounted both externalised costs and non-pecuniary benefits.

Few would argue that increased asthma rates cannot be translated into economic costs. But neither could many argue that the father who grew up fishing with his dad in the healthy lakes of the Adirondack Mountains of New York but cannot pass that tradition on to his children is paying a price; or that a family visiting Monticello today looking out at the Blue Ridge Mountains and seeing only a fraction of what Jefferson saw has not paid a price. For values that cannot easily be quantified, some would assign them the value of zero—the only number that is certainly wrong.

Indirect, non-pecuniary and hard-to-measure values can and should be made central to such analyses, because policy-making is ultimately a political and not a scientific exercise. Cost–benefit analysis in this context is simply a way of better understanding choices and making political decisions. Such analyses serve the policy-maker only if they take into consideration the greatest number of relevant factors, factors that may or may not be easily reduced to traditional economic analysis. When cost–benefit analysis is done correctly, 'markets', 'price', 'efficiency', 'optimality' and 'cost' can become part of the lexicon of the proponents of tough of environmental and conservation policies.

- **It's better to pick winners than losers**. Opposition to the government setting tough standards or rules is sometimes expressed in the hollow mantra that government should not pick 'winners and losers', despite the fact that making choices that affect people and markets is a central role for democratic government. For example, the US government decided that DDT was a 'loser'; it taxes tobacco and alcohol more heavily than it does baby food; US-flagged and US-crewed vessels can sail coastwise within the US but foreign-flagged vessels cannot. Presumably, such policies are designed precisely to favour or disfavour particular products, constituencies or industries because their favour or disfavour serves larger values and goals. In order to value clean air and clean water it may be precisely the goal of policy-makers to set rules and standards that will favour private-sector actors, technologies and practices that help reach those goals.

Furthermore, government policy that favours an economic non-incumbent over an incumbent is not necessarily an inappropriate usurpation of a market 'winner', since such an argument assumes that the incumbents were not themselves made 'winners' by direct or indirect acts of government. Such incumbent-sustaining government actions might be direct subsidies (such as oil depletion allowances) or indirect benefits (such as the military expenditures made to secure a stable flow of oil from the Middle East). Policies designed to further some environmental objective (such as subsidising research and deployment of alternative fuels) may not represent a new governmental interference in the marketplace as much as simply making a different choice.

3. The carrot and the sword—make compliance cheaper, easier and more attractive and make non-compliance costly

With the possible exception of lawyers and consultants, everybody wins when costs and burdens of meeting environmental and conservation goals are minimised. In fact, reducing the costs and burdens allows the setting of even stronger goals and standards than would otherwise be possible. Much of the energy and political capital of environmental protection have been spent catching and punishing cheaters. This is important, but from the perspective of environmental values it is, perhaps, more important to meet goals in the first place.

Thus, a new paradigm by which the design of environmental and conservation policy might metaphorically be understood as replacing the 'cattle prod' of command-and-control regulation with policies that incentivise and reward sound environmental practices yet threaten significant consequences for non-compliance. Representative government should decide what results are expected, minimise the burdens of meeting those goals (in part by minimising its own role), and render significant consequences if the goals are not met. This combination—the 'carrot' of incentives and cost minimisation, and a 'sword of Damocles' approach to enforcement—can rectify market failures, minimise private-sector costs and limit direct government intervention to disciplining the bad actors.

This is not the current model. Some environmental advocates equate flexibility and concern for private-sector costs as a weakening of environmental goals. The current fight over how to clean up old power plants is a fine example. The Clean Air Act, as interpreted and applied by the EPA, sets source-specific limits on emissions of some harmful pollutants from power plants and prescribes the investments, technologies and other remedial measures that must be taken by plants violating those limits. Thus, the government stipulates not only what the level of pollution should be but also dictates how to get there.

This is a classic command-and-control approach. Although it has bred conflict and litigation it has also achieved some very real improvements in air quality. But, by focusing so heavily on the 'control' side, the EPA and its supporters have in fact joined polluters in making the government's role the focus of the debate, such as whether EPA fairly interprets environmental legislation, and the economic costs of government-mandated microeconomic decisions. Instead, the focus of the debate should be on the 'command' (i.e. clean air), which is much harder for polluters to argue against. A better model and a better result would be for governments to set tough requirements for *all* harmful pollutants, establish a reasonable but aggressive time period for compliance, perform relatively non-intrusive monitoring functions, reduce compliance costs with tools such as emissions trading, but otherwise get out of the way. Even if the goals and standards are tough, reducing the costs and obstacles to meeting them while keeping the costs of failure significant would allow the private sector to figure out how to get to the desired result.

Energy expert Amory Lovins of the Rocky Mountain Institute likes to say that 'markets make a splendid servant, but a bad master and a worse religion' (Wolbarst 2001: 117). Market forces and market efficiencies are a tool, not an end. Encouraging the use of market mechanisms, such as emissions trading, and recognising that the private sector (once properly incentivised) is probably better than the government at figuring out how it can comply does not by any means suggest that the government should also let the market choose the objectives. Governments set the standards; markets help meet them. A true 'third way' approach to regulation neither exhibits slavish deference to markets nor relies on post hoc regulatory reversal of market results to achieve environmental and conservation goals.

A number of tools can be employed to better harness market forces and efficiencies in pursuit of environmental and conservation goals. While politically unpopular, many economists advise that the most efficient way to align economic and environmental incentives is often through the tax system. The infamous 'BTU (British Thermal Unit) tax', once pushed by the Clinton administration, was one politically clumsy but arguably bold and meritorious attempt to internalise the externalised costs of energy production and consumption. M. Jeff Hamond (1997) at the non-profit public policy organisation Redefining Progress has called for a more dramatic taxation approach that would create economically and environmentally preferable incentives by substituting taxes on work (payroll taxes and some income taxes) for taxes on 'waste' (i.e. inefficiencies such as emissions or over-consumption of public goods such as air and water). He argues that, fundamentally, we should be taxing the things we don't want more of (such as pollution) and taxing less the things we want more of (such as savings and income). The result, he persuasively argues, could be lower and more progressive taxes, greater wealth and greater environmental progress.

Besides direct taxation, other tools can lower costs, harness market efficiencies and vindicate environmental and conservation goals. Major steps have already been taken in the right direction by 'commoditising' environmental value in the form of things such as emission credits that can be bought, sold, borrowed against or donated. There may be future opportunities to apply these mechanisms to forest protection, water conservation and quality, and open-space conservation.

And, because the corollary to putting a more accurate price on environmental costs is that environmental improvements will create value, the next generation of policies can move toward the 'securitisation' of this value so that it is directly reflected in the price of capital and the value of enterprises. The fact that one out of every eight US dollars invested in the stock market today flows through some sort of 'socially responsible' screening shows that investors are willing to pay a higher price for equities reflecting non-traditional economic value. Even with the current mis-pricing of intangible environmental values, research further suggests that those companies that outperform their peers on a host of environmental metrics also tend to outperform them on traditional economic metrics (Coalition for Environmentally Responsible Economies 2002). Corporate managers and investors are beginning to realise that environmental performance is about more than avoiding costly fines; it is a source of value in itself.

However, for some environmental priorities, the profit motive alone could be enough to bring about real progress. Clean energy and environmental technology companies, economists, some environmental groups and former Vice President Al Gore have argued that vast economic opportunity lies in the wake of aggressive policies that will encourage investment in, and development and sale of, environmental technologies of all sorts. According to the President's Committee of Advisors on Science and Technology (1999), between now and 2050 the market in developing countries for new energy technologies will likely approach US$15–25 trillion, and that much of that market could be exploited by companies promoting clean, advanced technologies. The enticing conclusion is that we can make money, create jobs and solve environmental problems all at the same time—there is no need to choose between economic or environmental health. The political facility of promoting policies and investments to take advantage of such markets is clear and it is surprising there has not been more consensus and action to exploit such opportunities.

There are shortcomings to this 'get rich environmentalism', however. For example, it only works for some environmental challenges. Environmental policies that incentivise increases in energy efficiency (such as limitations on greenhouse gas emissions) can increase wealth on a net basis by creating new markets for energy efficiency technologies and saving money for the purchasers of the technology who reduce their energy expenses and, perhaps, sell emission reduction credits. But we might not be able to save the yellow-eared parrot from extinction by selling US-made technologies of one sort or another.

Furthermore, 'get rich environmentalism' is ultimately an industrial policy and not an environmental policy, and it would be a dangerous mistake to substitute industrial policy values for environmental and conservation values. It is true that new markets and economic opportunity can be a by-product of sound environmental policies; but that is not necessarily *why* we pursue them. President Clinton did not urge abandonment of the old ideas of conflict solely because it would lead to more economic prosperity. At the heart of his vision was an ethical foundation based on the recognition that it is the responsibility of our generation and our leaders to solve these problems; and it might not be as difficult as we thought.

Environmental advocates need not necessarily look at private-sector profit motives as obstacles to the fulfilment of environmental and conservation priorities. The private sector is, in many ways, the biggest potential ally in reaching those priorities. By better internalising costs and better aligning profit and environmental and conservation goals, more can be accomplished more quickly than by most other policy approaches. Such an approach can eliminate incentives for cheating, reduce government oversight and enforcement expenses, and bring private-sector efficiencies to the fight for the environment.

4. Build a broad and diverse coalition starting from the political middle

Tapping into varying yet reinforcing values and utilising creative, market-harnessing policy tools are important elements in establishing political primacy for conservation and environmental protection. But, grafted onto today's failed interest-group dynamic, these steps are not enough.

Again, consider the politics of social security. The foundation of its political support broadly straddles the political centre; the only 'battlegrounds' are well to the right (complete privatisation) and well to the left (a welfare-like wealth transfer system) rather than in the political middle. This is a recipe for political stability. For conservation and the environment, on the other hand, there are two centres of gravity (neither of which has any real likelihood of achieving firm political incumbency): on the right are the largely well-funded special interests inconvenienced by environmental protection and extreme 'property rights' ideologues, while on the left are the 'beltway elites' channelling the anger of grass-roots advocates in pursuit of goals that are often unrealistic in the current political milieu. The political middle, instead of being the calm foundation of political consensus, is constantly squeezed by both the left and right. Each side continues to court the edges of the middle on an issue-by-issue basis, occasionally pulling enough to their side to win marginal political victories.

If, on the other hand, those that favour strong environmental and conservation goals built a consensus at a fundamental level from the centre, and targeted incremental political progress outward toward the right and left of centre, the true opponents of environmental values could be severely marginalised.

- **Reconnect with natural allies.** The first step in this process is to bridge the gap between those natural allies who are already politically engaged. Speaking to the politically moderate Democratic Leadership Council several years ago on the frustrations of the environmental community with some Democrats, President Clinton said: 'You cannot expect any Members of Congress who come from rural districts that have a lot of poor people, or that rely on agriculture, to take a different approach [on environmental issues] unless there is a specific, clear and meaningful alternative that they can embrace.'[7] If such Members are forced to choose between the preferences of the Sierra Club and the Chamber of Commerce, that will be a tough choice for many. If, on the other hand, these Members are presented with a choice between the preferences of the National Mining Association on the one hand and Ducks Unlimited, the National Wild Turkey Federation or the Bass Anglers Sportsmen's Society on the other, the odds of environmental progress improve.[8]

7   Internal White House transcript.
8   Some discount the political importance of hunters and anglers by citing data that suggest the number of sportsmen and sportswomen in America is declining. First, even if that is true, they tend to be most populous in 'swing' political states and districts, and, second, the difference in outcome on environmental and conservation issues has proven to be quite small and a marginal change in political strength could make an enormous difference.

- **Focus on the real adversaries.** When parts of the traditional environmental community and more moderate conservationists can come together and bridge cultural differences, political histories and long-brewing animosities, the result could be to isolate those that threaten conservation and environmental protection. And this is possible. For example, there is growing agitation in the Rocky Mountain West with the destructive practices associated with coal bed methane extraction. Anti-development environmentalists have made an effort to reach out to non-traditional allies. One die-hard Republican rancher embroiled in this debate in Wyoming commented: 'Ranchers have never truly thought much of tree-hugging environmentalists, but with these methane boys on our land, we are starting to see these environmentalists as conservationists who want to help us preserve land for our kids' (*New York Times* 2002). Presumably, the environmentalists are also starting to see land owners or land users such as ranchers as critical conservation allies.

  In the Gunnison Valley of Colorado, long-time adversaries from the ranching and environmental communities have come together to fight developers and home builders. By working together to raise money for the purchase of conservation easements on family-owned ranch land, ranchers have been able to resist the temptation to cede their land to unbridled development and keep the land and their way of life for their children, while pleasing the field sports fraternity by preserving wildlife habitat. The ranchers sell the development rights to their land to a non-profit entity which holds the easement. Without development potential, the value of the land is greatly decreased, along with the ranchers' property taxes. In turn, the ranchers agree to certain stewardship practices such as streamside buffers and habitat creation for species such as the threatened Blue Grouse. This approach works because some environmentalists are able to table their desire for outright land acquisition and seek conservation progress in the face of very real environmental threats. It also works because of smart and creative federal policies such as the Farmland Protection Programme, which provides federal support for the purchase of such easements.

- **All environmental politics are local.** A common thread, and important lesson, from these two examples is that environmentalists, conservationists and non-traditional allies came to together at the *local* level. Environmental advocates will need to do a better job of encouraging local involvement, input and flexibility to build a politically powerful consensus. At a meeting of stakeholders to discuss the George W. Bush administration's plans to reconsider the Clinton administration's rule setting aside 56 million acres of national forest from road construction and other development threats,[9] a self-described socialist member of the Green Party and county commissioner from Colorado surprised nearly everyone in the

---

9 An act *The New York Times* called perhaps the greatest conservation achievement in modern history.

room by lambasting the rule and Clinton administration—not because he didn't support the protection of roadless areas, but because of what he saw as an even more egregious threat: the failure of the federal government and national environmental groups to adequately involve local communities in decision-making. As stated in a 1996 report by the President's Council for Sustainable Development (1996): 'Creating a better future depends in part on a knowledge that involvement of citizens [is critical] and on a decision-making process that embraces and encourages different perspectives of those affected by governmental policies.'

When a broad array of local stakeholders are courted and involved on behalf of strong environmental policy measures, whether in the form of federal or state law and regulations, there will likely be a more powerful political will for progress.

- **Cultivate new allies.** The final task is to broaden the coalition by reaching out to other allies who have not been politically active, who may be uncomfortable with the extremism of both sides to these debates or who may not fully understand the stake they have in the disposition of these issues. Specialist groups such as bird watchers, skiers, scuba divers and the industries that support them, as well as Boy Scouts, Girl Scouts, Garden Clubs and other politically significant groups can be better integrated in the political fabric of conservation and environmentalism. They have much more in common than differences. There is a fundamental commonality in the importance of environmental stewardship, but great dissimilarity in culture, style and methods. Again, groups such as gun owners are enormous potential political allies for conservationists and environmentalists. An approach using education, science, consensus-building and policy tools to attract broad support, so helping to solidify the political middle, can bring about fundamental political realignment.

Ultimately it will take successes to bind a broad coalition together and turn it into an unmovable political centre that demands political primacy for environmental and conservation issues. The conflict-oriented approach of the past and present is no longer yielding progress. The 'next' approach to environmental issues should be fundamentally about making *real* progress and getting beyond the gridlock of interest-group politics.

References

Ballentine, R., and J. Mazurek (2002) 'Clear Skies, Cloudy Climate', *Blueprint Magazine*, December 2002.

Carson, R. (1962) *Silent Spring* (New York: Houghton Mifflin).

Clean Air Task Force (2000) *Death, Disease and Dirty Power: Mortality and Health Damage Due to Air Pollution from Power Plants* (Boston, MA: Apt Associates).

Clear the Air/Physicians for Social Responsibility (2002) *Children At Risk* (Washington, DC; www.psr.org).

Coalition for Environmentally Responsible Economies (2002) *Value at Risk: Climate Change and the Future of Governance* (New York: Innovest Strategic Value Advisors Inc).

Emerson, R.W. (1836) *Nature*.

Gardner, G. (2002) 'Invoking the Spirit: Religion and Spirituality in the Quest for a Sustainable World', *WorldWatch Paper* 164 (December 2002).

Hamond, M.J. (1997) *Tax Waste, Not Work* (San Francisco: Redefining Progress).

Hawken, P., A. Lovins and L. Hunter Lovins (1999) *Natural Capitalism* (New York: Little, Brown).

Heal, G. (2000) *Nature and the Marketplace* (Washington, DC: Island Press).

Leopold, A. (1949) *A Sand County Almanac* (Oxford University Press).

Levy, J., S. Greco and J. Spengler (2002) *Health Impacts of Air Pollution from Washington DC Area Power Plants* (Cambridge, MA: Harvard School of Public Health, prepared for the Clean Air Task Force).

Miller, C. (2001) *Gifford Pinchot and the Making of Modern Environmentalism* (Washington, DC: Island Press).

Morris, E. (2001) *Theodore Rex* (New York: Random House).

National Environmental Trust (2002) *Toxic Beginnings: A Lifetime of Chemical Exposure in the First Year* (Washington, DC: National Environmental Trust).

Natural Resources Defense Council (1999) *Toxic Air Pollution: Risk of Top Carcinogens in Major Metropolitan Areas* (Washington, DC: Natural Resources Defense Council).

New York Times (2002) 'Ranchers bristle as gas wells loom on the range', *New York Times*, 29 December 2002: A1.

President's Committee of Advisors on Science and Technology (1999) *Powerful Partnerships: A Synthesis of a Report by the President's Committee of Advisors on Science and Technology* (Washington, DC: US Government Printing Office).

President's Council on Sustainable Development (1996) *Sustainable America: A New Consensus for Prosperity, Opportunity and a Healthy Environment for the Future* (Washington, DC): ch. 4; clinton2.nara.gov/PCSD/Publications/TF_Reports/amer-top.html.

Shen, S. (1995) 'Global Warming Elucidated', *World Resources Review* 7.1: 9.

University of Southern California Keck School of Medicine and the National Institute of Environmental Health Sciences (2001) 'Respiratory Effects of Relocating to Areas of Differing Air Pollution Levels', *American Journal of Respiratory and Critical Care Medicine*, December 2001.

Willhelm, M., and B. Ritz (2003) 'Residential Proximity to Traffic and Adverse Birth Outcomes in Los Angeles County, California, 1994–96', *Environmental Health Perspectives* 111.2: 207-16.

Wilson. E.O. (1992) *The Diversity of Life* (Cambridge, MA: Harvard University Press).

Wolbarst, A.B. (ed.) (2001) *Solutions for an Environment in Peril* (Baltimore, MD: The Johns Hopkins University Press).

3
Building environmental management systems focused on sustainability
THE INFLUENCE OF EMPLOYEES, COMPANY LEADERS AND EXTERNAL STAKEHOLDERS

Deborah Rigling Gallagher
Duke University, USA

> We are a new facility. We're brand new, starting from scratch. [And], we already have more than 100 standards to comply with. We are calling them 'technical guidelines'. We have a matrix with the owner of the programme—Environmental Protection Agency, state, county, city—and dates. We look each week, see what's coming up and see where we'll be. We saw the environmental management system as a tool that would help.
>
> *Environmental Engineer at Lambda Systems*

Facilities such as Lambda Systems face an ever-growing set of environmental rules and regulations. They increasingly rely on environmental management systems (EMSs) to build a path to compliance and beyond. In response, researchers have begun to examine EMSs. For example, Hamschmidt and Dyllick (2001) found that firms implementing EMSs have differing expectations of their potential benefits. Biondi *et al.* (2000) found that small and medium-sized enterprises (SMEs) implementing EMSs face barriers such as lack of environmental management skills. Kitazawa and Sarkis (2000) described the link between EMS implementation and continuous improvement of source reduction activities. In an exploratory study of New Zealand plastics firms Corbett and Cutler (2000) established that the existence of a total quality management programme prior to EMS implementation is beneficial. The link between EMS use and managerial goals in US firms (Switzer *et al.* 2000), its use on Native American reservations (Evers 2000) and the advantages to Brazilian firms of employing ISO 14001 (Maimon 2000) were described in Hillary 2000a. Hillary (2000b) linked SME use of EMSs with environmental benefits. Melnyk *et al.* (2003) found operational performance benefits due to implementation of ISO 14001 EMSs.

Internal and external benefits of EMS adoption (Rondinelli and Vastag 1996; Darnall *et al.* 2001) include increased employee involvement, improved document control, reduced regulatory surveillance and improved customer satisfaction. Morrow and Rondinelli (2002) examined US and German firm motivations to adopt EMSs and discovered that US firms were motivated to integrate systems, to improve regulatory performance and reduce costs, whereas German firms implemented EMSs to motivate employees, better document environmental impacts and reduce energy use. Chin and Pun (1999) found that firms implementing EMSs in the Hong Kong printed circuit board industry did so to improve environmental performance and obtain competitive advantage.

Researchers have also analysed the link between stakeholders and EMS implementation. EMSs have been shown to affect external stakeholder relationships positively (Tack 1999). External stakeholder expectations for EMS implementation (Bouma and Kamp-Roelands 2000), such as improved environmental performance and reduced environmental incidents, have been described. However, Freimann and Walther (2002) examined existing research on EMS implementation and concluded that more research is needed to discover the effect of organisational culture and broad stakeholder involvement on EMS outcomes such as progress toward sustainability. Indeed, to date, while EMS use increases, limited research has been conducted to explain the influence of stakeholder involvement on EMS design. This study, which examines data from a five-year study of US facilities implementing EMSs, responds to that need.

Environmental management systems

Businesses began using EMSs in the late 1980s to help them: comply with regulations; develop data for permit applications; identify, minimise and manage environmental risks; and achieve higher levels of environmental performance (NDEMS 2003; Florida and Davison 2001; Rondinelli and Vastag 2001; Chan and Li 2001). EMSs, like all quality management systems (Hackman and Wageman 1994), are designed to increase employee awareness of and involvement in environmental issues, and to create a culture focused on minimising environmental impacts.

Several templates are available to firms designing EMSs, including industry frameworks such as the American Chemical Council's Responsible Care programme and the American Forest and Paper Association's Sustainable Forestry Initiative. Beginning in the 1990s, several standards organisations developed EMS guidelines, as did the European Union (the EU Eco-Management and Audit Scheme [EMAS]) and in the British Standards Institution (BS 7750). The International Organisation for Standardisation (ISO) developed the ISO 14001 EMS framework in 1996 in response to a call for harmonisation of existing EMS standards. Currently it is the most widely adopted EMS standard, with over 36,000 organisations worldwide certified to date (ISO 2002).

The facilities participating in the research described herein developed EMSs using the ISO 14001 framework which includes five basic components: policy; plan;

implementation strategy; monitoring and corrective action system; and management review. With its 'closed loop' structure, in which data on performance is frequently monitored to update procedures, the ISO 14001 EMS framework provides a systems approach to continual improvement of environmental management practices. It also emphasises external communication and stakeholder involvement.

An ISO 14001-based EMS typically includes procedures to identify and manage the environmental impacts of operations, conduct facility inspections, measure and monitor impacts, keep records and report progress to facility management and regulatory agencies. ISO 14001 EMSs also include strategic components such as the facility's overall environmental policy, its long- and short-term environmental goals, targets and objectives and descriptions of personnel and management structures and processes to work with external stakeholders (Gallagher 2002). Finally, ISO 14001 EMSs incorporate the influences of internal and external stakeholders.

Stakeholder influences on EMS design

Internal stakeholders, such as employees, and external stakeholders, such as regulators, customers and local community members, may be involved in EMS design. Employee involvement in design and implementation of environmental management programmes increases the chances of programme success (Ramus and Steger 2000) and may be linked to increased environmental performance (Wehrmeyer 1996). As a total quality management programme derivative, ISO 14001 encourages the involvement of employees (Deming 1993). For example, Kitazawa and Sarkis (2000) found that greater benefits of ISO 14001 EMS implementation are realised when employees are involved. The ISO 14001 framework encourages the involvement of external stakeholders such as local community members in EMS design. As a minimum, organisations developing ISO 14001 EMSs must make their respective environmental policies available to external parties. External stakeholder involvement in EMS development is a significant strategic resource, increasing a facility's competitive posture (Delmas 2001).

In this study, a stakeholder theory perspective (Freeman 1984; Mitchell *et al.* 1997), is used to examine EMS design processes. Stakeholder influences have been shown to affect the development of specific EMS types (Gallagher forthcoming). EMS design is a form of first-order organisational change (Fox-Wolfgramm *et al.* 1998) in which modifications are made to existing environmental management programmes. Internal stakeholders such as facility leaders and boundary-spanning employees (Egri and Herman 2000), and external stakeholders such as regulators, customers and local community members, play a significant role in such change processes. In this study, evidence is presented to demonstrate how stakeholder influences within specific organisational contexts influence EMS design outcomes.

Methods

This study examines the influences of internal and external stakeholders, such as employees, regulators, customers and local community members, on ISO 14001-based EMS design outcomes at 41 US facilities, encompassing the electronics, metal finishing, chemical manufacturing, government operations and energy sectors. Survey and case-study data was used to determine the types of EMS designed, and to identify and describe stakeholder influences.

Data sources

Survey data

In 1996, the Multi-State Working Group (MSWG) was formed to examine the impact of EMSs on environmental performance. The US Environmental Protection Agency (EPA) funded a research programme, which included MSWG member-state EMS pilot programmes, the development of data collection protocols and a publicly accessible database, the National Database on Environmental Management Systems (NDEMS).

Data was collected from 83 facilities in 13 states through a series of three research protocols: baseline, EMS design and update. Baseline data included retrospective information about the three-year period prior to EMS adoption. EMS design data included descriptions of how facilities designed and implemented their EMSs. In addition to qualitative responses to a series of survey questions, facilities were asked to provide primary facility data on activities and associated environmental aspects and impacts, and on EMS objectives and targets. Quantitative data on EMS design costs and benefits was also provided during this phase. Update data included information on post-EMS implementation environmental and economic performance. Data collection protocols are available on the NDEMS project website.[1]

Three Microsoft Access databases were built to allow for data analysis. Once data was received from the facilities and entered into the databases, a detailed data quality control process was undertaken to verify collected data. This study was based on data from 41 NDEMS facilities, for which complete data was available at the time.

Case study data

Data was also acquired from case studies of nine facilities, selected to represent a cross-section of facility size, location and industry sector. This data was acquired to view facility-specific EMS design processes in greater detail and to present a fuller picture of how a variety of stakeholders in a variety of facility settings may influence EMS design. In this study three facility case studies were employed. Two (termed Kappa and Gamma) had participated in NDEMS as pilot facilities from MSWG member states. A third (Sigma) was recruited independently.

A case study protocol (Yin 1994), also available on the project website, outlined how facility tours were to be conducted, how participants were to be selected, what

1 ndems.cas.unc.edu

supporting EMS documentation was to be gathered, and which questions were to be asked of each interviewee. Employees at multiple levels within each facility, chosen to represent a specific step in the facility hierarchy, from worker to senior management, were interviewed at each site.

A team of two interviewers conducted the interviews, which were tape-recorded and transcribed. At each facility a minimum of five employees were interviewed. After conducting the interviews, researchers toured the facility and collected EMS policies and procedures, training manuals and progress reports.

Data analysis

Survey data

In this study, NDEMS survey data was analysed according to two EMS design dimensions: environmental management goal and nature of internal and external stakeholder involvement. These two dimensions are components of a three-dimensional EMS typology (Gallagher 2002), designed to serve as a strategic reference point (Fiegenbaum and Hart 1996) for facilities seeking to improve environmental performance through EMS use.

EMS objective/target data was analysed to determine the environmental management goals of facilities designing EMSs. Objective and target data describe the projects and programmes that facilities consider important for addressing environmental impacts. Objective/target pairs differed across facilities both in terms of the number included in the EMS (some facilities listed just five pairs while others had over a hundred) and in terms of environmental management focus.

To address these differences, facility objective/target pairs representing environmental management goals were coded on a continuum from compliance, through pollution prevention, eco-efficiency, product stewardship and, finally, environmental sustainability. These codes represent a progression of environmental management capabilities (Hart 1997). Facilities progress through environmental management stages as they acquire knowledge of, and experience in, managing environmental issues and as environmental goals move from conformance to voluntary (i.e. from compliance with regulations to reduction of environmental impacts) (Sharma 2000). For example, facilities first use environmental management capabilities to achieve compliance with regulatory requirements. Once compliance procedures have been put in place, facilities begin to reach higher, to articulate voluntary and proactive goals, the first of which is pollution prevention (Hart 1995; Christmann 2000).

As the company gains knowledge about the impacts of resource use on both its bottom line and the environment, eco-efficient processes, which use input resources cost-effectively and maximise production value, are employed (Ehrenfeld 2000). Next, facilities are poised to examine the environmental impacts of their products and services and, finally, to look towards environmental sustainability by addressing issues such as generational trade-offs and quality of life for local community members and workers (Hart 1997).

Three coders independently examined each facility objective/target pair. Coders then met to discuss the coding results and resolve any differences. Coders made identical coding decisions approximately 90% of the time and in all cases were able to agree on a coding decision. After individual objective/target pairs were coded according to the continuum described, facilities were assigned an overall environmental management focus, which reflected the highest-order objective/target pair listed. For example, a facility that listed three compliance-focused objective/target pairs—two focused on pollution prevention and one on eco-efficiency—was coded as designing an EMS with an overall environmental management focus on eco-efficiency. This progression was supported within the data—not one of the 41 facilities skipped a step in this environmental management goal hierarchy. (Gallagher 2002).

Data on stakeholder involvement was obtained from NDEMS survey responses and case-study protocol questions about the nature of participation in the EMS design process. Similar to the environmental management dimension, stakeholder involvement data was coded as a progression. This progression began with facilities whose EMSs are designed solely by in-house environmental health and safety (EHS) staff. Next in the progression, EHS staff and managers jointly design the facility's EMS. As facilities incorporate additional stakeholder input, EHS staff, managers and non-management employees are involved in EMS design. Following this, EHS staff, managers, non-management employees and formal non-governmental organisation (NGO) representatives design EMSs. Finally, at the last point in the progression, EHS staff, managers, non-management employees, formal NGO representatives and unaffiliated individuals, design the EMS. This progression accounts for the increasing sophistication of facilities in seeking the advice and counsel of actors outside its core EHS group whereby a broader sphere of external influence is incorporated (Freeman 1984). Facilities beginning EMS design depend on EHS staff and regulators. As a facility gains experience, non-EHS management employees from, for example, engineering, utilities, quality and human resources may be involved. Next, facilities involve non-management employees with knowledge of facility production. Finally, facilities seek input from external stakeholders (Gallagher forthcoming).

In this study, facilities were assigned an overall stakeholder involvement focus based on the highest order of stakeholder involvement reached. If a step in the hierarchy was skipped, the facility was assigned a focus based on the highest order of stakeholder involvement before that step. The use of such a path-dependent coding scheme is largely supported within the data: the three facilities that skipped a step within the hierarchy were required by their state pilot programme managers to incorporate external environmental group input into their EMS design, and did so without first involving non-management employees. These facilities were coded as influenced by non-EHS management employees.

Once each facility was assigned an environmental management and stakeholder involvement focus, patterns of stakeholder involvement/environmental management focus pairings were detected using a cluster analysis procedure. Facility EMS goal and stakeholder involvement scores were input into an agglomerative hierarchical cluster analysis procedure using Ward's method (1963) in which each facility, identified by its scores, begins as an individual cluster. Squared Euclidian distance between cluster centres are then measured and compared. Clusters are merged iteratively to minimise the increase in the total sum of squares of the distances between cluster centroids. Cluster formation continues until all facilities are associated with a single cluster. Facilities were found to cluster into three distinct EMS types (Gallagher 2002).

Case-study data

A common format guided the translation of transcribed notes into individual facility case studies, which were then reviewed by facility interviewees for accuracy and to increase the validity of findings. Case-study data collected from interviews, survey responses, archival sources and documentation was organised into a singular searchable database using QSR N5 software (Richards and Richards 1994).

Findings

EMS types

Three types of EMSs were evident in the sample of 41 facilities, referred to here as 'middle roaders', 'efficiency experts' and 'visionaries'. Twenty-two facilities designed middle-roader EMSs, 16 designed efficiency-expert EMSs and just three designed visionary EMSs.

Middle roaders

Environmental management goal
Middle roaders focused on compliance and pollution prevention. Most middle roaders' environmental management programmes consisted of pollution prevention planning or waste minimisation techniques before building their EMSs. EMS development was a way to build environmental management capacity within the facility. For the middle roader, the EMS was a means to achieve and maintain compliance, and to focus on pollution prevention through activities such as waste minimisation and recycling. Table 3.1 shows middle-roader objective/target pairs from the NDEMS database.

Stakeholder involvement
Most relied heavily on EHS staff augmented in some cases by consultants and state technical assistance programmes. Few sought help from facility managers and non-management employees. Some 20% of middle roaders reported that their EMS was designed wholly by the environmental manager with no other input. As one such manager explained, 'it was difficult to get employees involved in the [EMS] development process when the production schedule was so great'.

Efficiency experts

Environmental goals

Efficiency experts designed EMSs incorporating systems and procedures to increase the eco-efficiency of production processes. Eco-efficient processes use input resources, such as electricity and water, cost-effectively and maximise production or product value while minimising resource use and adverse environmental impacts.[2]

These facilities consistently complied with environmental rules and regulations, and had long relied on pollution prevention plans to achieve waste minimisation, recycling and resource substitution goals. Three-quarters of efficiency expert facilities had employed waste minimisation practices and pollution prevention planning for at least eight years, and over half had used compliance audits for over ten years. A third of the facilities had employed total quality management or best management practices for more than seven years and half had long used materials accounting practices. Table 3.1 shows examples of objective/target pairs included in efficiency expert EMSs.

Stakeholder involvement

Facilities building efficiency-expert EMSs emphasised an internal focus on efficiency rather than stakeholder inclusion. Efficiency experts engaged EHS staff and facility managers but did not involve non-management and external stakeholders in EMS design. Prior experience in environmental management, such as life-cycle accounting and compliance auditing, was leveraged and knowledgeable EHS staffs were relied on.

Corporate staff and customers also influenced EMS design at efficiency-expert facilities. One environmental manager described his facility's process as being 'shepherded' by corporate management, saying: 'Corporate environmental, health and safety staff led the . . . effort with input from various departmental experts.' If non-management employees were involved in EMS design, it was often after EHS staff and management had completed most of the upfront work. External stakeholder groups were rarely involved in efficiency-expert EMSs.

Visionaries

Environmental goals

Visionary facilities designed EMSs to achieve product stewardship and environmental sustainability goals. Like middle roaders, compliance and pollution prevention goals were incorporated and, like efficiency experts, eco-efficient process goals were included in visionary EMSs. However, they went farther by focusing on product stewardship and on impacts beyond the facility's boundary. Unlike some efficiency experts, visionaries did not necessarily possess long-standing environmental management programmes to build on in designing their EMS. One visionary facility had employed an environmental manager for just two years prior to developing its EMS. At this facility, prior environmental management programmes had included best

---

2 See 'Eco-efficiency', World Business Council on Sustainable Development, wbcsd.ch/ecoeff. htm, accessed 13 November 2000.

management practices, pollution prevention planning and compliance audits. Another facility's prior practices consisted only of life-cycle analyses and environmental reporting. However, these facilities used the opportunity of developing EMSs to incorporate ambitious goals. Examples of visionary facility objectives are described in Table 3.1.

Stakeholder involvement

Visionaries built their EMS with help from EHS staff, managers, non-management employees and external stakeholders. At one visionary facility, the environmental manager reported that 'an environmental committee was formed consisting of a member or members from each department and from the operator level to the foreman and manager level'. The environmental manager described the benefits of having such a team design an EMS: 'very interesting opportunities came up during the discussion . . . the operators and other people brought up some great points about the facility's operations that the facility had not commonly known before'.

One manager described the entire staff as being involved in an 'effort by breaking into small groups to determine objectives and targets'. Some visionaries used external auditors to measure the adequacy of their EMSs and provided opportunities for community groups to review audit results. Visionaries saw their EMS as a means of critically examining processes and products, and of considering impacts beyond the facility boundary.

EMS type	Objective	Target
Middle roader	50% reduction of inventory and/or use of hazardous chemicals in the R&D lab	Determine which chemicals can be reduced or eliminated
Middle roader	Obtain zero NPDES violations due to monitoring frequency criteria	Reduce number of violations by 50% from the previous year
Efficiency expert	Reduce energy use based on annual budgets	Achieve 10% reduction per engineering department budget
Efficiency expert	Reduce energy costs	Increase employee awareness of utility costs
Visionary	Reduce air emissions	Increase vehicle mileage 5% by 2002 through reduction on idling time of vehicles
Visionary	Flexible work hours	Schedule operations staff based on ten-hour shifts, thus reducing the number of commutes by 10%

NPDES = National Pollutant Discharge Elimination System

TABLE 3.1 Examples of facility objective/target pairs

Summary of EMS types

Middle roaders, efficiency experts and visionaries each focused on a unique set of environmental goals and involved a unique set of stakeholders in EMS design. Each type met the challenge of EMS development by leveraging their enthusiasm and experience in environmental management. For middle roaders that experience was limited, for efficiency experts it was long-held, and for visionaries enthusiasm mattered most

Middle roaders, the largest group identified in this study, represented a significant type of facility-level EMS. They were relative novices to environmental management and, for them, the EMS was a means of maintaining compliance, addressing relatively simple environmental management problems and, in the process, achieving cost savings. This EMS type is one to watch over time to determine if an EMS with its systematic focus on continuous improvement and external communication increases environmental management capabilities and provides opportunities for stakeholder involvement.

Efficiency experts also represented an important EMS type. They sought to build their EMS as efficiently as possible, and thus did not often involve non-management employees or external stakeholders in EMS construction. Efficiency experts focused on maintaining compliance, continuing pollution prevention progress and achieving greater production value by implementing eco-efficient processes. In building their EMSs, efficiency experts took advantage of internal environmental management capabilities and their long-standing experience in implementing environmental management techniques.

Finally, for visionaries, the process of designing an EMS served as an opportunity to gather together the collective expertise of environmental staff, facility managers, non-management staff and external stakeholders. This expertise was used both to examine the environmental impacts of their operations and to design a system that reached beyond compliance, pollution prevention and eco-efficiency objectives to tackle the difficult issues of product stewardship and environmental sustainability. These EMSs not only incorporated objectives and targets to achieve compliance, prevent pollution and increase the eco-efficiency of processes but also included objectives to address, for example, wider issues such as the effects of employee commutes and landscaping plants. Visionaries represent the environmental leaders that transform ecocentric values into organisational actions (Egri and Herman 2000). Table 3.2 shows the EMS types found in this study.

Case studies

Three case studies of middle-roader, efficiency-expert and visionary EMS design experiences are presented below. Their names are disguised to provide confidentiality. In each case study, physical setting, production processes, and facility strategy and structure are first described. Physical setting and production processes are described to show the operational challenges each facility faced in designing its EMS. Descriptions of facility strategy and structure are presented to show the role

EMS type	Environmental goals	Stakeholder involvement
Middle roader	Compliance and pollution prevention	EHS staff, regulators and consultants
Efficiency expert	Compliance, pollution prevention and eco-efficiency	EHS staff, management employees, corporate staff and customers
Visionary	Compliance, pollution prevention, eco-efficiency, product stewardship and sustainability	EHS staff, management employees, non-management employees, regulators and local community members

TABLE 3.2 EMS types

that interactions between and among employees, managers and external parties played in influencing EMS design efforts. Finally, the influences of stakeholders on the facility as it designed its EMS are summarised. Table 3.3 highlights the case study findings.

Facility	EMS type	Setting and products	Strategy and structure	Stakeholder influences on EMS design
Kappa Energy Technologies	Middle roader	Rural New England; energy transformers	Pollution prevention emphasis; small EHS staff manages programmes	Environmental group, vice president, quality manager, consultant
Gamma Industries	Efficiency expert	Rural south-east; photographic chemicals	Compliance and pollution prevention stressed; corporate oversight and total quality management	Environmental engineer, state regulator, facility and corporate leadership
Sigma Resources	Visionary	Suburban south-west; computer components	Environmental leader; teamwork and knowledgeable employees	Facility and corporate leaders, employees at all levels, regulators, local community members

TABLE 3.3 Case study summary

Middle roader: Kappa Energy Technologies

Kappa Energy Technologies (KET)'s EMS was designed with limited environmental management expertise and limited involvement outside of its small EHS group. The EMS focuses on compliance, pollution prevention and increased employee environmental awareness.

Physical setting

KET is a mid-sized manufacturer of energy distribution transformers located in a small, mostly rural community in northern New England. Initially a stand-alone private company, KET, while still privately held, has become a member of an international holding group of companies headquartered in Europe and with manufacturing facilities located across the globe. The company employs 350 people in manufacturing, assembly, research and development, and technical services.

Production processes

KET's production processes are organised into ten activity centres. Besides office support activities, KET's operations and facilities include materials procurement, product base manufacturing, laminating, a supply centre, product fabrication, shipping, recycling, maintenance and janitorial, and a laboratory. Two boilers provide energy. Base manufacturing, laminating and product fabrication are the heart of KET's production activities. These operations take pulp and fibre to produce fibreboard in a process similar to pulp and paper manufacture, but without toxic chemicals. Base components are laminated using compounds such as styrene and acetone. Laminated sheets are fabricated into energy distribution transformers. Boilers, base making, laminating and product fabrication make the most significant contribution to KET's environmental impacts. A small research laboratory tests product quality and recommends changes to inputs and production processes. Paper, plastics, metal scraps, laminated board scraps and other production by-products are collected for recycling.

Facility strategy and structure

For 30 years KET has emphasised compliance and pollution prevention. Because of KET's location in a region known for its unspoiled environment and environmental advocates, KET's philosophy has been to minimise waste products and to recycle as much as possible. Managers stress cost savings achieved through hazardous waste reduction. KET is concerned about maintaining and enhancing its environmental image and improving environmental performance. The company's formal environmental policy commits it to raising employee environmental awareness through training and communication, exceeding regulatory requirements, minimising pollution and achieving cost savings. The policy was developed by KET's environmental and safety manager, quality assurance engineer and laboratory chemist, with review and approval from the executive management committee.

Environmental activities at KET are managed by a small group of mostly professional employees, primarily the environmental manager, recycling shop operator and laboratory chemist. Most employees don't consider environmental issues in the workplace a primary concern, although many would consider themselves environmental advocates. KET's managers view the EMS as a means of increasing employee responsibility, accountability and involvement. As the company's total quality management system recently became certified to ISO 9000, KET managers felt that a systems approach to environmental management would be beneficial.

Influences on EMS design

KET's EMS design team was most influential. Information from training sessions and advice provided by a consultant influenced the core team's work. KET's new vice president, who had come to his job from one of the company's major customers, also played an important role. He raised environmental awareness and was an ardent EMS supporter and cheerleader for the team's efforts. Prior quality management systems experience also influenced EMS design. KET's quality engineer, an EMS design team member who had experience with ISO 9000 certification, influenced the development of a highly structured EMS.

Efficiency expert: Gamma Industries

Gamma Industries' EMS addresses compliance and pollution prevention and focuses on the efficient use of natural resources and energy. Gamma's EHS staff and facility management designed and implemented the EMS, with limited advice from non-management personnel. Gamma did not seek input from community stakeholders during EMS development.

Physical setting

Gamma Industries is a publicly traded, wholly owned subsidiary of Gamma Corporation, a large multinational headquartered in Tokyo. Gamma employs 350 people in a highly automated manufacturing facility. The company has won environmental performance awards from state regulators.

Production processes

Gamma manufactures photographic paper and emulsions. Three main production processes are employed: emulsion manufacturing, where the light-sensitive emulsion is prepared; coating, where it is applied to paper sheets and dried; and packaging, where coated paper is sized and packaged for shipment. Photographic emulsion manufacturing and paper coating processes have the potential to produce air and water emissions. Packaging processes have the potential to generate significant solid and hazardous waste. Utility boilers and chemical and hazardous waste handling also create environmental impacts.

Automated computer-controlled technology is used throughout Gamma's processes. Production rooms are controlled to offer specific environmental conditions. A tracking system is used to account for all chemicals used in manufacturing. The facility houses its own technical support centre for both quality assurance and some research and development activities.

Facility strategy and structure

Gamma makes local decisions on day-to-day operations through a management review board made up of senior managers. International headquarters' staff oversee long-term strategy and approve significant changes in production processes. Gamma's Japanese headquarters required all facilities to develop ISO 14001-certified EMSs. Gamma's EMS was the first to become certified to ISO 14001 and was used as a model for other US facilities within the company.

Employees are supported by numerous training and educational opportunities. They are encouraged to engage through regular participation in 'involvement teams' to exchange ideas and to take new jobs within the company to learn more about its operations. Gamma operates under a total quality control philosophy which relies heavily on statistical analysis of production data to improve effectiveness.

Gamma's environmental policy stresses compliance and pollution prevention, and provides guidance to Gamma employees on their environmental management responsibilities. Gamma's environmental and quality systems engineer and corporate environmental manager developed the policy, which was approved by senior management.

Influences on EMS design

Local and corporate senior management influenced EMS design at Gamma. Top management's influence came in two forms: first, the corporate directive to construct an ISO 14001-certified EMS and, second, the corporate philosophy of minimal sharing of information with parties outside the facility. The latter influenced the level of stakeholder involvement in Gamma's design process. Gamma's local president strongly supported the EMS efforts and participated in its design.

A state environmental agency employee who spent multiple days per week on-site teaching employees about EMSs and providing advice to the environmental group was critical to Gamma's design. However, the strongest influence on Gamma's EMS design was the environmental engineer. He shepherded the process, recruited employees to the environmental group and designed over 80% of the EMS.

Visionary facility: Sigma Resources

Sigma Resource's EMS design process engaged employees and external stakeholders to make its environmental vision a reality. Sigma involved management and non-management employees in EMS design and invited the public to participate. Sigma looked beyond compliance, pollution prevention and eco-efficiency to incorporate product stewardship and environmental sustainability goals in its EMS.

Physical setting

Sigma Resources is a large division of an international computer, networking and communications products manufacturing company. Located in the US south-west on the outskirts of a fast-growing city of just under 200,000, it manufactures semi-conductors and provides regional management and logistics support to the larger corporation. Sigma employs over 9,000 people on a 720-acre site.

Production processes

Sigma focuses on semiconductor assembly, testing and product development. Related functions include packaging development and design and marketing. Semi-conductor manufacturing requires large amounts of ultra-pure water and produces significant amounts of waste chemicals, particularly ethylene glycol and nitrates. To help supply the water needed for its operations, Sigma installed reverse osmosis processes to treat and re-use process water and has begun to re-use water from the on-site waste treatment processes, reducing water consumption by half.

Sigma's semiconductor manufacturing processes also generate volatile organic compound (VOC) air emissions. Cleaning and maintenance operations generate large amounts of solid and hazardous waste. Waste streams are hard-piped from manufacturing clean rooms to the facility's waste treatment plant.

Facility strategy and structure

Sigma's parent corporation is considered a world leader in environmental affairs and has produced an annual environmental report since 1992. Corporate environmental management programmes are headquartered at the Sigma site. Five employees provide on-site environmental management support, but all of Sigma's personnel are responsible for the environmental impacts of their activities as 'owners' of their processes. Individual environmental responsibility, described by one manager as 'cleanliness and leadership', is stressed, as is accuracy and zero tolerance of defects. Sigma's environmental programmes rely on teams, consistent environmental processes and employee awareness.

Influences on EMS design

Sigma's employees, from managers to waste management technicians, influenced the design of its environmental management programmes and EMS. Employees' environmental knowledge, enthusiasm and sense of personal responsibility as environmental stewards shaped Sigma's EMS.

Corporate environmental affairs staff and management played a role in guiding the development of Sigma's EMS. Corporate staff used tools such as benchmarking to assist in EMS design. Environmental staff applied knowledge gained from participation in environmental and trade organisation seminars. Local community members and regulators provided input. Finally, corporate environmental staff and company senior management communicated a clear vision that Sigma would continue to be an environmental leader.

Discussion

This study examined the EMS design efforts of 41 facilities in multiple sectors across the US. It explained how employees, company leaders and external stakeholders influence facilities to build distinct EMS types. To do so, environmental management goals and levels of stakeholder involvement were categorised. Facility objectives and targets were analysed to place EMS goals on a continuum from compliance to sustainability. Survey data describing the efforts of internal and external stakeholders was analysed to place facilities on a continuum of involvement beginning with in-house EHS staff and culminating in interaction with non-affiliated local community members.

Results showed that three distinct types of EMSs were designed: middle roaders, efficiency experts and visionaries. Middle-roader facilities possessed little experience in environmental management before designing their EMS. They built systems focused on compliance and pollution prevention with input primarily from their own EHS staff, consultants and regulators. Non-management employees and external stakeholders were rarely involved in designing middle-roader EMSs.

Efficiency-expert facilities possessed significant environmental management experience before designing EMS, having employed tools such as life-cycle analysis, environmental cost accounting and pollution prevention planning. They designed EMSs focused on the efficient use of resources such as water and energy, with input from EHS staff and facility management. Similar to middle roaders, non-management employees and local community members had little or no involvement in the design of efficiency-expert EMSs.

Finally, visionary facilities built EMSs focused on product stewardship and sustainable practices. But these facilities did not necessarily possess significant environmental management expertise prior to EMS design. They built EMSs with input from a diverse group of stakeholders, from EHS staff and management employees to non-management employees and local community members.

Implications for practitioners and policy-makers

Overall, results indicate that stakeholder influences are important in EMS design. While facilities may begin the EMS design process with varied levels of environmental management expertise, that expertise can be leveraged through interactions with a broad group of stakeholders to design EMSs focused on sustainability. Some facilities with limited systems-based environmental management experience, but who reached out to internal and external stakeholders, were shown to incorporate sustainability considerations, such as employee commuting or product life-cycle impacts into their EMSs.

The implications for public policy and for management practice relate to the importance of engaging stakeholders in EMS development, with companies encouraged to reach out to a diverse group of internal and external stakeholders. For example, the inclusion of local community members contributes a perspective on environmental impacts well beyond the production processes themselves. Factory floor workers provide practical knowledge of how impacts can be managed. Policy-makers can assist in increasing stakeholder engagement by creating links between facilities and external stakeholders and by providing opportunities for technical assistance and employee training.

Limitations and future research

This study is limited in two respects. First, due to the manner in which facilities were enlisted to participate in the NDEMS study, a likely environmental performance bias exists in the sample. State managers recruited facilities using two primary criteria: a record of high-level environmental performance and potential to benefit from technical assistance and training programmes. Thus, participating facilities were interested in improving their existing environmental management pro-grammes. This bias restricted opportunities to examine how facilities with limited environmental management experience and a focus on achieving basic compliance would be influenced by stakeholder participation during EMS design.

This study was also limited in time-frame. While it took place over a five-year period, the first year or so focused on establishing baseline environmental perfor-mance, the second and third years followed the EMS design process and the fifth examined post-EMS design performance. This time-frame was insufficient to exam-ine how EMSs and EMS design processes may have changed over time as facilities gathered more experience and expertise in systems-based environmental manage-ment. For example, the three EMS types examined in this study may represent a progression of environmental management practices from compliance to sustain-ability, with middle roaders representing facilities closer to a concentration on compliance and visionaries representing those approaching a sustainability focus.

Future research can build on the results of this study and address its limitations. While this study did not show facilities evolving from one EMS type to another, future researchers can consider whether an EMS progression occurs and, if so, how and why. Do facilities move from middle roader to efficiency expert to visionary as they gain EMS design and implementation experience and as they benefit from increased stakeholder influence? Do facilities incorporate more far-reaching envi-ronmental goals in their EMS or include a larger variety of internal and external stakeholders in EMS modifications as time progresses? Or do facilities design one type of EMS using a specific process and then stabilise, and in doing so fail to take advantage of the EMS's promise of continual improvement? In addition to stake-holder involvement and experience with systems-based management, factors such as facility leadership and organisational learning capacity, which may influence facilities to design increasingly far-reaching EMSs, can be considered.

Finally, research efforts can focus on examining the environmental management practices and EMS design efforts of 'laggard" facilities—those struggling to achieve or maintain basic compliance or those uninvolved in EMS pilot programmes and far removed from efforts to incorporate sustainable practices. By examining the use of EMSs in this under-studied population and the influence of stakeholders on them, researchers could contribute to an understanding of how facility-level progress toward sustainability can occur.

References

Andrews, R.N.L., N. Darnall, D.R. Gallagher, S.T. Keiner, E. Feldman, M. Mitchell and D. Amaral (2001) 'Environmental Management Systems: History, Theory and Implementation Research', in C. Coglianese and J. Nash (eds.), *Regulating from the Inside: Can Environmental Management Systems Achieve Regulatory Goals?* (Washington, DC: Resources for the Future): 31-60.

Biondi, V., M. Frey and F. Iraldo (2001) 'Environmental Management Systems and SMEs: Motivations, Opportunities and Barriers to EMAS and ISO 14001 Implementation', *Greener Management International* 29: 55-69.

Bouma, J.J., and N. Kamp-Rowlands (2000) 'Stakeholders' Perceptions of an Environmental Management System: Some Exploratory Research', *The European Accounting Review* 9.1: 131-44.

Chan, K., and X. Li (2001) 'A Study of the Implementation of ISO 14001 Environmental Management Systems in Hong Kong', *Journal of Environmental Planning and Management* 44.5: 589-601.

Chin, K., and K. Pun (1999) 'Factors Influencing ISO 14001 Implementation in Printed Circuit Board Manufacturing Industry in Hong Kong', *Journal of Environmental Planning and Management* 42.1: 123-35.

Christmann, P. (2000) 'Effects of "Best Practices" of Environmental Management on Cost Advantage: The Role of Complementary Assets', *Academy of Management Journal* 43.4: 439-58.

Corbett, L.M., and D.J. Cutler (2000) 'Environmental Management Systems in the New Zealand Plastics Industry', *International Journal of Productions and Operations Management* 20.2: 204-32.

Darnall, N., D. Gallagher and R.N.L. Andrews (2001) 'ISO 14001: Greening Management Systems', in J. Sarkis (ed.), *Greener Manufacturing and Operations: From Design to Delivery and Back* (Sheffield, UK: Greenleaf Publishing): 178-89.

Delmas, M. (2001) 'Stakeholders and Competitive Advantage: The Case of ISO 14001', *Productions and Operations Management* 10.3: 343-58.

Deming, W.E. (1993) *The New Economics for Industry, Government Education* (Cambridge, MA: MIT Center for Engineering Study).

Egri, C. P., and S. Herman (2000) 'Leadership in the North American Environmental Sector: Values, Leadership Styles, and Contexts of Environmental Leaders and their Organizations', *Academy of Management Journal* 43.4: 571-601.

Ehrenfeld, J.R. (2000) 'Industrial Ecology: Paradigm Shift or Normal Science?' *American Behavioral Scientist* 44.2: 229-44.

Evers, C.S. (2000) 'ISO 14001 and the American Indian Reservation', in R. Hillary (ed.), *ISO 14001: Case Studies and Practical Experiences* (Sheffield, UK: Greenleaf Publishing): 173-81.

Fiegenbaum, A., and S. Hart (1996) 'Strategic Reference Point Theory', *Strategic Management Journal* 17.3: 219-35.

Fisher, M. (1997) *Qualitative Computing: Using Software for Qualitative Data Analysis* (Aldershot, UK: Ashgate).

Florida, R., and D. Davison (2001) 'Gaining from Green Management: Environmental Management Systems Inside and Outside the Factory', *California Management Review* 43.3: 64-81.

Fox-Wolfgramm, S.J., K.B. Boal and J.G. Hunt (1998) 'Organizational Adaptation to Institutional Change: A Comparative Study of First-Order Change in Prospector and Defender Banks', *Administrative Science Quarterly* 43.1: 87-126.

Freeman, R.E. (1984) *Strategic Management: A Stakeholder Approach* (Boston, MA: Pitman).

Freimann, J., and M. Walther (2002) 'The Impacts of Corporate Environmental Management Systems', *Greener Management International* 36: 91-103.

Gallagher, D.R. (2002) 'From Coercion to Co-operation: Influences on Environmental Management System Design', unpublished doctoral dissertation, University of North Carolina at Chapel Hill.

—— (forthcoming) 'Environmental Management Systems and Sustainability: A Framework for Understanding Stakeholder Influence', in S. Sharma and M. Starik (eds.), *New Perspectives in Research on Corporate Sustainability: Stakeholders, Environment and Society* (Northampton, MA: Edward Elgar).

Hackman, J. R., and R. Wagemen (1995) 'Total Quality Management: Empirical, Conceptual and Practical Issues', *Administrative Science Quarterly* 40: 309-42.

Hamschmidt, J., and T. Dyllick (2001) 'ISO 14001: Profitable? Yes! But is it eco-effective?', *Greener Management International* 34: 43-54.

Hart, S.L. (1995) 'A Natural Resource-Based View of the Firm', *Academy of Management Review* 20.4: 986-1014.

Hart, S.L. (1997) 'Beyond Greening: Strategies for a Sustainable World', *Harvard Business Review* 75.1: 66-75.

Hillary, R. (ed.) (2000a) *ISO 14001: Case Studies and Practical Experiences* (Sheffield, UK: Greenleaf Publishing).

—— (2000b) 'The Eco-Management and Audit Scheme, ISO 14001 and the Smaller Firm', in R. Hillary (ed.), *Small and Medium-Sized Enterprises and the Environment: Business Imperatives* (Sheffield, UK: Greenleaf): 128-47.

ISO (International Organisation for Standardisation) (2002) *The ISO Survey of ISO 9000 and ISO 14001 Certificates. Eleventh Cycle: Up to and Including 31 December 2001* (Geneva: ISO).

Kitizawa, S., and J. Sarkis (2000) 'The Relationship Between ISO 14001 and Continuous Source Reduction Programs', *International Journal of Production and Operations Management* 20.2: 225-48.

Lee, T.W. (1999) *Using Qualitative Methods in Organizational Research* (Thousand Oaks, CA: Sage).

Maimon, D. (2000) 'Drivers and Advantages of Implementing EMSs: Brazilian Cases', in R. Hillary (ed.), *ISO 14001: Case Studies and Practical Experiences* (Sheffield, UK: Greenleaf Publishing): 297-307.

Melnyk, S.A., R.P. Sroufe and R. Calantone (2003) 'Assessing the Impact of Environmental Management Systems on Corporate and Environmental Performance', *Journal of Operations Management* 21.3: 329-52.

Mitchell, R.K.; B.R. Agle and D.J. Wood (1997) 'Toward a Theory of Stakeholder Identification and Salience: Defining the Principle of Who and What Really Counts', *Academy of Management Review* 22.4: 853-86.

Morrow, D., and D. Rondinelli (2002) 'Adopting Environmental Management Systems: Motivations and Results of ISO 14001 and EMAS Certification', *European Management Journal* 20.2: 159-71.

NDEMS (National Database on Environmental Management Systems) (2003) *Environmental Management Systems: Do They Improve Performance?* Project Final Report (Chapel Hill, NC: University of North Carolina).

Ramus, C.A., and U. Steger (2000) 'The Role of Supervisory Support Behaviors and Environmental Policy in Employee "Eco-Initiatives" at Leading Edge European Companies', *Academy of Management Journal* 43.4: 605-26.

Richards, T. J., and L. Richards (1994) 'Using Computers in Qualitative Analysis', in N. Denzin and Y. Lincoln (eds.), *Handbook of Qualitative Research* (Berkeley, CA: Sage): 445-62.

Rondinelli, D.A., and G. Vastag (1996) 'International Environmental Standards and Corporate Policies: An Integrative Framework', *California Management Review* 39.1: 106-22.

Sharma, S. (2000) 'Managerial Interpretations and Organizational Context as Predictors of Corporate Choice of Environmental Strategy', *Academy of Management Journal* 43.4: 681-97.

Switzer, J., J. Ehrenfeld and V. Milledge (2000) 'ISO 14001 and Environmental Performance: The Management Goal Link', in R. Hillary (ed.), *ISO 14001: Case Studies and Practical Experiences* (Sheffield, UK: Greenleaf Publishing): 262-72.

Tack, J. (1999) 'Environmental Management Systems and Stakeholders', *Greener Management International* 28: 50-58.

Ward, J.H. (1963) 'Hierarchical Grouping to Optimize an Objective Function', *Journal of the American Statistical Association* 58: 236-44.

Wehrmeyer, W. (ed.) (1996) *Greening People: Human Resources and Environmental Management* (Sheffield, UK: Greenleaf Publishing).

Yin, R.K. (1994) *Case Study Research: Design and Methods* (Thousand Oaks, CA: Sage, 2nd edn).

4

The relationship between environmental sustainability, environmental violations and financial performance

AN EMPIRICAL STUDY

Peter A. Stanwick and Sarah D. Stanwick
Auburn University, USA

Over the past 15 years, the relationship between environmental performance based on sustainability and economic performance has received an increased level of attention in the academic arena. With the recent conclusion of the 2002 World Summit on Sustainable Development in Johannesburg, the debate continues to focus on how businesses can focus on stakeholders' demands for environmental sustainability, while also addressing stockholders' demands on financial performance (Walley and Whitehead 1994).

The purpose of this study is to address the issue of whether organisational sustainability policies match sustainability-related organisational actions. This study will highlight similarities and differences between established policies and actions across US chemical firms. Previous research has examined the relationship between environmental policies and company actions from a number of different perspectives. Using data from the Investor Responsibility Research Center (IRRC), Dowell *et al.* (2000) examined multinational firms to determine whether their environmental standards were applied universally or were targeted to specific country demands. They explored the relationship between multinational enterprises (MNEs) and the establishment of a global environmental standard through MNEs' corporate environmental policy. The researchers found that MNEs that adopted a single comprehensive global environmental standard had a higher market value than those that used less stringent country standards. They concluded that countries that have less stringent standards attract companies that have a lower level of quality and are less globally competitive.

The IRRC accumulates a database on the environmental performance of firms by summarising information from government, non-profit and company sources. Government sources include the number of hazardous waste sites a company has listed on the Superfund's National Priority List. In addition, IRRC summarises the types of corrective actions required by companies that are on the Superfund list and the number of permits denied under the Resource Conservation and Recovery Act (Gerde and Logsdon 2001). Using IRRC, Hart and Ahuja (1996) were able to conclude that, when a company incorporates a policy of pollution reduction in its environmental strategy, it was able to reduce pollution emissions and increase profitability.

An area that has received limited focus, however, is comparisons between a company's stated commitment to sustainability with specific environmental violations identified by the US Environmental Protection Agency (EPA) that are associated with the company. In addition, previous research has not examined the link between sustainability reporting, environmental violations and the financial performance of the firm. The importance of including environmental violations in the relationship between sustainability reporting and financial performance is that it presents an important reflection of the firm's actions related to sustainability. Therefore, a major focus of this study is to examine whether firms are consistent in the development and implementation of their sustainability strategy.

The framework of this study is established around three relationships which examine the difference between sustainability policies and actions:

- Do firms in the same industry and who are members of the same voluntary association have comprehensive sustainability reports?

- To what extent are companies with comprehensive sustainability reports involved in illegal environmental activities?

- To what extent are the policies and actions pertaining to environmental sustainability associated with the financial performance of the firm?

As a result, this study addresses whether companies within the US chemical industry establish policies and commitments pertaining to environmental sustainability and whether they violate environmental regulations pertaining to sustainability. In other words, with respect to sustainability, do chemical companies both 'talk the talk' *and* 'walk the walk'? This study empirically examines whether chemical companies who are members of the industry's voluntary Responsible Care programme embrace the principles of the programme by describing their environmental commitment to sustainability, as well as by implementing actions pertaining to it.

Background to Responsible Care

Since 1988, the chemical industry in the US, through a partnership with the American Chemistry Council (previously known as the Chemical Manufacturers Association), developed the Responsible Care programme, which was adapted from a similar scheme in Canada. At the time of writing, the programme included 179 members from the industry.

When the Responsible Care programme was developed, approximately 13% of the environmental requirements needed to be a member of the programme overlapped with US federal government regulations. By 2002, almost 80% of the environmental requirements coincided with existing government environmental regulations.[1] From 1988 to 1999, the Responsible Care programme helped to reduce the pollution emissions of its members by 58% while seeing production increase by 18%. In addition, at the time of writing, approximately 300 Community Advisory Panels had been established to develop positive relationships between Responsible Care members and communities all over the US. The success of Responsible Care in the US has led to its adoption in over 46 countries, covering firms that produce over 85% of global chemicals production.[2]

The ultimate success or failure of a self-regulatory programme such as Responsible Care depends on what happens when members of the programme fail to abide by its guidelines. As King and Lenox (2000) found in their examination of Responsible Care chemical firms, self-regulation is only validated with the threat of explicit sanctions. They found that Responsible Care members have the opportunity to use their membership of the programme for opportunistic gains. For example, King and Lenox (2000) found that Responsible Care membership was heavily weighted towards heavy polluting firms, firms in heavy polluting industry and firms with a well-known brand name. As a result, the researchers concluded that firms used Responsible Care membership as an opportunistic action to improve their image. They warn that firms will not be committed to the Responsible Care guidelines unless there are explicit sanctions on such opportunistic behaviour.

The Responsible Care programme encourages chemical companies to accept and embrace industry standards pertaining to sustainability and the natural environment. These guidelines reach beyond the minimum standards required by the EPA for compliance with major federal environmental regulations, which include the Clean Air Act, the Clean Water Act, and the Superfund regime. In order to become a Responsible Care member and maintain membership, a chemical company must have:

- A Responsible Care management system in place

- Independent third-party certification of the Responsible Care management system

- A reporting mechanism to report publicly on performance based on various economic, environmental, health and safety measures

- A security code system to ensure security throughout the industry value chain

- By agreeing to become members, firms must agree to comply with the guiding principles shown in Box 4.1.

1   See www.responsiblecaretoolkit.com.
2   See www.americanchemistry.com.

The Responsible Care guiding principles

Our industry creates products and services that make life better for people around the world—both today and tomorrow. The benefits of our industry are accompanied by enduring commitments to Responsible Care® in the management of chemicals worldwide. We will make continuous progress toward the vision of no accidents, injuries or harm to the environment and will publicly report our global health, safety and environmental performance. We will lead our companies in ethical ways that increasingly benefit society, the economy and the environment while adhering to the following principles:

- To seek and incorporate public input regarding our products and operations.
- To provide chemicals that can be manufactured transported, used and disposed of safely.
- To make health, safety, the environment and resource conservation critical considerations for all new and existing products and processes.
- To provide information on health or environmental risks and pursue protective measures for employees, the public and other key stakeholders.
- To work with customers, carriers, suppliers, distributors and contractors to foster the safe use, transport and disposal of chemicals.
- To operate our facilities in a manner that protects the environment and the health and safety of our employees and the public.
- To support education and research on the health, safety and environmental effects of our products and processes.
- To work with others to resolve problems associated with past handling and disposal practices.
- To lead in the development of responsible laws, regulations and standards that safeguards the community, workplace and environment.
- To practice Responsible Care® by encouraging and assisting others to adhere to these principles and practices.

Box 4.1 The Responsible Care guiding principles

Source: www.americanchemistry.com, 2003

The performance metrics that firms are required to monitor and report in order to comply with the Responsible Care programme are shown in Table 4.1.

Theoretical foundation supporting participation in a voluntary environmental programme

An underlying rationale for companies to participate in a voluntary environmental programme is based on the core beliefs of stakeholder theory. Freeman (1984) asserted that there are a number of various interest groups called stakeholders who have a vested interest in the operations of the firm. In this framework, stakeholders can be both internal and external in nature and can include stockholders, employees, creditors, suppliers, governments, local communities and society at large.

Performance metric
Metrics reflecting Responsible Care environment, health, safety and security performance
1. Pounds of TRI—air, land and water releases (reported separately)
2. Number of reportable distribution incidents
3. Number of process safety incidents
4a. OSHA recordable incident rate—employees
4b. OSHA recordable incident rate—contractors
5a. Percentage of facilities completing security assessments based on Security Code schedule
5b. Percentage of facilities completing security enhancements/verification based on Security Code schedule
6. Certification of Responsible Care® Management System ('yes'/'no')
Metrics reflecting reputation, sustainable development, products and other initiatives
7. Greenhouse gas emissions (pounds of CO_2 equivalent net emissions per pound of production) indexed to base year
8. Energy efficiency (BTUs consumed per pound of production) indexed to base year

9. Industry economic performance:
    a. Total industry R&D investment
    b. Total number of industry employees
    c. Total value of industry payroll
    d. Total value of US industry net exports

10. Company has in place a documented process for characterising and managing product risk, and a summary of the process is available to the public ('yes'/'no')
11. Company has in place a process to communicate results of the risk characterisation and management process in an effort to facilitate public knowledge ('yes'/'no')

BTU = British Thermal Unit; CO_2 = carbon dioxide; OSHA = Occupational Safety and Health Administration; R&D = research and development

TABLE 4.1 Responsible Care performance metrics

Source: www.americanchemistry.com, 2003

Various researchers have extended stakeholder theory by arguing that the identification of all the relevant stakeholders is not only the 'right' thing to do, but is necessary to improve the financial performance of the firm (Clarkson 1995; Donaldson and Preston 1995; Jones 1995, Wood and Jones 1995; Jawahar and McLaughlin 2001) and that every stakeholder who has a vested interest in the firm has the right to place demands on it. Ruf *et al.* (2001) caution that, if a firm does not address the concerns of its various stakeholders, it may incur a negative image/reputation and potentially negative financial impact through lawsuits, fines and boycotts. Patrick ten Brink (2002) argues that voluntary environmental agreements can help share the responsibility of addressing environmental problems. Through programmes such as Responsible Care, various stakeholders have the ability to offer input and share responsibility for resolving sustainability problems.

Based on the work of the Environment Education Association and Shrivastava (1995) we define ecological sustainability as, 'the proper stewardship of resources that will benefit future generations including the protection and preservation of the diversity and the self-sustaining ability of the world's ecosystem'.

Another research area that links the voluntary actions of firms to their commitment to sustainability is 'resource dependence theory' (Pfeffer and Salancik 1978). Resource dependence theory is based on the premise that any company is dependent on resources available from various stakeholders. As a result, companies will actively manage the demands of the various stakeholders to ensure that resources are available when needed. Therefore, by identifying the impact of the demands various stakeholders may have on the firm, environmentally proactive firms will move beyond the minimum compliance requirements pertaining to sustainability. By volunteering to go beyond the minimum standards, companies can potentially develop a sustainable competitive advantage (Russo and Fouts 1997). An effective link between the firm and the resources available to it can generate a long-term and sustained competitive advantage (Dierickx and Cool 1989).

The benefit to the company is not only the ability to continue to differentiate its strategic position by focusing on sustainability issues but also the ability to distinguish it from its competitors by continuously improving its operations, from a technology perspective (Cohen and Levinthal 1990). As a result, firms that are proactive pertaining to sustainability may be able to extend the benefits of differentiation as a long-term competitive advantage. Therefore, participation in voluntary sustainability programmes allows firms to justify the necessary expenditures to maintain a long-term environmental competitive advantage (Stanwick and Stanwick 1999). In addition, by properly managing the resources available to the firm, managers may be able to increase profitability through cost reductions and/or revenue enhancement opportunities (Ruf et al. 2001). As Porter and van der Linde (1995) and Shrivastava (1995) highlight in their writings on the environment and competitive advantage theory, a company that incorporates ecological sustainability in its strategic orientation can be rewarded with increased levels of profitability by being more price-competitive and/or being able to more effectively differentiate its products.

In order to receive the full benefits of aligning the interests of its stakeholders with the action of the firm, the company must ensure that participation and commitment to the voluntary programme is communicated to the various stakeholders. As a result, it is expected that firms that view Responsible Care membership as a significant benefit to the firm would be more than willing to highlight this relationship in publicly available material. Therefore, it is expected that an overwhelming majority of Responsible Care firms develop descriptions of their respective environmental policies as these pertain to sustainability, as well as descriptions of how the firms have implemented their respective commitments to sustainability. Gray et al. (1996) list a number of incentives for environmental disclosures which include: helping to define the ethical conduct for employees; the ability to foster individual employee commitment to the programme; creating legal protection from litigation from various stakeholders; and the ability, potentially, to self-regulate the firm's industry as it pertains to various environmental issues.

Bullough and Johnson (1995) and Dechant and Altman (1994) argue that environmental reporting to stakeholders could be used to generate a positive image of the firm as well as to enhance its ability to create a sustained competitive advantage (Porter and van der Linde 1995). In addition, Stanwick and Stanwick (2000) found a positive relationship between the comprehensiveness of company environmental reporting and level of financial performance. The ability to present a positive image should encourage the company to allow widely available public access to its environmental policies and level of its environmental commitment.

Through the use of the Internet, companies now have a real-time and low-cost medium to present their environmental reporting to stakeholders all over the world. There is an incentive for firms to use the Internet because it allows them to present the information in a format over which they have complete control. As Brophy and Starkey (1996) state, using a public forum such as the Internet allows companies to present their approach to environmental issues. In his study on environmental disclosures, Cerin (2002) examined how firms in Sweden use the Internet to present relevant environmental information to the stakeholders. Cerin used Internet-based environmental reports since they allow stakeholders to retrieve information pertaining to the firm's environmental disclosures easily and quickly. Cerin (2002) found that firms in the traditional heavy polluting industries such as electricity generation, chemical, pharmaceuticals and forestry industries had the most environmental disclosures presented on their websites.

Returning to resource dependence theory, it is proposed that firms that have both a sustainability policy and a statement on commitment would have better financial performance by being able to secure additional resources from their various stakeholders. Therefore, the first hypothesis that will be examined is:

> *Hypothesis 1.* Firms that participate in industry voluntary sustainability programmes are more likely than not to publicise descriptions of their sustainability policies and their commitments.

The relationship between environmental sustainability and financial performance

Since the 1990s, the relationship between sustainability and economic performance has received an increased level of attention in both academic and practitioner literature. The traditionalist view of the relationship between environmental and economic performance is a negative one (Friedman 1970). The underlying assumption is that increases in environmental performance and sustainability, and their associated costs, outweigh the economic benefits (Walley and Whitehead 1994).

In contrast, Wagner (2000) and Wagner et al. (2001) presented an alternative view of a strong positive relationship between environmental and economic performance. This view is based on the foundation that firms that are proactive environmentally and that focus on sustainability issues are able to make significant gains in the marketplace and are able to yield positive financial returns from their environmental commitment. By differentiating its strategy through proactive environmental involvement and by focusing on long-term sustainability issues, a firm can distinguish itself from its competitors (Porter 1991; Porter and van der Linde 1995; Hart 1995; Reinhardt 1999a). In addition, improved environmental performance may also yield significant cost savings which will allow the firm to enhance its competitive position (Schmidheiny 1992; Reinhardt 1999a).

The strategic benefits of sustainability

By developing alternative manufacturing processes or by incorporating advanced technology in the process, firms are rewarded not only by increasing their compliance demands for improved environmental performance but also by attempting to ensure the long-term sustainability of their resources. In addition, firms are able to reduce production costs, increase efficiencies, reduce compliance costs and reduce future legal liabilities (Porter and Esty 1998; Reinhardt 1999b). Porter and van der Linde (1995) believe that pollution and waste products are inherent to an inefficient production process and that the hidden costs of pollution, such as wasted resources and employee effort, are not identified since they are buried within the life-cycle costs of the product. Porter and van der Linde (1995) state that the increase in the level of innovation through the adoption of proactive environmental strategies can lead to long-term competitive advantages that can more than offset the financial costs of such investments. In addition, firms are better able to serve the needs of their customers and other stakeholders by incorporating the most advanced technology in their operations. As a result, they are able to capitalise on the benefits of being first movers in their sector (Porter and Esty 1998).

Using event studies, White (1995) and Klassen and McLaughlin (1996) found a positive relationship between positive environmental practices, reflected by a comprehensive environmental management programme and stock returns, and a positive relationship between corporate environmental awards and abnormal stock returns, respectively. Cohen et al. (1995) also found a positive relationship between corporate environmental performance and profitability levels. This work of was extended by Hart and Ahuja (1996) who found that firms that reduce emissions and other pollution levels had higher levels of performance based on return on sales and return on assets within one or two years from when the pollution reduction strategies were implemented. King and Lenox (2002) discovered that firms that implemented waste prevention strategies not only yielded lower emission levels but also higher levels of profitability. These results built on the work of King (1995) and Majumdar and Marcus (2001) who claimed that waste reduction benefits companies by creating new learning opportunities.

Using a resource-based approach, Russo and Fouts (1997) found a positive relationship between environmental and financial performance. They also found that this relationship was moderated by the growth level of the industry. The positive relationship became stronger as the growth rate increased. King and Lenox (2001) concluded that industry was an important variable in this relationship. They found that higher environmental performance relative to others in the same industry sector had a positive impact on a firm's financial performance.

A new perspective on environmental sustainability

As Holliday *et al.* (2002) state, firms have developed a new lens through which to view sustainability. Thus, instead of seeing sustainability both as a cost and as a strategy that is difficult to implement, enlightened firms seek out the potential savings and new opportunities from their sustainable development activities. Instead of viewing information pertaining to the environment as proprietary, enlightened firms now have a more open and transparent perception of information. Instead of lobbying to try to minimise government regulations pertaining to sustainability for their industry, enlightened firms encourage a more open discussion with various sustainability-oriented stakeholders.

A resource-based focus on sustainability

Recent research on sustainability has focused on a resource-based perspective (Russo and Fouts 1997; Reinhardt 1998; Sharma and Vredenburg 1998; Christmann 2000; Buysse and Verbeke 2003). Christmann (2000) focuses on the internal factors that can impact the resources available to the firm. She examines whether the firm's 'complementary assets' impact the relationship between environmental activities and market competitiveness, defining complementary assets as resources that are necessary to acquire the assets needed to develop a strategy. Teece (1986) states that firms need complementary assets to capture the financial gains arising from the implementation of environmentally proactive strategies. Using comparative case studies in the Canadian oil and gas industry, Sharma and Vredenburg (1998) empirically tested resource-based theory and found that firms do have the ability to develop unique capabilities by incorporating resourced-based strategies with their proactive environmental benefits.

Furthermore, Aragon-Correa and Sharma (2003) argue that the ability of firms to manage business environment uncertainty, complexity and munificence allow the firm to develop a proactive environmental strategy which would also improve financial performance through the development of a more comprehensive competitive advantage. Therefore, it is proposed that firms that develop a sustainability strategy and are committed to its implementation will be associated with a high level of financial performance. As a result, the second hypothesis to be empirically tested is:

Hypothesis 2. Among firms that participate in their industry's voluntary sustainability programmes, firms with high financial performance will be more likely to have developed a sustainability policy and publicised their commitments than will those with low financial performance.

The relationship between environmental activities that do not comply with government regulations and environmental sustainability

An underlying assumption of previous research pertaining to illegal corporate activities is that the practice is widespread (McKendal *et al.* 1999; Kassinis and Vafeas 2002). It is also assumed that the result of this behaviour will lead directly to financial and social punishment in the form of financial penalties and a negative corporate reputation. It is also perceived that governments prosecute a very small percentage of potential cases that involve illegal corporate activities (Lipset and Schneider 1983; Gautschi and Jones 1987). For illegal activities to occur there must be motive, opportunity and lack of an effective monitoring system (Baucus 1994; McKendall and Wagner 1997; McKendall *et al.* 1999). Following this argument, a dominant motive to perform illegal actions is to enhance the level of profitability of the firm (Conklin 1977; Vaughn 1982; McKendal *et al.* 1999). Baucus (1994) asserts that the pressure from commercial competition and high environmental compliance costs can create a motive for firms to act unlawfully.

Opportunity occurs for company employees to carry out illegal environmental activities when there are no restrictions on their activities. In addition, such activities will occur when the interests of employees and/or the firm are put before the interests of other stakeholders (Vaughn 1982; Baucus 1994, McKendall *et al.* 1999).

Membership in the Responsible Care programme is contingent on a company having an environmental management system that is monitored by a third party. Therefore, it is expected that Responsible Care membership would greatly reduce the number of firms that have environmental violations and subsequent penalties filed by the EPA. In addition, the number of violating firms should be further reduced when firms have both sustainability policies and descriptions of their respective sustainability commitments which are communicated to the stakeholders. Therefore, the third hypothesis is:

Hypothesis 3. Firms that do not make publicly available sustainability commitments will be associated with a higher incidence of environmental violations than those that do.

Methodology

The firms in this study's sample were selected based on membership in the US Responsible Care programme, which is co-ordinated by the American Chemistry Council. A requirement for membership in the American Chemistry Council is an agreement to participate in the Responsible Care programme. All 179 members of the American Chemistry Council participate in the Responsible Care programme.

Criteria for the sample in the study

The criteria for firms to be included in this study sample were:

- Members of the Responsible Care programme

- Registered as a publicly traded company with financial information available

- Not identified as a division or subsidiary of a larger company (since this chapter examines corporate behaviour and not business unit behaviour)

- A viable entity, not merged or acquired by another firm

- Associated with an evaluation listed on the EPA's Enforcement and Compliance History Online (ECHO) system.

Sample measurements

The ECHO system allows users to examine compliance and enforcement information for an estimated 800,000 facilities in the US that are regulated by the EPA. Violations pertaining to the Clean Air Act, Clean Water Act, National Pollutant Elimination Discharge System and Resource Conservation and Recovery Act are included in the facility reports. The violations are classified into different categories by the EPA. The activities of the firms are classified as violations or significant violations. The activities of the EPA are classified as enforcement actions. The facility is considered to have a significant violation if the EPA had classified it as a high-priority violator under the Clean Air Act or it is currently in significant non-compliance with the Clean Water Act and/or the Resource Conservation and Recovery Act. ECHO also records whether a facility has at least one enforcement action taken against it in the previous two years.

Data on 62 firms in 2000 and 61 firms in 2001, including 1,014 facilities, were examined in this study.

The financial performance of the firms was measured as the ratio of net income–sales for 2000 and 2001, to control for the size of the firm. These two years were selected because the ECHO system currently examines the two years ending in 2002, but there is a lag between when the violation occurred and when the EPA reports it. Due to the small sample size, the firms were divided into three categories: high, medium or low performers based on their net income–sales ratio.

Classification of sustainability reports

Following on the work of Stanwick and Stanwick (2000), the sustainability reports were classified on the basis of:

1. Whether they contained any description of sustainability or issues pertaining to sustainability

2. Whether the firm had a sustainability policy; i.e a policy that refers to long-term sustainability issues

3. Whether the firm had a description of its commitment to sustainability

4. Whether the firm had both a sustainability policy and a description of its commitment to sustainability

The distinction between (2) and (3) above is subtle but important. Based on the results from the Stanwick and Stanwick (2000) study, it was observed that some firms do have a formal sustainability policy but do not have a description of how that policy is used to implement sustainability actions. This would be equivalent to the firm 'talking the talk' but not 'walking the walk'. In addition, some firms describe their sustainability activities yet do not have a formal policy as such. This would be equivalent to the firm 'walking the walk' but not 'talking the talk'.

Source of data collection

Information pertaining to sustainability was captured from each firm's website. The authors believe that such websites are an accurate source of information on sustainability issues since firms want stakeholders around the world to view this information (Cerin 2002) and they also enable companies to customise their corporate environmental reporting (Isenmann and Lenz 2001). It is expected that a company would be more than willing to describe its sustainability commitment via a corporate website since this provides a forum in which to present information pertaining to sustainability to all relevant stakeholders, and also presents a positive image of the firm (Jackson and Quotes 2002). However, a limitation of this criterion is that all firms with environmental disclosures may not be willing to provide these documents on their website due to concerns about releasing potential proprietary information.

The violations, significant violations and enforcement actions were also ranked based on a ratio calculated by the authors. The ratio used for each category was: violations–number of facilities; significant violations–number of facilities; and enforcement actions–number of facilities. The number of facilities was used as a denominator to control for the size of the firms. A number of firms in the sample had over 100 facilities included in ECHO, while others had only one facility, so it was appropriate to control for the size of the firm based on the number of facilities.

Use of the Wilcoxon test

Due to the small sample size, the data were grouped into categories (Siegel and Castellan 1988). The Wilcoxon Signed Ranks Test was used to analyse the data. This compares data pairs and assigns more weight to a pair that yields a large difference than to one with a small difference. This non-parametric test allowed the authors to compare the different categories of data.

Results

The descriptive statistics of the relevant data are shown in Table 4.2.

	Min.	Max.	Mean	Std dev.
Facilities				
Number of facilities	1	144	16.35	24.44
Environmental violations				
Number of violations	0	44	5.75	7.30
Number of significant violations	0	10	1.33	1.83
Number of environmental enforcements	0	20	2.59	3.55
Environmental penalties				
Number of environmental penalties	0	23	1.72	3.69
Dollar amount of environmental penalties	0	10.7M	0.464M	1.68M
Environmental violations/number of facilities				
Number of violations/number of facilities	0	1	0.42	0.22
Number of significant violations/number of facilities	0	1	0.12	0.17
Number of enforcements/number of facilities	0	0.77	0.18	0.17
Financial performance				
Net income/sales 2000	−1.22	24.71	0.45	3.14
Net income/sales 2001	−92.65	0.24	−1.50	11.86

M = millions   Std dev. = Standard deviation

TABLE 4.2 Descriptive statistics

The descriptive statistics highlight the significant variance in the data. The number of violations ranged from 0 to 44, the number of significant violations ranged from 0 to 10 and the number of environmental enforcements ranged from 0 to 20. The large variance in the amount of penalties will be addressed later on in this study.

The first hypothesis we empirically tested was our prediction that there would be more firms in the sample with a publicised sustainability policy and commitment than those without. The results support this hypothesis and are shown in Table 4.3.

2000				
Type of sustainability reporting				
Financial performance	*No P/C*	*P only*	*P and C*	*Total*
High performers	3	5	12	20
Medium performers	3	6	12	21
Low performers	4	10	7	21
Total	10	21	31	62

$Z = -3.717$; Significance = 0.000

2001				
Type of sustainability report				
Financial performance	*No P/C*	*P only*	*P and C*	*Total*
High performers	2	5	13	20
Medium performers	5	5	10	20
Low performers	2	11	8	21
Total	9	21	31	61

$Z = -3.799$; Significance = 0.000

No P/C: The firm has neither a sustainability policy nor a description of their commitment to sustainability.
P only: The firm has a sustainability policy.
P and C: The firm has both a sustainability policy and a description of its commitment to sustainability.
Note: No firm in the sample had just a description of their commitment to sustainability (C only).

TABLE 4.3 Type of sustainability reporting and financial performance for 2000 and 2001

Of the 62 firms in the study, 10 did not have a sustainability policy or a description of their sustainability commitment, 21 firms had a sustainability policy but not a description of their sustainability commitment, and 31 had both a sustainability policy and a description of their sustainability commitment. Therefore, half of the firms in the study had both a sustainability policy and a description of their sustainability commitment, and 83% had either an environmental policy or a description of their sustainability commitment or both.

Hypothesis 2 proposed that more firms with higher levels of financial performance would have developed both a sustainability policy and a description of their commitments than would those with low financial performance. The results for this hypothesis were supported for 2000 and 2001 using the Wilcoxon Signed Ranks Test and are shown in Table 4.3.

In both years, more high-financial-performance firms had both sustainability policies and descriptions of commitment than did low-financial-performance firms. Non-parametric analysis was used on the data due to the small sample size. Even though the authors started with 179 firms that were members of the Responsible Care programme, only 62 firms remained based on the criteria used in the study. As a result, there was not significant power in the sample size to warrant a parametric analysis of the results.

Hypothesis 3 states that there will be a higher incidence of environmental violations for firms that do not have a sustainability policy and/or a description of their sustainability commitment than firms that do. The results for this hypothesis were supported using the Wilcoxon Signed Ranks Test and are shown in Table 4.4. The Wilcoxon test can be used to compare any combination of pairs within a sample of two related variables. Therefore, even though the financial performance and sustainability reports are classified as three components, the Wilcoxon test is a valid statistical evaluation of the data (Siegel and Castellan 1988).

The results show that firms with both a policy and a commitment have consistent representation in all three violation categories (high, medium and low), firms without a policy or description of their commitment are clustered in the medium level of violations, while firms that only have a sustainability policy are more likely to either have a high or a low level of violations. The results for significant violations are also shown in Table 4.4.

Hypothesis 3 proposes that firms without a publicly available sustainability commitment would have higher levels of environmental violations. The results shown in Table 4.4 partially support this hypothesis. But, for the relationship between sustainability reports and EPA environmental violations, the results do not support the hypothesis. Only 20% of the firms that did not have a sustainability policy or a description of their sustainability commitment had a high level of environmental violations.

However, hypothesis 3 is supported for significant violations. Of the ten firms with a policy or commitment, 60% had a high level of significant violations, while only a third of firms with a sustainability policy had a high level of significant violations. In addition, only 23% of firms that had both a policy and a description of their commitment had a high level of significant violations.

The results for sustainability reports and enforcement actions also support hypothesis 3. Again, 60% of the firms without a policy or commitment had a high level of enforcement actions, while only 38% of firms with a policy and 23% of firms with a policy and a description of their commitment had a high level of enforcement action.

EPA environmental violations and type of sustainability reporting by the firms

Level of EPA environmental violations

Type of sustainability report	High	Medium	Low	Total
No P/C	2 (20%)	6 (60%)	2 (20%)	10
P only	8 (38.1%)	5 (23.8%)	8 (38.1%)	21
P and C	11 (35.5%)	10 (32.3%)	10 (32.3%)	31
Total	21	21	20	62

$Z = -3.976$; Significance = 0.000

Significant violations and type of sustainability reporting by the firms

Level of significant violations

Type of sustainability report	High	Medium	Low	Total
No P/C	6 (60%)	3 (30%)	1 (10%)	10
P only	7 (33.3%)	3 (14.3%)	11 (52.4%)	21
P and C	7 (22.6%)	13 (41.9%)	11 (35.5%)	31
Total	20	19	23	62

$Z = -4.060$; Significance = 0.000

Enforcement actions and type of sustainability reporting by the firms

Level of enforcement actions

Type of sustainability report	High	Medium	Low	Total
No P/C	6 (60%)	3 (30%)	1 (10%)	10
P only	8 (38.1%)	4 (19%)	9 (42.9%)	21
P and C	7 (22.6%)	14 (45.2%)	10 (32.3%)	31
Total	21	21	20	62

$Z = -4.352$; Significance = 0.000

No P/C: The firm has neither a sustainability policy nor a description of their commitment to sustainability.
P only: The firm has a sustainability policy.
P and C: The firm has both a sustainability policy and a description of its commitment to sustainability.
Note: No firm in the sample had just a description of their commitment to sustainability (C only).

TABLE 4.4 EPA environmental violations, significant violations and enforcement actions in relation to type of sustainability reporting

Discussion

This study has highlighted a number of interesting results. One of the results from empirically testing hypothesis 1 was that 10 of the 62 firms had neither a sustainability policy nor a description of their commitment to sustainability. This is surprising since it is expected that membership in the Responsible Care programme would generate an incentive for firms to publicise its approach to sustainability.

The empirical support of hypothesis 2 demonstrates that there *is* a relationship between sustainability and financial performance. The firm's sustainability performance is represented by the its sustainability policy and description of commitment. In the sample, half of the firms had both a sustainability policy and a description of their sustainability commitment. The motivation for such an approach could be that such firms are trying to satisfy various stakeholders, including stockholders, employees, customers and regulators.

Since the US chemical industry has traditionally been a major focus for the EPA, it is not surprising that the firms in the study try to present a comprehensive stream of environmental information. The study results also support the significant inverse relationship between level of violations and sustainability reporting. Again, this was expected, since membership in the Responsible Care programme implies that these firms should try to be good corporate citizens as environmental violations impact their environmental and sustainability performance. The results show that even Responsible Care membership is not enough to ensure legal compliance. The existence of internal documentation by way of a policy or a description of their commitment helps direct the firm toward consistent legal behaviour. This supports the view of Stead *et al.* (1998) who state that environmental and sustainability commitment must be institutionalised within the company. This helps not only in reducing legal and social liability of legal non-compliance, but can also have a positive impact on the financial performance of the firm. Therefore, it seems that most firms in the sample are 'walking the talk' as Holliday *et al.* (2002) proposed. However, some Responsible Care members appear to be using membership as an opportunistic action to create a positive image without being committed to the programme.

In conclusion, this study has highlighted the complex relationship between sustainability policies and commitment, illegal environmental activities and financial performance. The results show that firms having publicly available comprehensive guidelines on sustainability are associated with better financial performance and are less likely to be involved in illegal environmental activities.

The study has highlighted the complex relationship between corporate sustainability activities and financial performance. The results show that not all firms are fully committed to the self-regulatory principles inherent in a voluntary industry initiative. Since ten firms in the study did not have a sustainability report, they may be members of Responsible Care only in order to reduce the level of scrutiny by various stakeholders.

This study has shown that firms view self-regulation from different perspectives. Some firms in the sample not only accept but embrace sustainability issues in their strategic orientation. They are considered the 'visionaries' who view the natural environment and sustainability as a business opportunity rather than a business cost. However, there are also firms in this study who view membership of Responsible Care as the only requirement to consider sustainability issues. These firms are not utilising the full potential benefits of membership in the programme. As a result, it is the responsibility of stakeholders to see the true commitment of these firms to sustainability.

References

Aragon-Correa, J., and S. Sharma (2003) 'A Contingent Resource-Based View of Proactive Corporate Environmental Strategy', *Academy of Management Review* 28.1: 71-88.

Baucus, M. (1994) 'Pressure, Opportunity and Predisposition: A Multivariate Model of Corporate Illegality', *Journal of Management* 20.4: 699-721.

Brophy, M., and R. Starkey (1996) 'Environmental Reporting', in R. Welford (ed.), *Corporate Environmental Management: Systems and Strategies* (London: Earthscan Publications): 177-200.

Buysse, K., and A. Verbeke (2003) 'Proactive Environmental Strategies: A Stakeholder Management Perspective', *Strategic Management Journal* 24: 453-70.

Bullough, M., and D. Johnson (1995) 'Corporate Environmental Reporting in Practice', *Business Strategy and the Environment* 4.1: 36-39.

Cerin, P. (2002) 'Characteristics of Environmental Reporters on the OM Stockholm Exchange', *Business Strategy and the Environment* 11: 298-311.

Christmann, P. (2000) 'Effects of "Best Practices" of Environmental Management on Cost Advantage: The Role of Complementary Assets', *Academy of Management Journal* 43.4: 663-80.

Clarkson, M. (1995) 'A Stakeholder Framework for Analyzing and Evaluating Corporate Social Performance', *Academy of Management Review* 20.1: 92-117.

Cohen, M.A., S.A. Fenn and J. Naimon (1995) *Environmental and Financial Performance: Are They Related?* (Nashville, TN: Owen Graduate School of Management, Vanderbilt University).

Cohen, W., and D. Levinthal (1990) 'Absorptive Capacity: A New Perspective on Learning and Innovation', *Administrative Science Quarterly* 16.1: 128-52.

Conklin, J. (1977) *Illegal But Not Criminal* (Englewood Cliffs, NJ: Prentice-Hall).

Dechant, K., and B. Altman (1994) 'Environmental Leadership: From Compliance to Competitive Advantage', *Academy of Management Executive* 8.3: 7-27.

Dierickx, I., and K. Cool (1989) 'Asset Stock Accumulation and Sustainability of Firm Performance', *Management Science* 35: 1,504-14.

Donaldson, T., and L.E. Preston (1995) 'The Stakeholder Theory of the Corporation: Concepts, Evidence, and Implications', *Academy of Management Review* 20.1: 65-91.

Dowell, G., S. Hart and B. Yeung (2000) 'Do Corporate Global Environmental Standards Create or Destroy Market Value?', *Management Science* 46: 1,059-74.

Freeman, R.E. (1984) *Strategic Management: A Stakeholder Approach* (Boston, MA: Pitman).

Friedman, M. (1962) *Capitalism and Freedom* (Chicago: University of Chicago Press).

—— (1970) 'The social responsibility of business is to increase its profits', *New York Times Magazine*, 13 September 1970: 33.

Gautschi, F., and T. Jones (1987) 'Illegal Corporate Behavior and Corporate Board Structure', in J. Post and L. Preston (eds.), *Research in Corporate Social Performance and Policy* (Greenwich, CT: JAI Press): 93-106.

Gerde, V., and D. Logsdon (2001) 'Measuring Environmental Performance: Use of the Toxics Release Inventory (TRI) and Other US Environmental Databases', *Business Strategy and the Environment* 10: 269-85.

Gray, R., D. Owen and C. Adams (1996) *Accounting and Accountability* (London: Prentice Hall).

Hart, S. (1995) 'A Natural-Resource-Based View of the Firm', *Academy of Management Review* 20: 986-1,014.

—— and G. Ahuja (1996) 'Does it Pay to be Green? An Empirical Examination of the Relationship between Emission Reduction and Firm Performance', *Business Strategy and the Environment* 5: 30-37.

Holliday, C., S. Schmidheiny and P. Watts (2002) *Walking the Talk: The Business Case for Sustainable Development* (Sheffield, UK: Greenleaf Publishing).

Isenmann, R., and C. Lenz (2001) 'Customized Corporate Environmental Reporting by Internet-Based Push and Pull Technologies', *Eco-Management and Auditing* 8: 100-10.

Jackson, R., and P. Quotes (2002) 'Environmental, Social and Sustainability Reporting on the Web: Best Practices', *Corporate Environmental Strategy* 6.2: 193-202.

Jawahar, I.M., and G.L. McLaughlin (2001) 'Toward a Descriptive Stakeholder Theory: An Organizational Life Cycle Approach', *Academy of Management Review* 26.3: 397-414.

Jones, T.M. (1995) 'Instrumental Stakeholder Theory: A Synthesis of Ethics and Economics', *Academy of Management Review* 20.2: 404-37.

Kassinis, G., and N. Vafeas (2002) 'Corporate Boards and Outside Stakeholders as Determinants of Environmental Litigation', *Strategic Management Journal* 23: 399-415.

King, A. (1995) 'Innovation from Differentiation: Pollution Control Departments and Innovation in the Printed Circuit Industry', *IEEE Transportation Engineering Management* 42: 270-78.

—— and M. Lenox (2000) 'Industry Self-Regulation without Sanctions: The Chemical Industry's Responsible Care Program', *Academy of Management Journal* 43.4: 698-716.

—— and —— (2001) 'Lean and Green: Exploring the Spillovers from Lean Production to Environmental Performance', *Production Operations Management* 10: 244-56.

—— and —— (2002) 'Exploring the Locus of Profitable Pollution Reduction', *Management Science* 48: 289-99.

Klassen, R., and C. McLaughlin (1996) 'The Impact of Environmental Management on Firm Performance', *Management Science* 42: 1,199-214.

Lipset, S., and R. Schneider (1983) *The Confidence Gap: Business, Labor, and Government in the Public Mind* (New York: The Free Press).

Majumdar, S., and A. Marcus (2001) 'Rules versus Discretion: The Productivity Consequences of Flexible Regulation', *Academy of Management Journal* 44: 170-89.

McKendall, M., and J. Wagner (1997) 'Motive, Opportunity, Choice, and Corporate Illegality', *Organization Science* 8: 624-47.

——, C. Sanchez and P. Sicilian (1999) 'Corporate Governance and Corporate Illegality: The Effects of Board Structure on Environmental Violations', *The International Journal of Organizational Analysis* 7.3: 201-23.

Pfeffer, J., and G. Salancik (1978) *The External Control of Organizations: A Resource Dependence Perspective* (New York: Harper & Row).

Porter, M. (1991) 'America's Green Strategy', *Scientific American* 264.4: 168.

—— and D. Esty (1998) 'Industrial Ecology and Competitiveness: Strategic Implications for the Firm', *Journal of Industrial Ecology* 2.1: 35-43.

—— and C. van der Linde (1995) 'Green and Competitive: Ending the Stalemate', *Harvard Business Review*, September/October 1995: 120-34.

Reinhardt, F. (1998) 'Environmental Product Differentiation: Implications for Corporate Strategy', *California Business Review* 40: 43-73.

—— (1999a) 'Bringing the Environment Down to Earth', *Harvard Business Review* 77: 149-57.

—— (1999b) 'Market Failure and the Environmental Policies of Firms', *Journal of Industrial Ecology* 3: 9-21.

Ruf, B., K. Muralidhar, R. Brown, J. Janney and K. Paul (2001) 'An Empirical Investigation of the Relationship between Change in Corporate Social Performance and Financial Performance: A Stakeholder Theory Perspective', *Journal of Business Ethics* 32: 143-56.

Russo, M.V., and P.A. Fouts (1997) 'A Resource-Based Perspective on Corporate Environmental Performance and Profitability', *Academy of Management Journal* 40.3: 534-59.

Schmidheiny, S. (1992) *Changing Course: A Global Perspective on Development and the Environment* (Cambridge, MA: The MIT Press).

Sharma, S., and H. Vredenburg (1998) 'Proactive Corporate Environmental Strategy and the Development of Competitively Valuable Organizational Capabilities', *Strategic Management Journal* 19: 729-54.

Shrivastava, P. (1995) 'The Role of Corporations in Achieving Ecological Sustainability', *Academy of Management Review* 20.4: 936-61.

Siegel, S., and N. Castellan, Jr (1988) *Non-parametric Statistics for the Behavioral Sciences* (New York: McGraw-Hill, 2nd edn).

Stanwick, S.D., and P.A. Stanwick (1999) 'Exploring Voluntary Environmental Partnerships', *Journal of Corporate Accounting and Finance* 10.3: 111-25.

—— and —— (2000) 'The Relationship between Environmental Disclosures and Financial Performance: An Empirical Study of US Firms', *Eco-Management and Auditing* 7.4: 155-64.

Stead, E., M. McKinney and J. Stead (1998) 'Institutionalizing Environmental Performance in US Industry: Is it Happening and What if it Does Not?', *Business Strategy and the Environment* 7: 261-70.

Teece, D. (1986) 'Profiting from Technological Innovation: Implications for Integration, Collaboration, Licensing, and Public Policy', *Research Policy* 15: 295-305.

Ten Brink, P. (ed.) (2002) *Voluntary Environmental Agreements: Process, Practice and Future Use* (Sheffield, UK: Greenleaf Publishing).

Vaughn, D. (1982) 'Toward Understanding Unlawful Organizational Behavior', *Michigan Law Review* 80: 1377-402.

Wagner, M. (2000) 'The Relationship between the Environmental and Economic Performance of Firms: What Does Theory Propose and What Does Empirical Evidence Tell Us?', paper presented at the ESST (European Inter-university Association on Science and Technology) Annual Conference, Strasbourg, May 2000.

——, S. Schaltegger and W. Wehrmeyer (2001) 'The Relationship between the Environmental and Economic Performance of Firms: What Does Theory Propose and What Does Empirical Evidence Tell Us?', *Greener Management International* 34: 95-108.

Walley, N., and B. Whitehead (1994) 'It's Not Easy Being Green', *Harvard Business Review,* May/June 1994: 46-52.

White, M. (1995) 'The Performance of Environmental Mutual Funds in the United States and Germany: Is there Economic Hope for "Green" Investors?', *Research in Corporate Social Performance and Policy* Supplement 1: 325-46.

Wood, D.J. and E.J. Jones (1995) 'Stakeholder Mismatching: A Theoretical Problem in Empirical Research on Corporate Social Performance', *International Journal of Organizational Analysis* 3.3: 229-267.

5

Social system complexity
NEW FORMS OF US FEDERAL
AGENCY INVOLVEMENT*

Christopher P. Durney
ICF Consulting, USA

J. Glenn Eugster
US National Park Service

John W. Wilson
US Environmental Protection Agency

The leaders of US federal agencies who need to plan their programmes in a wide range of areas—environment, health, emergency preparedness and community development, among others—face a dilemma. Current developments—the demand for speed and responsiveness driven by the Internet, the growing role of empowerment in programme implementation and the recognition that sustainable programme implementation can occur only at the level of the specific borough, town, city and county—are forcing US federal agency leaders to recognise that more of their programmatic activity must take place within the target community. But this

---

* Many of the insights in this essay were first developed during a programme evaluation, conducted by two of the authors, of EPA's involvement in South Florida's ongoing initiative to protect the Everglades, looking at the period 1995–99. The initiative continues to evolve, however (see Case Study A). Another author was directly involved in EPA's environmental efforts on the Delmarva Peninsula. These efforts at environmental awareness and restoration eventually merged with the broader Save the Bay activities sponsored by the Chesapeake Bay Program (see Case Study B). We also conducted discussions with participants in a wide range of US federal agency projects that relied on voluntary community participation in some critical way. Among these projects were the Department of Housing's Neighborhood Networks programme, designed to provide low-income communities with access to electronic government services, the Federal Emergency Management Administration 's Project Impact, aimed at increasing the disaster resistance of US communities and the EPA's Energy Star and Commuter Choice programmes, both voluntary participation programmes intended to contribute to better air quality.

focus on the local community—fostering private–public partnerships, working as one member of a widely diverse team, dealing with different local conditions, concerns and resources—challenges the top-down, control, regulation and enforcement approaches that traditionally characterise US federal involvement. Managers responsible for community-based programmes must find new strategies to deal with these new realities.

Trends driving the need for a new approach

For at least the last three decades, the standard model for US federal action has been top-down control and regulation, with predictable, uniform implementation and enforcement. This intervention model, based in large part on a linear, mechanistic view of human behaviour that holds that specific actions will yield specific predictable results (Burns 2002; Mathews *et al.* 1999; Kiel 1997), has resulted in significant community, quality-of-life and environmental improvements over the years, and is still the backbone of most of the core programmes at US federal agencies such as the Environmental Protection Agency (EPA), the Departments of Energy (DOE), Housing and Urban Development (HUD), Agriculture (USDA), Transportation (DOT), Justice (DOJ), the Treasury and the Federal Emergency Management Administration (FEMA).[1]

However, the achievement of additional societal and environmental gains now requires a new, complementary blueprint for federal involvement. Several societal and technical changes are driving this need for a new approach.

First, the speed, power, reach and adaptability of the Internet require faster, more informed responses to stakeholder demands and force organisations in all sectors—public, private and non-profit—to become more customer-oriented to meet clients' growing expectations.[2] In response, leaders in some US government agencies have been trying to shed their traditional regulatory mode in favour of community-centred, deeply involved approaches to fulfilling their missions.

Second, the last 20 years have seen an increasing decentralisation of information in practically all areas of human endeavour. Once privileged information is now available to anyone who wants it. The US federal agency role as the central information provider, a role that brought power and influence when information was hierarchically managed, can no longer justify an agency's existence.

---

1 There is also a record of US federal involvement at the local level, of course. However, this involvement more often consists of the offering of technical assistance to individual and groups or organisations receiving federal grants or other funds under tightly controlled programme protocols.

2 Attention to the use of electronic means to reach a wide range of stakeholders quickly and effectively is reflected in the initiatives outlined in President Bush's 2002 Management Agenda (*The President's Management Agenda*, Executive Office of the President, Office of Management and Budget, FY 2002–03) which identified accountability, electronic government and service to US citizens as critical concerns for his administration.

Third, the concept of 'empowerment'—the strategy to push decision-making down to the most appropriate, local level possible, where the knowledge, information and experience to make the best, quickest and most responsive decisions resides—is becoming central to management thinking, including to some US government approaches. Leaders within these centralised, bureaucratic organisations are learning they cannot mandate change but must work with local citizens to make change happen. Local empowerment brings collaborative strategies onto centre stage since no single player has all the necessary knowledge, authority, energy or resources (Chrislip and Larson 1994).

Fourth, social activists are recognising that sustainable change in societal and environmental conditions must take root at the local level, since the source of these conditions always lies in the actions and decisions of the individual actors in the local populace. And each locality has its own irreducible combination of concerns, knowledge, experiences, people, history, culture and geophysical conditions that demands a unique response (Innes and Booher 1999a; Kiel 1994).

Fifth, the last 20 years have seen increasing pressure on US federal agencies to 'behave in a more business-like way'. While government is importantly different from a 'business' and has its own mission, purpose and values, this pressure has led at least to a focus on greater fiscal responsibility and accountability for federal managers.[3]

Advantages of a complex adaptive system perspective

Based on our experience with community-based federal projects—the EPA's involvement with South Florida's efforts to protect the Everglades (see Case Study A), the efforts of communities on the Delmarva Peninsula to save the Chesapeake Bay (see Case Study B), the EPA's Energy Star and Commuter Choice voluntary participation programmes, FEMA's efforts to improve disaster readiness in US communities and HUD's efforts to bridge the digital divide in low-income neighbourhoods, among others—we have begun to see the advantages of seeing a local community as a complex adaptive system (CAS).

A CAS is a richly connected web of independent, interacting, intelligent agents, each of which operates according to its local knowledge and conditions. Through this interaction, these agents create a system-wide ability to learn, respond and evolve to environmental changes that is greater than the sum of their individual abilities. Such an approach to community involvement—based on the concepts of non-linear, dynamic systems—stands in fairly sharp contrast to traditional modes of US federal agency involvement, based as they are on the more traditional linear, mechanistic view of systems.

3   President Clinton's Reinventing Government initiative during his administration and President Bush's Management Agenda initiatives are examples of the trend in US government to address fiscal accountability, productivity and best value as critical concerns for federal agencies.

In the next section, we describe the characteristics of a CAS and, using examples from our experiences, illustrate how the local community fits these characteristics.[4] Next, we describe three tactics, based on CAS concepts, that leaders in US federal agencies can use to help them work more effectively at the local community level. Finally, we suggest new perspectives and approaches that leaders in US federal agencies need to adopt in order for them to take advantage of the benefits to be gained from viewing the local community from a CAS perspective.

Traditional approaches versus complex adaptive systems

Interest in CASs has grown significantly in the physical and biological sciences over the last two decades (Holland 1995, 1999; Capra 1996; Kaufman 1995; Lewin 1993; Waldrop 1992; Gleick 1987). Since the mid-1990s, the literature that applies CAS thinking to management challenges has been growing. While efforts to apply the CAS model to organisations acknowledge the differences between physical natural systems and social systems, many authors have found the concepts underlying CAS helpful in analysing social system interactions (Van Uden *et al.* 2001). Efforts to apply CAS concepts to organisations tend to fall onto either the quantitative side, with mathematical modelling of organisational processes as a basis (Kiel and Seldon 1998; Costanza *et al.* 1993; Priesmeyer 1992), or the qualitative side, in which the characteristics of the CAS model are used in metaphorical and analogical ways (Dent 2003; Burns 2002; Wheatley 1999; Innes and Booher 1999a, 1999b). Our approach in this chapter takes this latter, qualitative approach, in the belief that future work in social networks, communication channels and other modelling of social systems will provide a quantitative validation of our analysis.

A CAS has definable characteristics that make it different from traditional, mechanistic systems (see Table 5.1).

A CAS is composed of multiple independent agents acting together

Traditional management models and approaches are generally based on a mechanistic view of systems as assemblages of parts, with each part best understood separately and individually (Innes and Booher 1999a; Morgan 1986). No matter how complex the system, as the properties of each part are known, the purpose and functioning of the whole becomes clear. When changes occur in the external environment, managers within the mechanistic organisation will reassemble its parts into new structures in the hopes that the redesign will meet the new challenges.

In a CAS, however, each 'part' is an individual agent acting in parallel with other agents to create a result greater than any individual part (Pascale *et al.* 2000; Holland 1992). For instance, in South Florida's Everglades initiative (see Case Study A), multiple players—beginning with the thousands of citizens involved, but at various levels of aggregation, including dozens of local communities, five counties, multiple state and federal agencies (with both headquarters and regional offices),

---

4   See Case Study A for a description of the South Florida project and Case Study B for a description of the Delmarva Peninsula project.

CAS model	Mechanistic model
System is composed of multiple independent agents acting together.	System is composed of multiple parts, each with a specialised role to play.
Performance is a result of the whole system. Focus on improving parts could lead to sub-optimisation.	System performance results from improvement of parts.
System evolves by learning and adapting to changes in the external environment.	System changes only through the imposition of desired change by forces outside the system itself.
The multiple independent agents in a CAS always act on local knowledge and conditions.	The parts in the mechanistic model act on information from the central source.
Cause and effect are distant, non-proportional: the 'butterfly effect'.	Cause and effect are well known; outputs are proportional to inputs.
Over time, change is non-linear. System moves through periodic state shifts.	Over time, change is linear. Behavioural changes are incremental and predictable.
Control is dispersed; no one agent is in charge.	Control is centralised; a designated group of parts controls the whole.

TABLE 5.1 CAS model versus mechanistic model

and a variety of not-for-profit organisations—came together to ensure a healthy future for the Everglades and its surrounding communities. Each player had its own vision and mission, and its own reason for becoming involved. In addition, various discrete 'named' initiatives, such as Eastward Ho! Brownfields Partnership, the Brownfields Showcase Community Designation and the Governor's Commission,[5] also existed as independent agents within the larger Everglades movement, with overlap of resources and people.

---

5   The Eastward Ho! Brownfields Partnership, established in February 1997, had a wide range of signatories (among them were Miami-Dade, Palm Beach and Broward counties, a number of non-profit groups, the Florida Department of Environmental Protection, several regional planning councils and the City of Miami) who committed to work together to restore and redevelop brownfield sites in South Florida. The goal was to redevelop sites that would contribute directly in implementing the Eastward Ho! vision, which was to make the eastern corridor a more attractive development alternative, thus taking some of the development pressure off the Everglades. The Governor's Commission for the Everglades, which was composed of representatives from state agencies, businesses, including agriculture, the tribes and non-profit organisations, was created by Governor Jcb Bush in June 1999 to serve as a forum for improving decision-making and public participation in Everglades' restoration and South Florida economic and community sustainability. The Brownfields Showcase community programme was started by the EPA in 1998, making funds and technical assistance available to communities who applied and met the criteria for designation. A partnership of more than 15 federal agencies with interests in brownfields redevelopment designated 16 Brownfields Showcase communities throughout the US, including South Florida.

Performance of a CAS is not reducible to its constituent parts

While individual agents can be analysed on their own terms, what matters is their contribution to producing the desired behaviours. Too strong a focus on improving individual parts can lead to either sub-optimisation or the destruction of the emerging order (Holland 1992). In South Florida, several perturbations were observed during which one player, such as a county with a specific environmental goal to achieve or a regional planning commission with a growth plan to implement, would attempt to impose its own limited point of view without consensus from the whole partnership. Inevitably, this behaviour led to countervailing actions by other partners—public protests from minority groups, behind-the-scenes attempts to influence project direction or outright withdrawal of crucial resources—that threatened the viability of the overall vision.

A CAS evolves by learning and adapting to changes in the external environment

In the mechanistic model, the individual parts are fashioned from the beginning to play a specific role and perform a specific function. If new learning takes place, it occurs outside the system and change is introduced through the design of new parts or the re-engineering of old ones. In a CAS, the parts are independent agents that can learn from and adapt to environmental changes (Innes and Booher 1999a; Capra 1996; Waldrop 1992). This is not necessarily conscious learning in the human sense; for instance, a colony of ants adapts to changes in the external environment (Pascale *et al.* 2000). As one of the staff involved in South Florida commented to us:[6]

> Have a sense of where you want to go, but this will evolve over time. You need to be alert to new learning in order to make sure you get to a place you want to be. For instance, we weren't really thinking about how important the transportation issue was at the beginning of the project, but we learned that without accounting for how people will travel through the corridor, we won't be successful in changing their behaviours. We realised we had to reach out and involve the transportation planners in our efforts.

Under the right conditions, this learning can lead the system to successively higher states of self-organisation (Holland 1995). In South Florida, early, small, isolated efforts helped to increase the availability of information about the current and future state of the Everglades under the escalating pressure of expanding land use. Over time, the development and sharing of this information through conferences, meetings, publications and so on helped the various initiatives recognise their common purpose. The initial efforts began to combine in various ways—

6   This quote, and others in this essay, are from South Florida residents who were interviewed as part of the programme evaluation of the EPA's involvement in South Florida. During the programme evaluation, approximately 30 in-depth interviews were conducted with stakeholders in the EPA and in South Florida (using a standard interview protocol and analysis methodology). The formal interviews were supplemented by informal conversations with approximately 20 additional stakeholders in those initiatives that were supported by EPA involvement. Interviewees were promised anonymity as part of the interview process.

smaller groups came together to form fewer larger groups, creating successively more integrated levels of organisation. This kind of evolution was visible in the region's application for EPA's Brownfield Showcase Community Designation which, if successful, would make the region eligible for significant federal aid. In order to make the strongest case possible to the EPA, the majority of the existing smaller units joined with larger ones to present a unified regional vision. In a CAS, these higher forms of organisation are frequently temporary, breaking apart and reverting to smaller, more cohesive groups when turbulence is experienced and then recombining as conditions change. This type of fluctuation continues even today in South Florida as the comprehensive Everglades restoration plan moves forward (Clarke 2003).

In the Delmarva case (see Case Study B), learning gained in one locality—for instance, through the development and implementation of a heritage plan—was quickly passed to neighbouring communities, with the result that additional players sought entry into the growing system.

The multiple independent agents in a CAS act on local knowledge and conditions

The parts of a mechanistic system react as programmed to specific stimuli, which are either sent by the central processing unit—that is, the senior management team—or received from outside the system (Kiel 1994). In contrast, the multiple individual agents that comprise a CAS act on the basis of their internal perception of the local conditions and priorities. The people interviewed in the South Florida programme evaluations were, unsurprisingly, acting in their own self-interests. One woman in South Florida remarked:

> Saving the Everglades is nice. But I'm involved [in Save the Everglades activities] because I want to make sure that, when they build on the empty corner by my house, they put in a supermarket and not another high-rise.

The lesson here is that in a CAS efforts to control every aspect of the system's behaviour from some centralised 'nerve centre' will often be frustrated. A strong central authority can attempt to dictate a specific course of action for the whole, but unless the multiple independent agents can recognise their own goals and motivations within that common action, eventually they will revert to their own individual courses.

In a CAS, cause and effect are distant, non-proportional

Within a CAS, constant, iterative feedback turns small changes in the initial condition of the system into disproportionately larger-than-expected consequences. Otherwise known as **sensitive dependence on initial conditions** this 'butterfly effect' teaches that, through the internal amplification caused by constant feedback within a CAS, small interventions can have surprising, dramatic results. For example, during one of the initial meetings in South Florida, an EPA official was asked a simple question, 'What is a brownfield?' Attempting to answer the question, the official proposed a regional conference on the topic. Ultimately, a series of regional conferences were held which, in turn, generated a number of unprecedented collaborations between citizens and politicians that led to a new multi-county effort for restoration and economic development. In such a system, setting linear performance measures can be almost impossible, since the end results are often unpredictable.

Over time, change is non-linear: a CAS moves through periodic state shifts

A CAS moves through periods of 'bifurcation' in which it jumps through a series of definable behavioural states, ranging from equilibrium to chaos (Holland 1992; Kaufman 1995; Wheatley 1999). One particular state, known as being 'far from equilibrium' or on the 'edge of chaos', is key to generating new ideas and new levels of self-organisation (Pascale *et al.* 2000). Complex systems seem to adapt effectively to rapid environmental changes only when the systems demonstrate a great rate of internal turbulence and shifting relationships while still maintaining their identity as systems. The 'edge of chaos' state is contrasted with the 'equilibrium' state on the one hand—the organisation has achieved some temporary, stable accommodation with the external environment so that growth or innovation rarely occur—and the 'chaotic' state on the other—a state so unstructured that dissolution is a more likely outcome than survival (Pascale *et al.* 2000). Projects near the 'edge of chaos' may frustrate the federal manager looking for control and order, but will ultimately produce more energy and creativity than a project that is kept in a highly controlled state. In the South Florida and the Delmarva Peninsula initiatives, periods of turmoil generally heralded periods of increased self-definition, as lessons learned about the whole permeated the behaviour of the system.

In a CAS, control is dispersed; no one agent is in charge

Because the individual agents in a CAS act on local knowledge and conditions, control of a CAS's actions will be dispersed throughout the system. While individual agents can influence the shape and direction of the CAS, no one agent is in full control. The recommendations detailed below indicate some of the ways by which individual actors can influence the orientation of the CAS.

The traditional mechanistic model of federal agency intervention assumes top-down control and direction by the lead agency. In contrast, the distributed character of authority and power that characterises CAS is easily observable in community-based projects such as the ones in South Florida and on the Delmarva Peninsula. Multiple components—transportation, health and human services, power and infrastructure management, and others—must interact successfully to sustain the long-term health of large ecosystems, such as the Everglades and Chesapeake Bay, or to create long-term changes in a community's economic decision-making patterns. These components, when viewed at the micro-level, devolve into thousands of individual decisions and actions.

For instance, land use is a critical component of environmental asset management. While certainly subject to top-down policy and regulation, land use is essentially the cumulative result of many small decisions made by individual actors (singly or in groups), all of whom generally act in their own perceived best interests, whether favourable to the environment or not. Of course, environmental degradation can result just as easily, and perhaps more insidiously, from the countless small decisions taken every day by ordinary people acting on limited information and interests than from the single-source environmental abusers who get the most attention. Even land-use decisions in support of unarguable societal benefits such as: better, more affordable housing; attractive landscaping; efficient transportation; productive agriculture; and access to consumer goods, can contribute to losses of environmental assets. Therefore, any economic growth that aims to be environmentally friendly must integrate these various dimensions into a system of accommodations and balances. In turn, this integration requires the co-operation of organisations with multiple viewpoints.

New perspectives for US federal agencies working in communities

Change is non-linear and responsive to evolving conditions. Communities, with their many players and complex interactions, demonstrate the characteristics of the CAS model—no single source of control but, rather, many individuals and groups acting independently (although still as part of the same system) and resisting separation into distinct, mechanistic parts that follow predictable laws. In the face of such complexity, it is impossible for federal (or local, for that matter) agencies to engineer a single, standard approach to societal issues. Federal agencies thus need a new approach to accomplishing their missions.

Traditional US federal action works best when directed toward the control of relatively certain and fairly generalisable functions, such as waste-water discharge, drinking water purification, home-building methods, food-processing approaches and solid waste management. These functions, all falling within the responsibility of local governance, have specific, national parameters based on prior learning—water quality standards, construction safety and material composition standards, landfill regulations and the like—that can inform and regulate local practices. But the plethora of social problems now demanding attention are much less homogenous at the national level and also vary considerably from one community to the next. These problems include the health of large ecosystems, children's educational levels, potential class disparities created by the digital divide, a community's exposure to natural disasters and the threat of domestic terrorism, among others. Such problems are much less amenable to nationwide programmes with a single mission focus, requiring direct involvement from the local communities that are affected by them.

Furthermore, the basic history, structures, operations, industries and concerns that influence the day-to-day behaviour of each individual community are different, often significantly, from those in communities just a few miles away, not to mention those in other parts of the country. The ways in which decisions are made, implemented and monitored, and the ways in which a local community interacts with the state, the federal government and other interested parties also differ from locality to locality. While there are similarities from which agencies can learn, when we analyse the behaviour of any specific place it appears complex, unpredictable and unique.

Given the need to work effectively at this individual, local level, federal agencies must find ways to work within a CAS context. The new ways may borrow liberally from voluntary community initiatives—such as community policing, literacy initiatives and environmental activists—from which many of the lessons of collaborative leadership have been learned (Chrislip and Larson 1994). The new modes of involvement in such situations—based on insights offered from the study of the CAS—complement each agency's more traditional roles, which still can and should be applied when they make sense. But the new approach is required if agencies are to achieve maximum success when working at the local community level. This new model will, in turn, require new skills and attitudes on the part of agency staff involved in working in communities.

Agency perspectives under the mechanistic model

In the mechanistic model, the federal agency is given discrete objectives, often tied directly to budgetary line-items approved by Congress. Each specific objective is accomplished by precisely defining—often in legal language—the 'products' or 'deliverables' that need to be produced by the agency and then by designing an organisational apparatus to produce each product. Such an apparatus consists of well-designed organisational parts that function together with effectiveness and precision (Innes and Booher 1999a). For instance, a grants management apparatus for an organisation with grant-making responsibility is designed to ensure that the right number of grants are awarded in the right amount of time and that the money is spent according to proper rules of accountability and stewardship.

When something goes awry, lack of performance by some part of the apparatus is generally blamed. When a new product or mandate is required, the organisation tends to create a new mechanism for its production. Improvement in this model has to do with redesigning the structure of the mechanism and then 're-engineering' the parts—for instance, retraining the people in the new structure—to execute more effectively (Kiel 1997). Frequent reorganisations of the various divisions and departments within federal agencies are visible signs of this tendency to re-engineer the parts of the organisation in response to perceived inefficiencies.

The traditional federal agency demonstrates a command-and-control perspective through which decisions are made by senior managers and then passed down to the various parts for execution. This hierarchical communication structure is typical of bureaucracies and is very difficult to change, even when events strongly point to the need for more horizontal forms of communication to supplement the vertical channels. For instance, following the space shuttle *Challenger* disaster in 1986, the panel analysing the causes of the accident noted that the command-and-control structure within the National Aeronautical and Space Agency (NASA) limited the flow of information, particularly from low-level engineers, about potential problems. NASA was encouraged to develop a more open culture in which every voice would be heard without prejudice. Seventeen years later, the board investigating the space shuttle *Columbia* disaster concluded that, despite these previous recommendations, despite the consequences that could result from lack of open communication, especially where safety concerns were involved, and despite the assurance of senior managers that such free communication was supported, there remained a very strict hierarchical communication system that prevented concerns from those lower in the structure from being heard higher up the organisation where key decisions are made (Langewiesche 2003).

When the object of focus is outside the agency itself—for instance, managing an environmental asset such as clean air—the outside world is also addressed through the mechanistic language of laws, formulae, standards and outputs. Even innovative voluntary participation programmes, such as the EPA's Energy Star and Commuter Choice, which invite partnership and collaboration are expected to translate the results of these collaborative efforts into quantitative pollution reduction goals in order to secure government funding (Heslin 2001). The traditional agency's approach to involvement with stakeholders is also characterised by the mechanistic perspective, often focusing on linear policy-making, regulation and enforcement, usually imposed from a distance (although the agencies are, by law, required to 'propose' new regulations and to invite the public to comment on them before publishing them in the federal record).

Such thinking is in keeping with the traditional perspective in which Congress allocates specific resources to federal agencies for the management and control of discrete social concerns, such as air quality, marine fish stocks, illicit drug trafficking, emergency preparedness or air traffic control, and often even names the specific pollutant, type of fish or drug, and expects (at least from a political position) to receive a quantifiable return on the 'investment'. Furthermore, this return on investment must occur within a limited time span. Unless the designed organisational apparatus can produce measurable, short-term returns, it must be revised and redesigned. Solutions that take many years to produce results—and in the case of systemic social challenges, this is nearly always the case—are often seen as intractable by both Congress and US federal agencies.

For example, the questions that EPA managers wanted answered through our programme evaluation of the agency's involvement in South Florida were: 'What value did the EPA gain from the resources it spent in South Florida? What evidence was there that the expenditure of federal dollars contributed in a real way to the accomplishment of stated EPA goals and objectives?' In answering these questions, South Florida stakeholders were predominantly positive, pointing out ways in which EPA involvement had strengthened the Save the Everglades initiative by:

- Bringing the perspective of a national organisation to help balance national and regional points of view

- Demonstrating a commitment to diversity by ensuring that appropriate stakeholder groups were included in the process

- Providing education and information such as Showcase Community information and the Brownfields conferences

- Providing communication infrastructure with teleconferencing capabilities, funds to facilitate meetings, website support and newsletters.

- Providing money and other resources

Senior EPA managers, however, were reluctant to accept the judgment of success-ful involvement without a more linear assessment of return on their investment—what visible successes could be pointed to that the EPA could claim as its own?

Agency perspectives under the CAS model

In the CAS model, the basic perspective of the federal agency would be one of adaptation and co-evolution with its environment. The agency still must produce products and deliverables that create some additional inflow of resources (addi-tional budgets from Congress, mainly), but the focus of the agency is on its suc-cessful adaptation to changing political, social and economic realities.[7]

In accomplishing this purpose, agency management attention will embrace the performance of the organisation as a whole. When something goes wrong with the agency's outputs, the functioning of the system as a whole is explored rather than simply the reliability of each individual part. For instance, by examining the quality of system inputs, the interactions and communications between sub-groups, the learning ability of the employees and so on, the organisation looks to find 'butter-flies'—points of leverage in the system that can improve overall system behaviour (Kiel 1997). When a new function is received, the individual agents within the organisation are educated in the new function (not necessarily re-engineered or rearranged) to respond to the new need.

The ability of employees to play more than one role (redundancy of function) is the organic organisation's hedge against possible shifts in user demand (Morgan 1986). The traditional mechanistic organisation must maintain a cadre of extra employees (redundancy of parts) to guarantee the same resiliency.

Since many community-based projects—for example, the Everglades initiative, efforts to encourage 'smart growth' or to help communities become more disaster-resistant, or strategies to help specific groups overcome the growing digital divide—are concerned with sustained changes in the health of a specific place, they often require sustained action, sometimes over decades, to protect existing resources and allow for continued development and change (Environmental Advisory Coun-cil to the Swedish Government 2002). This long-term point of view requires that agencies find a way to provide consistent support over long periods—an extremely difficult perspective to master given the shifts of programme focus inherent in the frequent turnover of senior agency managers.

When working at the community level on systemic social issues, command-and-control approaches are not always appropriate. No single agency, especially when operating remotely (as is often the case), can 'control' the dozens of independent local agents—state and local governments, non-profit organisations, other federal and state agencies and individual citizens—that make up a large-scale social action. In fact, such an action, as it gains momentum, interest and, most importantly,

7   The current mandate for federal agencies to adopt e-government is a good example of this organic impulse. Rather than specifying products, such as grant applications or disaster insurance funds, that can be delivered in a mechanistic way, the e-government agency must find ways to take advantage of the emerging electronic environment to create new relation-ships with the agency's communities and stakeholders.

resources, will often appear to be near the edge of chaos, as the various agents come together and then separate in pursuit of their own goals and interests.

In such situations, an individual agency is not 'in control' in any real sense. Although the agency may become involved in the community, either through invitation from local participants or through its own provision of a requested service or assistance, the agency is not in a position to control the local activity. In fact, it is often hard to conceive just what activity could be controlled in the first place. In South Florida, the EPA was invited to participate in the growing efforts to save the Everglades through the investment of analytic resources and personnel time. On the Delmarva Peninsula, the EPA brought the monetary resources, a template for heritage preservation planning and the capability to develop relationships between disparate projects. Neither of these situations constituted a 'controlling' interest for the agency.

The mechanistic model of organising has, of course, resulted in many gains for both organisations and individuals. However, as some have suggested, the model has become so ingrained in our thinking about organisations that it has become difficult to think about organising in any other way (Morgan 1986). Overcoming this reluctance to think differently about organisations becomes increasingly important in an age characterised by accelerated change, since the mechanistic model may no longer meet the needs of federal agencies as they strive to respond to increasingly rapid changes in their environments. The CAS model, however, provides new insights for federal managers and employees into the present and future of federal action.

New tactics for federal employees working at the community level?

In addition to the two EPA cases in South Florida and on the Delmarva Peninsula, we have discussed the issues central to this essay with team members from EPA's Energy Star and Commuter Choice voluntary participation programmes, HUD's Neighborhood Networks and FEMA's Project Impact for building disaster-resistant communities, among other programmes. Our discussions compel the conclusion that working within such complex situations requires new tactics on the part of the involved federal agency employees, including, of course, the agencies' leaders.

We suggest three tactics for working in community-based programmes: **sustained nudging, design and discovery** and **incremental co-evolution**. These tactics take advantage of CAS characteristics, thereby helping involved employees work in concert with the complexity of the situation rather than becoming confused and frustrated by it. While some of the specific skills that comprise the tactics are familiar to managers of large projects—negotiation skills, for instance, are taught in many federal leadership and management development programmes—the particular slant here is on the use of these skills in a way that takes advantage of the characteristics of complexity in our communities.

Sustained nudging through collaboration management

The 'butterfly effect' suggests that small changes in initial conditions can have disproportionately large effects further down the road. If the key leverage points within the complex system are known, then significant changes in outcome can be produced by fairly small inputs. As Douglas Kiel (1994: 193) says:

> Knowing that unstable systems often require small *nudges* rather than heavy-handed control may help managers think in terms of changing relationships, altering processes, and examining the dynamics of time series.

These nudges can have either an amplifying effect, identifying new possibilities for growth and expansion, or a damping effect, monitoring threshold variables to keep behaviour from sliding too far out of a desirable range (Pascale *et al.* 2000). Amplification acts to keep the CAS away from equilibrium in which no change takes place; damping serves to keep the CAS from sliding into chaos.

Even the suggestion of such a possibility should be welcome news to federal managers challenged with delivering more with fewer resources. When effectively positioned within the local community, the federal employee can 'nudge' the situation here or there by carefully introducing new information, additional money and other resources, finding and introducing new independent agents who could have a stake in the action (as in the case of using a small grant to increase the diversity of the group), or increasing the number of connections and information channels among existing players (by providing a communications infrastructure, for instance). The effects of these amplifying nudges can then be monitored to check that the resultant increases in self-organisation seem to be leading toward the stated goals. A series of such nudges over time may be necessary to create the kind of sustained self-organisation within the community that will move the community steadily toward the accomplishment of its (and the federal agency's) goals.

Leverage points for nudging community-based initiatives include:

1. Help establish a 'good enough' evolving vision.

2. Infuse timely, fitting information.

3. Identify opportunities for increasing diversity.

4. Encourage multiple points of focus.

5. Favour decisions that build local capacity.

6. Provide a communication infrastructure.

7. Provide money.

Nudging requires intimate knowledge of the situation. Federal employees must spend time on the ground, listening to local leaders and citizens and facilitating the building of relationships. Nudging also takes a good deal of patience on the part of agency leaders back in Washington, since it may appear for periods of time that little progress, if any, is taking place and because the outcomes of these nudges will be hard to measure in a traditional, linear, return-on-investment sense.

However, our observations indicate that nudging works. Many points of leverage were noted as key to EPA accomplishments in South Florida and on the Delmarva Peninsula. First, the multiple independent agents in a community-based project were working on partial information sets, many of which contained potentially conflicting data. A goal in South Florida was to build coherence among the core group—a coalition of approximately 30 state and local officials who were meeting fairly consistently to discuss the Everglades issue—to help harness the group's energy and reduce communication overheads. The EPA employee assigned to the project encouraged the group to create an overarching 'vision' of where the initiative needed to go (Kouzes and Posner 2002; Stacey 1992). Examples of visions that had worked in other communities were provided and the core group was encouraged to arrive at a 'good enough' vision that people could generally agree on. It was important that the vision responded to local concerns since it is only through responding to such concerns that a broader, big-picture awareness is able to develop. The resulting vision for the Eastward Ho! initiative produced constructive discussion and created a focal point for self-organising activity.

A second important point of leverage in South Florida and on the Delmarva Peninsula was the introduction of timely and fitting information into the system. While EPA was neither in control nor initiated the work in South Florida and on the Delmarva Peninsula, EPA employees were able to bring unique information from their perspective as a national organisation, such as the availability of grants, significant opportunities for peer-matching with other communities, or even international programmes that support planning. Information that seemed particularly important to the stakeholders in South Florida were lessons learned that EPA provided from other communities throughout the nation that were dealing with similar issues and concerns.

Third, support for additional diversity within the South Florida core planning group enhanced the initiative's ability to address a broad range of stakeholders. In a successful CAS, the system's internal variety should match the variety in the external environment (Morgan 1986). In other words, if minority populations play a significant role in the overall community (the external environment) they should also play a significant role on the project team. An outside perspective in South Florida helped identify additional opportunities for increasing internal diversity that might otherwise have been overlooked.

A fourth way that the EPA nudged the system was by encouraging the initiative to establish more than one point of focus. This proved particularly important since the Everglades initiative covers such a broad geographical area. People involved in South Florida told us they 'wanted to see something concrete happen'. It seemed important to local leaders to be able to point to real improvements in their own neighbourhoods as signs that the overall Everglades initiative would create tangible benefits. A neighbourhood building project, a riverbank reclamation and the development of an integrated transport plan were all sponsored by the Eastward Ho! initiative, with each initiative building credibility for the overall effort. On the Delmarva Peninsula, simultaneous activities within regions, and even across regions, were supported in order to bring as many people into the project as possible. As long as the core vision of the initiative stays intact and each area of focus is seen as contributing to the overall project, then multiple focal points allow more stakeholders to feel closer to the project as a whole.

Working within the community, US federal employees can also nudge decisions that help build local capacity. Successful environmental action often requires long-term commitment and federal agencies cannot provide the energy needed to sustain a decades-long movement throughout its full life-cycle. Therefore, the initial federal involvement must contribute to a self-sustaining situation within the local community which requires the intentional building of local capacity in every resource decision. This was a lesson learned after-the-fact in South Florida. For one of the conferences, a nationally recognised expert from halfway across the country was brought in to give one of the key talks. Later, the team recognised that it may have been more valuable to use an expert who taught at one of the local colleges who, although not nationally known, understood the specifics of the South Florida situation far better and who, as a member of the local community, would have then become a local resource for the movement, a role the more distant lecturer could not fill as effectively.

The communication infrastructure is another point of leverage in a complex system. The federal government has significant resources in terms of existing communication infrastructure—often including videoconferencing, teleconferencing, and Internet resources—that can serve as a communications backbone for a community-based project. In South Florida, the EPA provided and managed a communication infrastructure—primarily email and voice mail—that allowed people from various areas, localities and regions to share ideas and decisions in a collaborative way. This collaboration extended to other federal agencies and EPA played a role in tying various agencies efforts together for the stakeholders.

Finally, a little money at the right time can provide the perfect push in certain circumstances, if focused on providing some concrete, definable contribution. On the Delmarva Peninsula, in addition to technical assistance, EPA's interventions included small financial grants, with each grant tied to a specific project approved by the 'circuit rider' (see Case Study B). In South Florida, EPA contributed funds for a variety of very specific purposes, such as sponsoring the brownfields conferences and providing small grants for community diversity groups to become involved in the Everglades efforts.

Design and discovery

An interesting aspect of our experience with working in communities has been the dynamic interplay of two salient features that appear to work together to create progress—a general emphasis on designed approaches complemented by an openness to discovery (Seymour 1994).

By 'design' we mean the use of tools, methods and approaches developed and proven outside the community and brought in to respond to specific issues or concerns. Good designs can be applied repeatedly in very different geographic, social and environmental situations. For instance, on the Delmarva Peninsula, discussions with stakeholders led to the circuit rider's suggestion that the community develop a local heritage protection plan. This process, which had already been applied and refined in other places, followed a set of structured steps from the initial goal-setting, through the identification and prioritisation of local environmental heritage concerns, to the development of action plans for protecting the highest-priority assets. The use of a designed process provided a defined path for people to begin getting involved in environmental stewardship activities.

On the other side of the implementation coin is 'discovery'—the emergence of locally conceived and instituted actions to meet local needs. These opportunities may already exist, but on the Delmarva Peninsula they often surfaced during the implementation of the designed process. There, the development of the first heritage protection plan for the Lower Eastern Shore led to discussions with the mayor of one of the participating towns who was considering whether or not to outsource the town's small marina. Although generally not the type of issue that usually gains EPA attention, the federal employee on site agreed to support the investigation. Surprisingly, the effort led to the identification of environmental benefits that would accrue to the local community only if the town continued to manage the marina as part of a larger heritage tourism effort, a finding that eventually solidified local support and sealed the decision not to outsource the marina.

Discovery is the commitment to the local place and local goals that allows the active participants to uncover the internal logic of the local challenge and respond to that, rather than to some dictated issue or entry pathway (the design) that may not get to the point. Discovery challenges design—indeed, it challenges the traditional mechanistic model that suggests that activities should be carefully engineered to produce reliable results—by requiring an adaptive, intuitive response to unique stimuli, challenges and opportunities. Discovery is decentralised and unique in the sense that it arises out of a specific situation and requires a willingness to bend a design to respond to new ideas, needs and opportunities in the community that will contribute to progress.

Thus, design and discovery interact. Implementing a designed activity—the heritage protection plan—on the Delmarva Peninsula led to the discovery of the mayor's dilemma with the town's marina and a number of other opportunities for interaction. Some of these discoveries will be limited to the specific time and place. However, as the circuit rider on the Delmarva Peninsula realised, in some circumstances the learning done during a discovery encounter can be captured, categorised and turned into a design itself, available when the specific stimuli reappears under new conditions. The provision of heritage visitor centre assistance, an outcome of one of the earliest heritage protection plans, became the template for a designed activity that was repeated numerous times throughout the circuit rider's assignment.

Incremental co-evolution

Equilibrium is a threat to a CAS (Pascale *et al.* 2000). No evolution or new self-organisation can take place in an equilibrium situation. One way to stifle a community-based movement swiftly is to impose too much organisational structure on it; such structures have a way of becoming their own rationale for continued existence and so drain the movement's energy. On the other hand, death of a social movement can also result from too much unfocused energy. Without any structure, the movement's energy eventually dissipates in random activities without having accomplished any project goals.

The way a CAS can survive and evolve is to attain the edge of chaos, maintaining its existence there without either falling back into a comfortable equilibrium (disguised sometime as 'orderly' progress) or sliding completely into chaos (Pascale *et al.* 2000). By continually taking in new information from other systems in the external environment and passing new information back to those systems, a CAS can co-evolve with its external environments in a relationship that can be sustained.

Co-evolution is the co-ordinated and interdependent evolution of two or more systems within a larger ecological system (Kauffman 1995). Feedback between or among the systems occurs in terms of competition or co-operation and different utilisation of the same limited resources. Community-based social movements can co-evolve as conditions change both within the systems with which the movement interacts and also within the external environment as a whole (Environmental Advisory Council to the Swedish Government 2002). In fact, this co-evolution can provide a constant source of energy to keep the CAS slightly disturbed, never quite settling into equilibrium (Kauffman 1995).

From afar—for instance, from the perspective of a federal agency's headquarters in Washington, DC—the appearance of constant turmoil can seem chaotic and, ultimately, frustrating. Several of the EPA managers reviewing their South Florida involvement told us that they believed that 'South Florida is a bad example for other projects because there are too many local governments involved. Better to work with a single government', and that 'Good things have happened, good tools have been shared, and South Florida is happy to have the help. But there is not a good sense of where we're supposed to be in two years and what kind of key decisions are going to be made and how the environment will be affected. Also, South Florida is very large and very expensive and doesn't give any evidence of a structured kind of involvement.'

But the view from within the situation—the view of the involved stakeholders— senses this edge-of-chaos situation as energy for new learning, new opportunity and new growth.

Although this co-evolutionary aspect underlies all great social transformations, it is often hidden, since it takes place slowly over long periods (Environmental Advisory Council to the Swedish Government 2002). Incremental co-evolution requires not only continual learning but also patience. Several of the scientists participating in the efforts to restore the Everglades feel that it may take as long as 50 years before the learning being achieved within the various Everglades-related activities makes its way back into the general populace and the safety of the Everglades is truly assured. Similarly, the Chesapeake Bay programme, the largest conservation organisation dedicated to the restoration of the Bay, has set restoration targets in the Delmarva region for the years 2010 and 2050.

Federal agency employees involved in communities can aid this kind of co-evolution in a number of ways. Federal agencies have access to lessons learned from around the nation and beyond. Functioning as a 'national knowledge manager' in their assigned areas, federal agencies can give their employees 'on the ground' a wide range of valuable lessons to use within the local setting. Examples of successful projects in other parts of the country can elicit creative responses from a community struggling to move toward the achievement of a social goal.

The federal agency employee can also remind the group than an entrepreneurial, public outreach-oriented component is important for a fully functioning social movement. After all, 'Save the Everglades' bumper stickers and 'Save the Bay' licence plates function as information pulses introduced into the external environment to begin the gradual changes that lead to long-term sustainability.

Implications and summary:
taking advantage of new forms of involvement

Much of what US federal agencies do, and the means by which they do it, will not change in the near future. The traditional structure of standards, research and enforcement provides the basis for much effective federal action in defining and supporting national goals for the environment, education, housing and so on. In fact, the system of standards and typical efforts to meet them are essentially the design components of federal involvement and, in themselves, provide a rich and valuable resource. However, some changes will be required in order for the leaders and employees of US federal agencies to take full advantage of the insights emerging from complexity science, especially when working in the field at the local community level.

The US federal agency system of measurements and rewards will have to change to accommodate longer time-frames and new definitions of success. Significant change on the local level can rarely be accomplished within the artificial periods of an annual budget cycle or a four-year period presidential administration. In turn, US federal managers' ability and willingness to 'take the longer view' will depend on new budgetary tools—accounts established and funded to span fiscal years and administrations.

Discovery and adaptation can work only if an agency is a respected partner in the local community. Respect and partnership come more from listening than from commanding. As one of the South Florida stakeholders told us: 'When we heard EPA was getting involved, we assumed they would come in and try to boss us around. They didn't. They listened to us instead. Some of us were really amazed.' If the federal agency hopes to be effective in achieving national goals, its employees have to be where they are needed when they are needed, and they must be prepared to listen and learn to what the local populace is telling them.

Once established as a partner in the local community, the federal agency can then help keep the work moving forward by suggesting directions and outcomes (the design), facilitating the provision of information, money and other resources that contribute to the larger good, encouraging internal diversity to build the resilience of the initiative and providing a communication infrastructure that supports consensus.

However, constrained by budgets that are always under the threat of reduction, federal agencies cannot afford to assign their employees to permanent, local offices in every community that has a social challenge. How, then, can an agency choose those places where there is not only a significant challenge but also a likelihood that the community will be receptive to this 'on the ground' approach?

We believe that, as a minimum, two conditions, need to be present:

1. A 'significant' regional or national issue

2. A level of concern, turbulence, opportunity and momentum already present in the community

A 'significant' issue can be a unique natural resource, a region with a large or special human or natural community at risk or a situation such that, if a successful approach could be demonstrated, it could be repeated in many other similar places without significant federal involvement. Both South Florida and the Delmarva Peninsula had the following characteristics that could be used as a guide to 'significance' in the area of environmental management:

1. An endangered ecosystem or cultural landscape that is a recognised regional (and international) asset

2. A history of concern for the ecosystem

3. Clear impact on the asset from the encroaching development

4. An urban area experiencing stress in several areas: sewage, water, transportation, energy, poverty

5. A fairly well-accepted assessment of future growth that suggests continued stress on the area

6. A significant amount of activity focusing on the challenges

7. A political climate growing more inclined to support the project

The second condition acknowledges that without local energy, concern and leadership a federal agency cannot come in from outside and make it happen. EPA, FEMA or HUD cannot start local work from scratch. To use the insights from CAS, the elements of the CAS have to already exist. This may be a case where conflict, confusion and turmoil in a community is actually an opportunity rather than a barrier—indicating a situation on the edge of chaos that may be ripe for a new approach.

Federal agencies will continue to regulate, inspect and enforce. However, many of our social challenges—ecosystem restoration, cultural landscape protection, the improvement of educational systems, overcoming the digital divide—are unresponsive to these traditional, top-down responses. To begin to address many of these challenges, the federal agency must find ways to become creatively engaged at the level of the local community without exerting command-and-control attitudes. Our experiences in South Florida and on the Delmarva Peninsula offer examples of how federal employees can work effectively at these local levels. We believe that the emerging study of CAS provides a theoretical structure that will help us understand the dynamics at work in these situations so that the lessons discovered by federal employees in one area can be made available as proven designs to employees working in other places.

Case Study A: Protecting the Everglades

In 1997, the Governor's Commission for a Sustainable South Florida came to a startling conclusion. With 1,000 new residents a day and an expected doubling of its population in the next 30 years, growth in new areas outside the historically urbanised zone from West Palm Beach to the Keys was eating up the buffers around the Everglades. Without steps to redirect the expansion of human settlement on the East and, eventually, the West coasts, the massive state and federal effort to save the Everglades would fail.

The proposed response was to direct as much new growth as possible to already developed areas, away from the remaining natural areas. This 'new urbanism' approach depended on higher-density development in communities with restored amenities such as low crime, good schools, quality services and public transportation. Multiple local, state and federal agencies became involved in the effort, including the EPA.

The EPA did not have a specific authority, regulatory or otherwise, to dictate the shape of its involvement. Instead, the complexity of the situation—multiple federal and state agencies and local groups were involved—suggested that a more adaptive approach, responsive to local needs was appropriate. EPA's initial response was to place a full-time member of staff in the South Florida community to facilitate the involvement of its regional and headquarters EPA offices, as well as other federal agencies. The presence of a full-time staff member, willing to work in collaboration with the various state and local leaders to strengthen local capacity, was seen as the best way to ensure co-ordination between on-the-ground efforts and federal direction.

Over the course of the next two years, through their employee on the ground in South Florida, the EPA provided information, education, communication support and targeted resources. For instance, it provided a small grant to include a local interest group in an effort to expand the diversity of the core team. Through a combination of providing resources at critical times, using its visibility to convene meetings and support committee work, and bringing expertise and support from the entire federal agency family when local issues arose, EPA was able to work in South Florida in a new way. While tracking specific administrative tasks or completions of programmatic activities was not possible, the work in South Florida supported the ultimate achievement of the much larger effort to protect the Everglades.

Our programme evaluation of EPA's involvement in South Florida concluded that success should not be measured by the traditional, linear measure of return on investment. Instead, the evaluation concluded that, based on the testimony of numerous key people within the 'Save the Everglades' movement, the EPA's work in support of the Everglades had been a success. As one of the local officials commented to us at the close of our interview with her:

> We would not be as far along as we are if we had not had EPA involvement. There's no question about it. EPA provided energy, direction and education. They helped bring things together that otherwise would have just faded away and been lost. And they brought some good fiscal resources too.

Case Study B: Maintaining natural and cultural heritage through design and discovery on the Delmarva Peninsula

The Delmarva Peninsula is fragile low-lying land set between the Chesapeake Bay to the west and the Atlantic Ocean to the east, and including coastal sections of Delaware, Maryland and Virginia. Famous for a rural lifestyle of farming, fishing and recreation, the area is under significant pressure from the ever-expanding population centres of the mid-Atlantic states.

In the mid 1980s, the EPA decided to initiate the development of a heritage protection plan (HPA) as a means of preserving some of the unique features of the landscape and the culture of the area. The idea for a HPA was derived from other similar efforts across the country and, in traditional form, follows a set approach of assessment, planning and approval in a good, but essentially top-down, approach to preservation. From the beginning, the effort did not gain much traction locally and languished. Other issues, such as the request for a new marina, issues regarding a waste dump and local pollution concerns dominated the attention of the local stakeholders.

Starting in the late 1980s, EPA personnel began to take a new approach to the whole area. Rather than seeing each of these local issues as separate concerns that could potentially divert attention from the larger regional planning effort, EPA staff working in the area began to use the separate local issues as a means of building awareness for conservation on a larger scale. They began to identify different paths for involvement that could be followed in parallel, using a combination of structured approaches (previously proven designs) and adaptive responses to emerging needs (discovery of new opportunities for involvement). Multiple 'circuit riders' were assigned to work within the local communities, trying to identify opportunities for EPA and other government or private-sector involvement. Figure 5.1 attempts to capture the experience of one EPA route rider using a combination of previously proven, structured approaches and discovery of new opportunities.

In 1988, a grant to assist in Pocomoke River clean-up activities was provided to a local group. Contacts developed during this activity quickly led to a subsequent opportunity for providing technical assistance to develop a 'heritage plan' for the lower eastern shore. The development of these heritage plans followed a structured format with definable objectives and milestones, which we consider an involvement using a previously proven design. Stemming from these initial two involvements, numerous other opportunities (shown as the stems emerging from the trunk activities on the chart) were discovered and pursued within the same general area and populace.

Many of the discovered opportunities for involvement required a new attitude on the part of EPA personnel. In a traditional top-down involvement strategy, the federal agency was often perceived as 'telling' local people how the federal dollars or technical assistance could be used. Instead, the discovery mind-set of the route riders allowed local people to inform EPA personnel about issues that were most important at the local level. Federal staff could then find a way to respond, or to

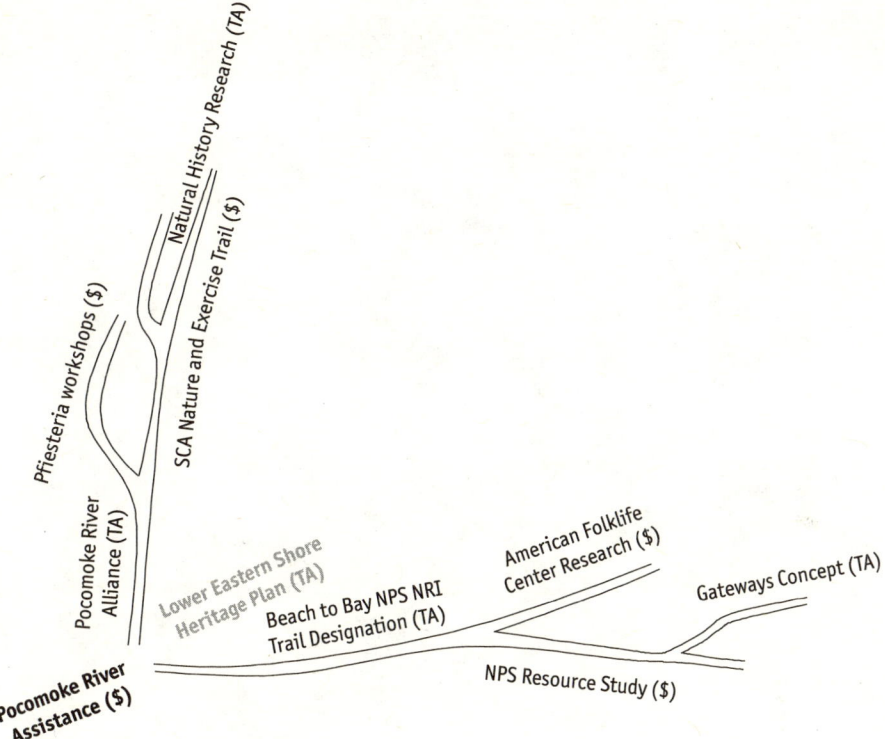

$ = financial assistance; TA = technical assistance; grey text = design approach

FIGURE 5.1 Chesapeake Bay land, growth and stewardship assistance: initial efforts 1988–92

decline involvement politely, as sometimes was required when no adequate connection between the local concern and the federal agency mission could be discerned.

As these discovered activities expanded, news of the circuit rider's activities began to spread throughout a wider region. This news led to requests from other specific localities for support.

In Figure 5.2, the trunk of the graphic is composed of EPA involvements that, read from left to right, indicate the sequential spread of one circuit rider's involvement on the Delmarva Peninsula from 1988 through 1992. Each trunk activity represents a movement into either a new, expanded geographical scope or a new, adjacent geographical area. In turn, each trunk activity gave rise to additional opportunities for involvement within the new geographic area. The side branches stemming from each of the trunk activities represent these additional involvements. Activities along each branch are related in that activities closer to the trunk contain the seeds of the activities farther out from the trunk.

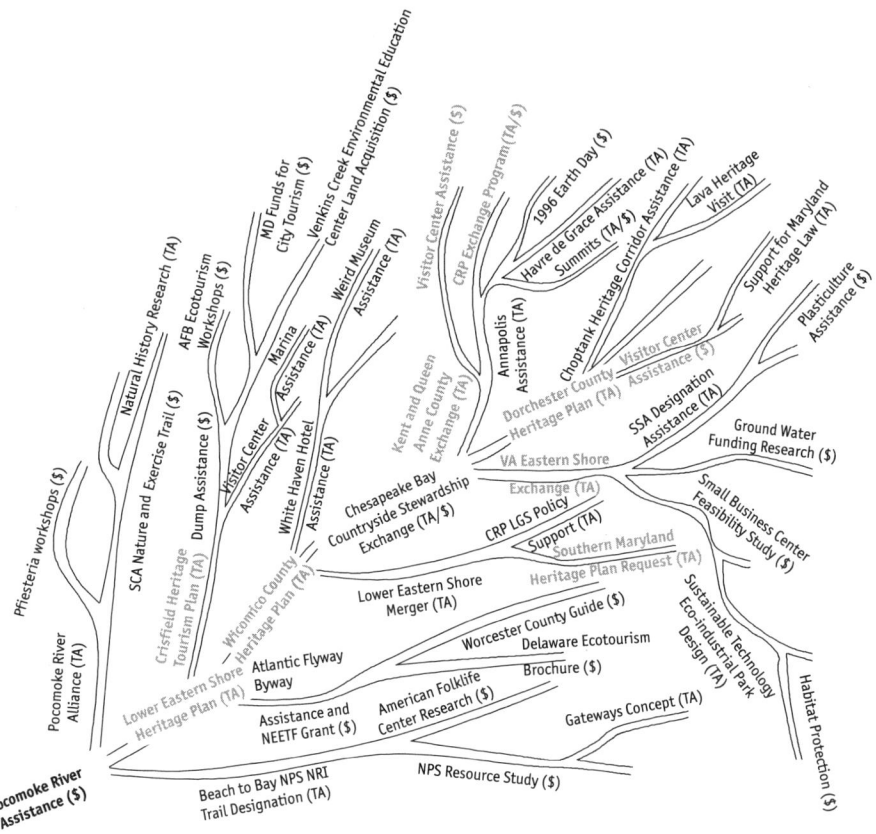

$ = financial assistance; TA = technical assistance; grey text = design approach

FIGURE 5.2 Chesapeake Bay land, growth and stewardship assistance 1988-96

Three aspects of the design and discovery approach become clear from the chart. First, discovered needs in one area can become designed approaches that can be repeated in other areas. For instance, heritage visitor centre assistance, which was discovered as an outgrowth of the lower eastern shore heritage plan, became more of a designed involvement as it was repeated in subsequent areas. Similarly, information exchange programmes became more structured as they were repeated in multiple geographical locations.

Second, each trunk activity spawned multiple offshoots, and these offshoots continued to generate follow-on opportunities long after the initial involvement was over. Furthermore, these offshoots proceeded concurrently in many places, with each activity adding to the local capacity to deal constructively with their watershed issues.

Third, because core EPA environmental values were at the heart of the activities depicted, the spread of the activities over time might be read as the growing penetration of environmental awareness over an increasingly large geographic area. In fact, we might hypothesise that this pattern of involvement—repeated in other Chesapeake watershed areas by other groups discovering the same self-organising properties of community involvement—has been one of the major contributors to the growth in public concern and federal and local commitment to restoring the health of the Bay.

References

Burns, J.S. (2002) 'Chaos Theory and Leadership Studies: Exploring Uncharted Seas', *Journal of Leadership and Organizational Studies* 9.2: 42-57.

Capra, F. (1996) *The Web of Life: A New Scientific Understanding of Living Systems* (New York: Anchor).

Chrislip, D.D., and C.E. Larson (1994) *Collaborative Leadership* (San Francisco: Jossey-Bass).

Clarke, A.L. (2003) 'Introduction to Special Issue. Restoring the Florida Everglades: Balancing Population and the Environment', *Population and Environment* 24.6 (July 2003): 451.

Costanza, R., L. Wainger, C. Folke and K.-G. Maler (1993) 'Modeling Complex Ecological Economic Systems', *Bioscience* 43.8 (September 1993): 545-55.

Dent, E. (2003) 'The Complexity Science Organizational Development Practitioner', *Organizational Development Journal* 21.2 (Summer 2003): 82-86.

Environmental Advisory Council to the Swedish Government (2002) *Resilience and Sustainable Development: Building Adaptive Capacity in a World of Transformation* (Stockholm: Ministry of the Environment).

Gleick, J. (1987) *Chaos: Making A New Science* (New York: Viking).

Heslin, K. (2001) 'EPA's Energy Star Program Pays Dividends', *Energy User News*, www.energyusernews.com/CDA/ArticleInformation/features/BNP__Features__Item/0,2584,19253,00.html, January 2001.

Holland, J.H. (1992) 'Complex Adaptive Systems', *Daedalus* 121.1 (Winter 1992): 17-30.

—— (1995) *Hidden Order: How Adaptation Builds Complexity* (Reading, MA: Addison-Wesley).

—— (1999) *Emergence: From Chaos to Order* (New York: Perseus Book Group).

Innes, J.E., and D.E. Booher (1999a) 'Metropolitan Development as a Complex System: A New Approach to Sustainability', *Economic Development Quarterly* 13.2 (May 1999): 141-56.

—— and —— (1999b) 'Consensus Building and Complex Adaptive Systems: A Framework for Evaluating Collaborative Planning', *APA Journal* 65.4 (Autumn 1999): 412-23.

Kauffman, S.A. (1995) *At Home in the Universe: The Search for the Laws of Self-organization and Complexity* (New York: Oxford University Press).

Kiel, L.D. (1994) *Managing Chaos and Complexity in Government* (San Francisco: Jossey-Bass).

—— (1997) 'Embedding Chaotic Logic into Public Administration Thought: Requisites for the New Paradigm', *Public Administration Management: An Interactive Journal* 2.4.

—— and B.J. Seldon (1998) 'Measuring Temporal Complexity in the External Environment: Nonlinearity and the Bounds of Rational Action', *American Review of Public Administration* 28.3 (September 1998): 246-65.

Kouzes, J.M., and B.Z. Posner (2002) *The Leadership Challenge* (San Francisco: Jossey-Bass, 3rd edn).

Langewiesche, W. (2003) 'Columbia's Last Flight', *The Atlantic* 292.4 (November 2003): 58-87.

Lewin, R. (1993) *Complexity: Life at the Edge of Chaos* (Chicago: University of Chicago Press).

Mathews, K.M., M.C. White and R.G. Long (1999) 'Why Study the Complexity Sciences in the Behavioral and Social Sciences?', *Human Relations* 52.4: 439-62.

Morgan, G. (1986) *Images of Organization* (Newbury Park, CA: Sage).

Pascale, R.T., M. Millemann and L. Gioja (2000) *Surfing the Edge of Chaos* (New York: Three Rivers Press).

Priesmeyer, H.R. (1992) *Organizations and Chaos: Defining the Methods of Nonlinear Management* (Westport, CT: Quorum Books).

Stacey, R. (1992) *Managing the Unknowable: Strategic Boundaries between Order and Chaos in Organizations* (San Francisco: Jossey-Bass).

Seymour, F.J. (1996) 'Are Successful Community-Based Conservation Projects Designed or Discovered?', in D. Western and R.M. Wright (eds.), *Natural Connections: Perspectives in Community-Nased Conservation* (Washington, DC: Island Press).

Van Uden, J., K.A. Richardson and P. Cilliers (2001) 'Postmodernism Revisited? Complexity Science and the Study of Organizations', *Tamara: Journal of Critical Postmodern Organization Science* 1.3: 53-68.

Waldrop, M.M. (1992) *Complexity: The Emerging Science at the Edge of Chaos* (New York: Simon & Schuster).

Wheatley, M. (1999) *Leadership and the New Science* (San Francisco: Berrett-Koehler, 2nd edn).

6
Honda Insight
DEVELOPMENT AND LAUNCH
OF A HYBRID ELECTRIC VEHICLE

Melissa A. Schilling
New York University, USA

James Johng
Tishman Speyer Properties, USA

Yong-Joo Kang
PricewaterhouseCoopers, USA

Jane Sul
Samsung Securities Company Limited, South Korea

Masayuki Takanashi
Sumitomo Mitsui Banking Corporation, Japan

In 1997, the Honda Motor Company introduced a two-door gasoline–electric hybrid vehicle—the Insight—to Japan. The Insight's fuel efficiency was rated at 61 miles per gallon (mpg) in the city and 68 mpg on the highway, and its battery did not need to be plugged into an electrical outlet for recharging. By 1999, Honda was selling the Insight in the US, and winning accolades from environmental groups. In 2000, the Sierra Club gave Honda its Award for Excellence in Environmental Engineering and, in 2002, the Environmental Protection Agency (EPA) rated the Insight as the most fuel-efficient vehicle sold in the US for the 2003 model year.

Developing environmentally friendly automobiles was not a new strategy for Honda. In fact, the company's work on developing cleaner transportation alternatives had begun decades earlier (see Box 6.1). Gaining mass-market acceptance of such alternatives, however, had proven somewhat more challenging.

1970   **Efficient start:**
The lightweight and fuel-efficient N600 is the first Honda car sold in America.

1971   **The world's first:**
Compound vortex controlled combustion technology is announced by Honda. In 1975, this led to the world's first engine to comply with the 1970 Clean Air Act emission requirement without a catalytic converter.

1973   **Marine engines:**
Since 1973, Honda has manufactured only four-stroke outboard motors which are about 90% cleaner, 50% more fuel-efficient and 50% quieter than typical two-stroke outboard motors which release oil directly into the water.

1977   **Fuel-efficiency leadership:**
The Honda Civic CVCC is ranked first in fuel efficiency in the EPA's first-ever list of the top ten fuel-efficient cars.

1986   **50 plus:**
The Civic CRX-HF is the first mass-produced four-cylinder car to break the 50 mpg fuel-economy mark.

1988   **Redefining the possible:**
The foundation technology for Honda's achievements in high performance, low emissions and high fuel efficiency is announced: the VTEC™ (variable valve timing and lift electronic control) automobile engine.

1989   **Solvent-free:**
Honda becomes the first car maker in America to use solvent-free waterborne paint in mass production.

1995   **Continued leadership:**
Fuel-economy leadership puts four Honda models on the EPA's list of the top ten fuel-efficient cars.

The first LEV:
The 1996 Honda Civic is the first gasoline-powered car to meet California's low-emission vehicle (LEV) standards, reducing smog-related hydrocarbon pollutants by 70% below federal standards.

1996   **Solar power:**
Honda's two-passenger solar car, the Dream, breaks World Solar Challenge records.

1997   **Getting to zero:**
Honda announces a virtually pollution-free, gasoline-powered internal-combustion engine, the ZLEV (zero-level emission vehicle).

EV plus:
With an EPA-rated city driving range of 125 miles, Honda begins leasing the first four-passenger electric vehicle with advanced battery technology to consumers.

1998   **Cleanest in the world:**
Production begins on the 1998 Honda Civic GX natural gas vehicle. Manufactured with a sealed evaporative-fuel system, the GX is recognised by the EPA as being the cleanest internal-combustion engine in the world.

Box 6.1 Honda's environment and technology timeline (continued opposite)

1999 **Hyper:**
Honda introduces the HYPER VTEC four-stroke engine in the CB400 motorcycle in Japan, lowering emissions and increasing fuel efficiency, while also improving performance. Honda has committed to producing motorcycles and scooters with only four-stroke engines for on-road use by the year 2002.

Honda's hybrid technology:
Honda develops a fuel-efficient low-emission hybrid engine that achieves 61 mpg city/70 mpg highway (EPA fuel economy estimates), with a gasoline engine and an electric motor.

2000 **SULEV Accord:**
The 2000 Accord is the first gasoline vehicle to meet CARB's super ultra low emission (SULEV) standard.

2001 **Fuel efficiency:**
For the third straight year, the Honda Insight is named the most fuel-efficient car in America by the EPA.

2002 **Civic hybrid:**
The Honda Civic Hybrid ushers in a new era of hybrid technology, and Honda becomes the first car company to mass-produce the hybrid powertrain to the consumer market.

Fuel cell certification:
The FCX from Honda is the first fuel-cell vehicle in the world to receive government certification. Honda again proves its commitment to a cleaner environment by paving the way for the commercial use of fuel-cell vehicles.

'Green' facility:
Honda opens a 212,888 ft^2 warehouse, designed, constructed and now operating using environmentally friendly products and practices. Honda's new 'green' facility will supply parts to nine US western states and act as a training centre and zone office in Gresham, Oregon.

Box 6.1 (from previous page)

History of Honda

Honda was founded by Mr Soichiro Honda (1906–91) in 1946 as the Honda Technical Research Institute. The company began as a developer of engines for bicycles and by 1949 it had produced its first motorcycle, the Dream. In 1959, Honda entered the US automobile and motorcycle market by opening the American Honda Motor Company. A few years later, in 1963, Honda released its first sports car, the S500, in Japan.

Honda Motor Co. Inc. grew rapidly to become one of the world's largest automobile companies. Its global strategy of building factories that would meet the needs of local customers resulted in a total worldwide presence of more than 100 factories in 33 countries. Furthermore, while other car manufacturers engaged in a frenzy of merger and acquisition activities in the late 1990s, Honda steadfastly maintained its independence. In 2002, it was Japan's third largest car manufacturer (after Toyota and Nissan), and the world's largest motorcycle manufacturer, with sales of more than US$55 billion (see Table 6.1). In 2002, it was ranked 41 in *Fortune*'s Global Most Admired Companies.

2002 sales

	$ millions	% of total
North America	32,330	46
Japan	28,600	41
Europe	4,529	7
Other regions	4,164	6
Adjustments	(14,370)	–
Total	55,253	100

2002 product breakdown

	$ millions	% of total
Automobiles	44,501	80
Motorcycles	7,114	13
Financial services	1,571	3
Other	2,205	4
Adjustments	(138)	–
Total	55,253	100

TABLE 6.1 Honda's 2002 sales: geographic and product breakdowns

Source: www.hoovers.com

Honda's environmental orientation

At Honda, being an environmental leader means never uttering the words, 'It can't be done'. That's why, for more than two decades, Honda has led the way in balancing what consumers want with what the environment needs. Technologies change over time—but our commitment to the environment never will.

Honda corporate website, August 2003

In 1972, Honda introduced the Civic, which became an immediate success, ranking first in US fuel economy tests for four consecutive years starting in 1974. Throughout the 1980s and 1990s, Honda made a number of advancements in environmentally friendly transportation. In 1986, it developed the first mass-produced four-cylinder car that could break the 50 mpg barrier, the Civic CRX-HF. In 1989, it became the first car manufacturer in the US to use solvent-free paint in its mass production facilities. In 1996, Honda introduced a record-breaking solar powered car (a prototype not designed for commercial production) and in 1998 it introduced a completely electric vehicle. Although the electric car was not a commercial success, the process of developing it created a foundation of expertise that Honda would later employ in its development of fuel cell technology. Fuel cells were considered to offer great potential for the eventual replacement of combustion engines.[1]

Honda's environmental strategies also extended into its factory design and alternative transportation initiatives. The company's Green Factory programme to increase the re-use of materials, reduce emissions and promote recycling drove down its chemical emissions by 63% per car produced between 1995 and 1998 (see Fig. 6.1).

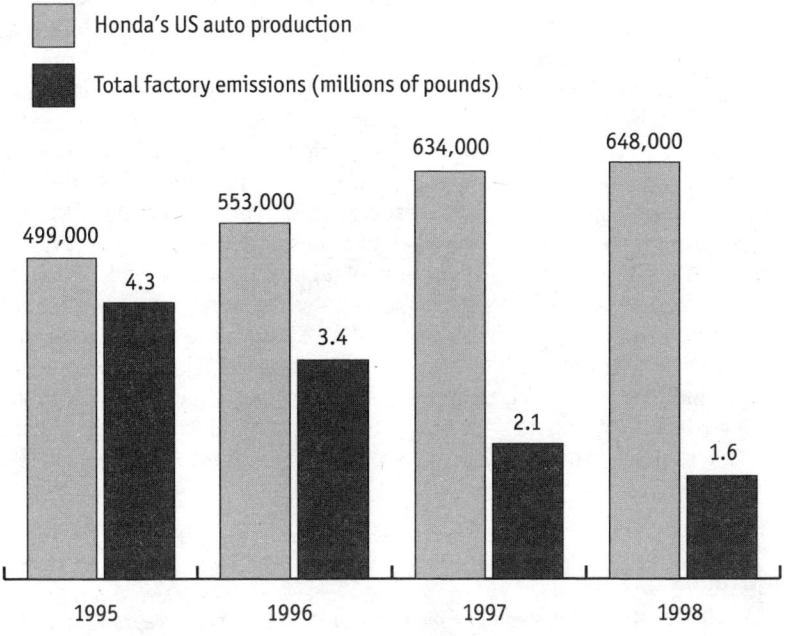

FIGURE 6.1 Honda's US auto production and total factory emissions 1995–98

Honda also worked with Bay Area Rapid Transit, CalTrans, University of California Davis and University of California Riverside to develop innovative car sharing programmes called CarLink and Intellishare. Both of these encouraged individuals to share the use of fuel-efficient Honda models for commuting and personal errands. These projects were developed with the intention of developing a greater understanding of whether such programmes would be effective and what would be the obstacles to their implementation.

1   National Renewable Energy Laboratory website, www.nrel.gov/vehiclesandfuels/hev, accessed 7 November 2004.

Hybrid electric vehicles

By the 1980s and 1990s, under growing pressure from organisations such as the EPA, a few automobile manufacturers had introduced electric vehicles (EVs) (see Box 6.2 on page 144 for an interesting history of the electric vehicle). None of these vehicles achieved widespread acceptance or commercial success, however. The EV's limited range and its need to be plugged into an electrical outlet for recharging were obstacles to mass-market adoption. However, by the late 1990s, automobile manufacturers were experimenting with hybrid vehicles that offered a compromise between the combustion engine's environmental impact and the electric vehicle's awkwardness. Both Honda and Toyota introduced hybrids (the Insight and Prius, respectively) in Japan in 1997. After some initial commercial success, both companies brought their hybrid models to the US in 1999.

Hybrid electric vehicles (HEVs) are electric vehicles that use another source of energy besides the battery used by EVs. In most cases, the alternative power source is the internal combustion engine. In such cases, the HEV combines the internal combustion engine with a battery and electric motor, creating a vehicle that is able to provide at least twice the fuel economy of a gasoline-only vehicle. Basically, the HEV is able to utilise the benefits of both power systems by providing the fuel economy and environmental friendliness of an EV with the torque and range of a gasoline vehicle. This results in a 'best of both worlds' vehicle. While some industry experts argue that HEVs are a temporary solution that would give way to vehicles with better battery technology in the future, others believe it will be a long time before other 'clean cars' would provide real competition to the hybrids (Reuters 2002a).

Advantages of HEVs

HEVs have several advantages over gasoline vehicles, notably regenerative braking capability, reduced engine weight, lowered overall vehicle weight, increased fuel efficiency and decreased emissions. The regenerative braking capability of HEVs helps to minimise energy loss and recover the energy used to slow down or stop a vehicle. This means that engines can be sized to accommodate average loads instead of peak loads, significantly reducing engine weight. In addition, the special lightweight materials that are used to manufacture HEVs further reduce the overall vehicle weight of the vehicle. Finally, both the lowered vehicle weight and the dual power system greatly increase the HEV's fuel efficiency and reduce its emissions. The 2003 models of the Honda Insight and Toyota Prius released an average of 3.5 and 4.1 tonnes of greenhouse gas emissions per year respectively. By comparison, gasoline-only compact cars emitted 7–10 tonnes of greenhouse gases per year.

In developing HEVs, automobile manufacturers kept in mind that consumers were most concerned with four specific attributes—performance, reliability, safety and fun—when purchasing cars (American Honda Motor Co. Ltd 2001). Since the performance of the HEVs was in most cases on par with or better than that of conventional vehicles, consumers were presented with a very competitive substitute. In addition, since the feel and drive of the HEVs were designed to be very similar to gasoline vehicles, the new vehicles required almost no education of the consumer. As Thomas G. Elliot, executive vice president of North American Honda, said: 'Hybrids are the kind of car that most consumers can live with. The technology is almost transparent to them' (*Business Week Online* 2000). Thus, for the driver, the HEV offered similar or superior performance compared to a conventional vehicle and, at the same time, provided a practical way for consumers to lessen their impact on the environment and still take advantage of the added benefits of fuel cost savings and government tax incentives.

The only downside to the HEV was its price. As of mid-2002, HEVs in the US cost around US$4,000 more than equivalent standard models. Many believed that the lacklustre growth in sales of HEVs would soon change once the cost issues were resolved. As Ted Miller, a senior official at the US Advanced Battery Consortium (USABC) put it: 'If you can deliver a hybrid vehicle to a customer for nearly the same price as a typical [non-hybrid] vehicle, demand can be fairly significant' (Reuters 2002b).

The Insight

The Insight is a two-door two-seater hybrid gasoline–electric car that can run up to 70 miles a gallon on the highway and 61 miles in the city. The Insight's fuel efficiency was achieved in two primary ways. First, the car's electric motor produced its power from a nickel metal hydride battery pack that was continuously charged by regenerative braking. Regenerative braking permits energy that would be wasted by braking to be recaptured for future usage. Second, the vehicle's body was light and aerodynamic. The frame and body were constructed mostly of aluminium, shaving almost 40% off a car's typical weight. Aluminium is both lighter and more rigid than traditional steel.[2] The Insight's fenders were made of recyclable plastic. It also employed aluminium alloy wheels, a magnesium oil pan and plastic front head cover, which allowed the Insight to tip the scales at only 1,850 lbs. All this helped to improve the vehicle's energy efficiency while also increasing its rigidity. The teardrop-shaped body, enclosed rear wheel wells and an under-car cover resulted in a coefficient of drag (Cd) of only 0.25, the lowest Cd of any production car.[3]

Competition in the HEV industry

As of early 2002, only two companies, Honda and Toyota, had successfully penetrated the hybrid market. Compared to their Japanese rivals, the 'big three' US car makers—General Motors (GM), Ford and DaimlerChrysler—were lagging well behind. Although most US car manufacturers had schedules to release their own HEVs in the near future, Honda and Toyota were quickly positioning themselves as the car makers of the future. Honda, in particular, was perceived to be a leader in

2   Honda had acquired extensive expertise in the design of aluminium car bodies with its pioneering work on the Acura NSX sports car.
3   Insight Central website, www.insightcentral.net, accessed 2 November 2002.

technology by many, such as Daniel Becker, director of global warming policy at the Sierra Club, who said that Honda 'started the race for hybrids' and 'put on vehicles fuel-saving technologies that Detroit only keeps on the shelves' (*New York Times* 2002a).

Although Honda and Toyota were unlikely to be without competition for long, their lead enabled them to gain valuable experience in the production of environmentally friendly cars with consumer appeal (Raeburn 2002). In fact, both companies had stepped up schedules to release more HEVs in an effort to maintain their position. For example, in mid-2002, Honda released a hybrid version of its very popular Civic and in late 2003, Toyota released its improved Prius.

Toyota

While the Toyota Prius and the Insight had much in common, there were some interesting differences between them in terms of format, features, technologies employed and performance. Although the two cars could be seen as rivals within the environmentally friendly vehicle market, they nevertheless appealed to different segments of this market. This was partly as a result of the strategic direction the two companies decided to adopt when they entered the market in order to differentiate themselves, and partly a result of moves made early on in the development of the two vehicles and the technologies available to their developers.

Like the Honda Insight, the Toyota Prius utilised advanced engineering to combine a gasoline engine with an electric motor to create an environmentally conscious, fuel-efficient, hybrid sedan rated at 60 mpg in the city and 51 on the highway. While the Insight achieved better efficiency than the Prius in both city and highway driving, the Prius was unique in that its city-driving-rated efficiency was better than its highway efficiency. In addition, unlike the Insight, the Prius was a four-door mid-sized sedan with back seats for extra passengers, something the two-door Insight lacked. Thus, the Prius made more sense for people who regularly travelled with more than two people and could serve as the one and only car for a family.

Other competitors

Together with the US Department of Energy, the 'big three' US automobile manufacturers formed a partnership to develop and produce HEVs as possible competitors to the Honda Insight. GM developed the Gen2 Stirling HEV in 1998 and was planning on further enhancing its design in order to release another concept car called the GM Precept. Although GM did not have a hybrid car commercial available as of 2002, it was scheduled to release an electric version of its Chevy Silverado in 2004 (Raeburn 2002). Ford had also developed several prototypes through the partnership programme, such as the Ford P2000 and the Ford Prodigy, and was a little further along in releasing a HEV vehicle than GM. The Ford Escape, a sports utility HEV vehicle, was scheduled for release in late 2004 to capitalise on both the move towards cleaner cars and the popularity of sport utility vehicles. Although the Ford Escape was unlikely to compete directly with the Insight, it served to show that other competitors were near to releasing viable commercial HEV vehicles. Similarly, DaimlerChrysler was also working on a commercially viable HEV vehicle. Through its development of the ESX2 and ESX3, DaimlerChrysler had developed and showcased a hybrid version of its popular sport utility vehicle, the Jeep® Liberty, with its patented through-the-road (TTR) hybrid system. The Liberty HEV achieved a 30% improvement in fuel efficiency compared with the conventional six-cylinder Liberty without sacrificing utility, comfort or performance (Raeburn 2002).

In addition to these three manufacturers, several other companies, such as Volvo and Mazda, had also expressed intentions of entering the HEV market. Flexible fuel automobiles from Volkswagen and alternative-fuel cars from Mitsubishi were also soon to be introduced.

Other stakeholders

HEVs were subject to pressures from other key players such as federal and state government agencies and environmental organisations. Governmental pressures on automobile manufacturers to develop cleaner vehicles came in the form of regulations, partnerships and tax incentives, while environmental organisations exerted pressure through the media and lobbying legislators. Each player was significant in its own right in driving the development of HEVs.

Department of Energy

The Department of Energy began its HEV programme in 1993. Developed as a five-year cost-shared partnership between the department and the big three US car makers, the programme called for the companies to develop production-feasible HEV engines by 1998, first-generation prototypes by 2000 and market-ready HEVs by 2003. The goal of the programme was to produce vehicles that achieved at least twice the fuel efficiency of today's cars. Ideally, the goal was to develop an automobile that delivered 80 mpg and had performance, safety and cost levels comparable to internal combustion engines. As the programme progressed, the goals began to merge with the goals of the Partnership for a New Generation of Vehicles (PNGV).

PNGV and FreedomCAR

In 1993 the Clinton administration established the PNGV—a US$1.5 billion programme, funded by the government, to help the 'big three' develop energy-efficient vehicles. The goal of the project was to develop an affordable family car (to seat five) that could get 80 mpg. Despite the bold goals of the PNGV, US car makers were much slower than their Japanese rivals to bring alternative vehicle technologies to market (Belton 2000). In February 2003, the Bush administration scrapped the PNGV programme in favour of one called FreedomCAR. Under this programme, the government would spend US$1.7 billion on helping US automobile companies develop cars based on hydrogen fuel cells. Critics were sceptical as to whether FreedomCAR would be any more successful than the PNGV, and pointed out that both Toyota and Honda had developed profitable energy-efficient cars without such help.

California

California was the only state allowed under the Clean Air Act in 1967 to set its own tough emissions limits, a loophole that existed because of the previously extreme levels of smog around Los Angeles. Despite fierce opposition from the car and oil industries, in July 2002, California became the first US state to regulate emissions of the greenhouse gas carbon dioxide from motor vehicles through the passing of the California Climate Bill (*New York Times* 2002b). The law granted the California Air Resources Board (CARB) power to set 'economically feasible' maximums on emissions standards for gases such as carbon dioxide. Those standards would be set by 2005 and were required in automobiles sold by 2009 (*New York Times* 2002b). Because the Clean Air Act allowed any state to adopt California's strict emissions standards in place of weaker federal rules, a number of states, including New York, Massachusetts, Maine and Vermont followed in California's footsteps. It was believed that the law would ultimately force the car industry to focus more on fuel-efficient vehicles, including HEVs.[4]

Internal Revenue Service

In August 2002, the US Internal Revenue Service (IRS) made the Prius the first hybrid car for which buyers could claim a US$2,000 clean-burning fuel federal income tax deduction (Reuters 2002c). Honda also applied for certification and attained approval from the IRS in September 2002 to make the Insight and the hybrid version of its Civic model eligible for the same tax break (Reuters 2002d). Such tax incentives were expected to be available to almost all future HEVs on the market in an effort to popularise and make them more affordable.

The Sierra Club

The Sierra Club was extremely active in the push for more environmentally safe vehicles. They praised the efforts of Honda and Toyota by honouring both companies with Awards for Excellence in Environmental Engineering, making it the first time in the Club's 108-year history that an automobile manufacturer had been so honoured (Raeburn 2002). Viewing the hybrid cars as the 'wave of the present', (Raeburn 2002), the Club was focused on trying to push the 'big three' into releasing their HEVs. In fact, in June 2002, the Club announced the launch of a three-year campaign to urge the 'big three' to improve the fuel economy of their vehicles.

---

4   *Financial Times* environment news service, accessed 22 July 2002.

Besides pressuring them directly, the Sierra Club also used publicity campaigns to indirectly pressure US car makers. Public opinion surveys showed that consumers wanted vehicles with better fuel economy, indicating that Americans wanted to reduce the country's dependence on foreign oil, save money at the fuel pump and cut pollution. The Sierra Club hoped that its publicity campaigns would encourage consumers to ask car dealers for a Freedom Option Package, a set of fuel-saving components which could be added to most standard models. If this proved success-ful, the fleets of the 'big three' would be improved to gasoline mileages of 40 mpg or more. In addition, such campaigns would mobilise the Club's 700,000 members across the country to hold events at local auto dealers, highlighting public demand for these fuel-saving technologies. Such pressures would only bring about further development of environmentally friendly vehicles, such as HEVs, and spur the auto-mobile industry into adopting stricter standards for vehicle emissions.

Other players

Besides those mentioned above, agencies such as the EPA were also fighting for tougher emissions standards that would force car makers to produce 'clean cars' such as HEVs. Oil companies, such as BP, ExxonMobil and Shell, were also key players in the future of environmentally friendly automobiles such as the fuel-cell cars.[5] In fact, the oil companies were participating in many clean-car initiatives and collaborative research that could significantly affect the future of HEVs.

Insight strategies

New product development process

Honda's new product development process for the Insight was characterised by three distinct stages—concept, pre-production and production.

Concept: J-VX

At the 1997 Tokyo motor show, Honda showed its ambition for a hybrid gaso-line–electric car in the form of the J-VX concept car. The J-VX was presented as a super-efficient sports car. Much of the focus was on the model's sporty side, with special emphasis on the use of light materials giving the J-VX the 'quick, agile handling only available in lightweight sports cars'.[6] Nonetheless, the J-VX was designed to achieve a new level of efficiency and low emissions with a fuel effi-ciency of 30 km per litre (70 mpg).

---

5   Electric Vehicles Association of the Americas, 'ExxonMobil Corporation Joins California Fuel Cell Partnership', news release, 26 March 2001, www.exxonmobil.com/corporate/newsroom/ newsreleases/corp_xom_nr_260301.asp, accessed 8 July 2005.

6   Insight Central website, www.insightcentral.net, accessed 2 November 2002.

The J-VX had a stereotypical concept car design with its primary colour design and air belts (seatbelts that inflate much like airbags). In addition, its entire roof was made out of tinted glass. Rather than batteries, J-VX's IMA (integrated motor assist) powertrain utilised an ultra-capacitor for storing charge in the form of electrons. A capacitor has the advantage of a virtually unlimited lifetime, and the ability to discharge its power very quickly, although this could prove very dangerous, particularly in an accident.

Pre-production: VV

While Honda's production car was based on the J-VX with the same 30 km per litre fuel efficiency level, changes had to be made to the J-VX concept to ensure the creation of a more practical product that consumers would want to buy. According to Kazuhiko Tsunoda, chief engineer of the Insight project, the Insight had to be 'a real world product for the global market'. Honda had made advances with previous products such as the Natural Gas Civic GX, but did not receive favourable reviews from customers. Thus, Honda set the following goals:

- To create the most world's most efficient production car, and to achieve extremely low emissions

- To make the car fun to drive

- To achieve the levels of safety and comfort that consumers expect

- To be able to sell at reasonable prices

On 4 January 1999, Honda unveiled its pre-production prototype hybrid at the North American international auto show in Detroit. The VV coupe at this time was very similar to the final production car. The car was to achieve 70 mpg, weigh less than 2,000 lbs and meet ULEV (ultra-low emissions vehicle) emissions levels. The hybrid propulsion system remained much the same, but a battery was used for energy storage rather than a capacitor. The prototype's internal combustion engine underwent much development to reduce weight and friction further while improving emissions.

With further investment in body technologies, the VV coupe enjoyed even better aerodynamics. Although hybrid gasoline–electric powerplant was an integral part of the final production car, Honda considered that body technology was just as important as energy efficiency. The aerodynamics and lightweight aluminium construction of the body were to play a big role in reducing the prototype's energy requirements. Rear seats were eliminated to give more cargo area, better aerodynamics and further weight savings. The glass roof also disappeared, as it increased both the weight and cost of the car. With the elimination of the rear seats and glass roof, the Insight began to take on similarities with the last generation Honda. The car was no longer a sports car. More emphasis was put on efficiency and low emissions. However, its fun-to-drive sporty nature was still important.

Production: Insight

The production car, the Insight, was almost identical to the VV coupe in technology and engineering. Honda had made a few minor cosmetic and functional developments to ensure a product ready for full production. The headlight shape was refined, the aluminium wheels lost their plastic covers, a rear wiper was added and the interior appearance was modified slightly. In addition, the entire engine bay's plastic cover was removed to make room for additional sound insulation in the hood.

Market entry

Toyota's Prius had been the world's first hybrid car when it was released in 1997. However Toyota made the strategic choice to release the Prius only in Japan. Honda responded by quickly introducing the Insight and being the first to bring a HEV to North America. Honda made a considerable commitment to get this title of 'first to the (American) market'. In the words of an engineer involved in the development of the Insight: 'We [Honda] were particular about becoming first' (AP Newswire 2002). This strategic move helped Honda reinstate its prominence in the development of environmentally friendly vehicles.

Since its release, sales of the Honda Insight in the US have been better than expected, reaching a total of 10,730 by the end of 2002. Many industry analysts, however, questioned whether Honda's timing was more a result of 'serendipity, not strategy' (Welch and Armstrong 2000). Both the Insight and the Prius hit the US market at a time when gasoline prices were rising, averaging around US$1.65 a gallon nationwide and over US$2.00 in the Midwest (Welch and Armstrong 2000). The debate regarding the Insight's timing has been argued both ways by different camps. But, whether the success of the product was due to planning or luck, Honda's move appeared to have paid off. The success of the Insight in penetrating the US market was particularly notable given that the technology was new for most consumers and small cars were usually the industry's slowest sellers (Welch and Armstrong 2000).

Marketing

Comparisons between the Honda Insight and the Toyota Prius were inevitable. Technologically, the two were among the most advanced cars ever offered to consumers, and were both marketed as 'green'. In order to differentiate between them, Honda and Toyota used very different marketing strategies. Toyota decided to build interest in its car through a demonstration programme for its US introduction. Basically, a Prius was given to several families in each of the larger metropolitan areas and they were allowed to drive it around free for four weeks. This initiative not only improved consumer awareness of the product, but it also gave the Prius visibility and credibility among the public. The Toyota president Fujio Cho volunteered to promote the sale of the Prius by switching his luxury, black-coated company car to a white Prius (AP Newswire 2002).

Honda, on the other hand, decided to rely solely on its existing brand image as a forward-thinking car maker, capitalising on its 'first-mover' status. Honda felt that its main marketing task was to educate the consumer and address some of the misconceptions associated with hybrid vehicles. Hence, the television commercials and other advertisements used by Honda highlighted the 'Insight's industry-leading fuel economy and that the car's battery did not need to be "plugged-in" for recharging' (*Automotive Intelligence News* 2001).

Realising that the typical buyer of a hybrid vehicle was an environmentalist and technophile who yearned for the latest in automotive gadgetry, Honda's Insight advertising strategy targeted 'techies' (Guyer 2001). Robert Bienenfeld, Insight marketing manager, observed: 'The typical Insight buyer is a male engineer in his mid-40s who is interested in technology' (Welch and Armstrong 2000). Given this fact, Honda used a small budget for its national TV and Internet advertising, since most of the Insight buyers were thought to search out information about the Insight independently. Most of Honda's marketing budget was used to develop materials that could be used by dealers in their local advertising media (Littman 2000). Art Garner, a spokesperson for American Honda, explained that training 'dealers to talk about the Insight with the local media was the best way to take advantage of the interest generated by rising gasoline prices without spending more on a national effort' (Littman 2000: 96).

In keeping with Honda's philosophy of making environmental technology accessible to consumers, Honda priced the Insight at less than US$20,000, with a full complement of standard comfort and convenience features added in. Although Honda was actually incurring a loss on each Insight that it sold, it felt that hybrid technology could become profitable in the long term. Honda felt that the real-world experience that it would build up by working with hybrid technology and the continuance of its 'green' car company image were strong enough motivations to sell the Insight at a loss for the first few years.

Manufacturing and distribution

The Insight was produced in Japan at the Takanazawa plant, 80 km north of Tokyo. The Takanazawa plant produced other low-volume, unique-technology vehicles such as the Acura NSX. On a daily basis, only about 20–30 Insights were manufactured, much fewer than the Civic or the Accord. Honda adopted a limited production volume strategy for the Insight initially, as the market demand for hybrid vehicles was uncertain. But, after receiving an enthusiastic response in the US market, Honda increased its sales target for the US from 4,000 to 6,500 vehicles for 2002.

Forgoing partnerships

Car makers all over the world witnessed a global realignment of the industry during the 1990s. This led to partnerships and acquisitions such as Nissan Motor Co.'s partnership with Renault SA and Mitsubishi Motor Corporation's tie-in with DaimlerChrysler AG, all in an effort to seek foreign investment in order to survive

(AP Newswire 2002). Even among all this realignment, Honda and Toyota decided to keep their independence. In fact, Honda president Hiroyuki Yoshino ruled out the possibility of his company forging a partnership with a foreign auto-maker, saying: 'It's better for a person to decide about his own life rather than having it decided by others' (AP Newswire 2002). Thus, Honda decided on solo development of the hybrid vehicle.

With its stable financial condition and its core products, the Civic and the Accord, maintaining their leadership in the global markets, Honda had the funds and technology to develop the hybrid vehicle alone. However, even Honda's strongest competitor, Toyota, was considering co-operative development by 2002. Toyota president Fujio Cho said that, although Toyota is 'not thinking of a capital tie-up with foreign carmakers', it was considering 'the possibility of establishing co-operation with a wide spectrum of makers in the areas of technology and production' (AP Newswire 2002).

Standing firm on environmental issues

By June 2002, Honda was the only major car manufacturer who was not a member of the Alliance of Automobile Manufacturers, the industry trade group leading the fight against tougher fuel and emissions standards. According to Thomas Elliot: 'We (Honda) cannot agree with the alliance on several issues' (*New York Times* 2002a). By holding itself to a higher standard, Honda stood to carve itself a position as the technological leader in environmentally friendly automobiles. Compared to other car makers, Honda devoted the highest percentage of its revenues to research and development into improving technologies (see Fig. 6.2). Honda's effort to position itself as the environmental leader in automobile manufacturing appeared to be paying off, as evidenced in a statement by Daniel Decker, director of the global warming policy for the Sierra Club: 'The only hope I see for a future with cleaner cars is Honda' (*New York Times* 2002a).

The future of HEVs

In 2003, HEVs were widely believed to have the potential to allow continued growth in the automotive sector, while also reducing critical resource consumption, dependence on foreign oil, air pollution and traffic congestion. However, the success of hybrids was far from assured. While the technology's capabilities held great promise, the widespread penetration of hybrids hinged on the economics of producing a complex hybrid power system. The hybrid's complexity, and the fact that some of the necessary complementary technologies (such as storage and conversion systems) still had room for improvement, caused opinions to be mixed on the hybrids' ultimate impact in the marketplace.

Complicating matters was the fact that many in the industry had their sights set on a different environmentally friendly technology—fuel cells. Fuel cells offered much greater energy efficiency when converting fuel to electricity than the combi-

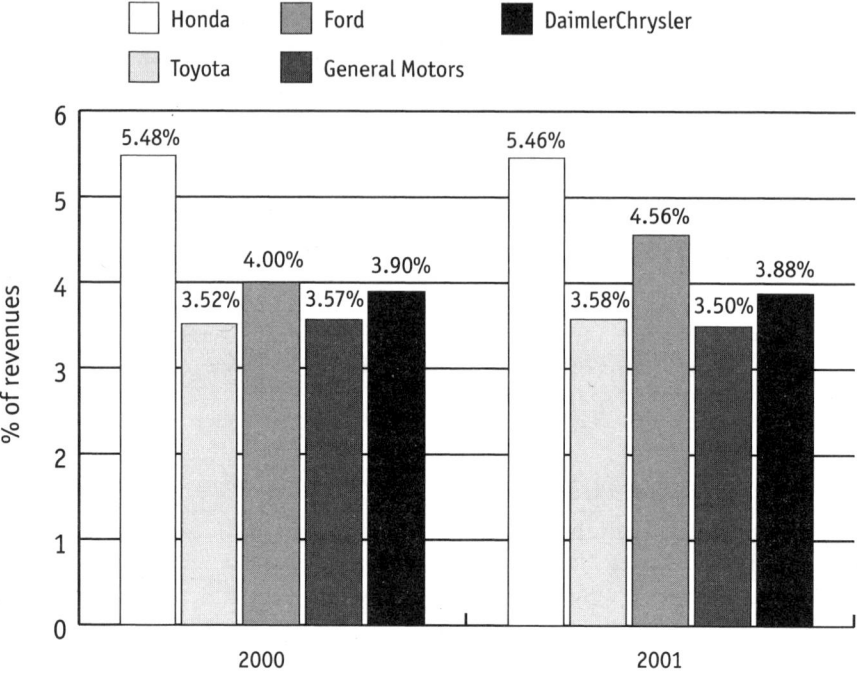

FIGURE 6.2 R&D expenses comparison

nation of an internal combustion engine with a battery. By converting chemical energy directly into electrical energy, fuel cells had been known to achieve a conversion efficiency greater than 50%, twice that of internal combustion engines (Morrison and Eccles 2001). In July 2002, Honda succeeded in manufacturing the first fuel-cell vehicle to receive certification by the CARB and the EPA by meeting all applicable standards. This new fuel-cell vehicle, called the FCX, was certified as a 'zero emission vehicle' by the CARB and as a Tier-2 Bin 1 national low-emission vehicle (NLEV) by the EPA, the lowest national emission rating.[7] However, most fuel-cell developments were based on hydrogen as a fuel source. This meant that widespread adoption of fuel cell vehicles would first require building an almost entirely new fuel infrastructure. Furthermore, many speculated that fuel-cell vehicles would be dangerous since the hydrogen fuel (a highly combustible substance) would have to be stored under great pressure. Although there appeared to be an industry-wide move towards creating environmentally friendly cars, which of the technologies would dominate remained highly uncertain.

7   *Financial Times*, news.ft.com/home/rw, accessed 6 November 2002.

Discussion

Honda's development and launch of the Insight demonstrates the company's serious commitment to both environmental progress and technological leadership. It is also interesting to note that Honda chose to use several strategies that might at first seem counterintuitive: examining these strategies is instrumental to understanding environmental innovation strategy and product deployment. Below, we discuss several key issues that emerge from Honda's approach.

Innovation strategy

Honda has consistently invested in technology development projects that were well in advance of any expectation of commercial deployment. It has also forgone forging partnerships or alliances despite a frenzy of such activity among other players in the auto industry. Each of these decisions stands in contrast to much of the popular opinion regarding new product development strategy.

Technology project choice

Honda introduced a solar vehicle in 1996, an all-electric vehicle in 1997 and fuel-cell vehicles in 2002, knowing full well that such vehicles were ahead of their time and would not be commercially viable in the near future. Although such projects are unlikely to generate an economic return in the short term, they are investments in Honda's long-term capabilities and technological leadership. All of Honda's product mix draws on its exceptional expertise in developing engines—this is one of the firm's primary distinctive competencies. To sustain a leadership position and reinforce this competence, Honda has consistently invested in engine and energy projects that have been leading-edge. By developing technologies ahead of their time, Honda ensures that, when the marketplace is ready for such technologies, it will have the experience to deploy them rapidly and efficiently. Even if some are never commercially viable, the insight and learning they yield can be leveraged into other, related technologies.

Partnerships and alliances

Despite recent consolidation and alliance activity in the auto industry, Honda has steadfastly maintained its autonomy and independence. It has also relied, almost solely, on internal development of technologies rather than external acquisition, and it has resisted joining the Alliance for Automobile Manufacturers. While alliances may enable firms to acquire capabilities or access to new markets quickly, and to exert market or political power, they also impose constraints that a firm such as Honda has been unwilling to bear.

Independence allows Honda the freedom to pursue projects that may be at odds with other car makers' efforts to prevent the imposition of much tougher emissions regulations. Independence ensures that Honda is never pressured to compromise its identity as an environmental leader.

Deployment strategies

Honda chose several unique deployment strategies for the launch of the Insight. These include its timing of entry, pricing and marketing strategies.

Timing of entry

Both Toyota and Honda were intent on being the first to introduce HEVs: although Honda did not beat Toyota to the Japanese market it was first to bring the HEV to the US market. There are both advantages and disadvantages to being first to market. While the early mover may gain reputation effects and pre-emptively capture resources such as key dealership commitments or consumer 'mindshare', being early also imposes costs and risks. First, the early mover often bears the bulk of the technology development costs. Developing radically new technologies usually involves exploring a number of different alternatives before an appropriate solution mix is found; the later mover can capitalise on this early development effort and focus only on recreating those technology features that have worked. Second, customer requirements are often highly uncertain when the early mover enters the market. The early mover may have to spend a considerable amount on customer research and customer education—essentially performing 'missionary work' for the industry. Later movers, by contrast, can watch the customer response to the early mover and refine their products and strategies accordingly.

As of 2003, the environmentally friendly vehicle market was in an 'era of ferment', and it was unclear which technology would emerge as a dominant design (Anderson and Tushman 2000). During such periods, many companies in high-technology industries will deliberately wait to observe which technology will emerge as dominant. IBM, for example, has explicitly chosen a 'second mover' strategy in several product markets. However, Honda and Toyota both made the decision to pioneer HEVs, gambling that they could turn these innovative cars into a commercially viable product.

Pricing

In deciding on price, Honda had to assess how best to ensure it would both recoup its development costs and promote a market movement to alternative-energy vehicles. In the end, Honda chose to use a penetration price of less than US$20,000, sacrificing profits in order to build volume. Although Honda would lose money on the car initially, building volume could lead to economies of scale and learning-curve savings, and could be key to making the Insight viable in the long run. In addition to the competitive price, Honda lobbied the IRS to give hybrid-vehicle customers a tax deduction, which ultimately led to a one-off US$2,000 tax break. Honda believes that such efforts have not only increased sales for the Insight but will also lead to increased market awareness when selling future HEVs.

Marketing

Honda chose to rely almost entirely on word of mouth, dealer advertising and its reputation as an environmentally sound company in promoting the Insight. Although most new technologies are often accompanied by intensive marketing campaigns to kick-start adoption, Honda believed that its target market was a relatively small and select group of individuals (environmentally motivated technophiles) that would seek out information about the vehicle on their own. Honda would thus be able to rely largely on free publicity from the popular press and the educational efforts of dealers who would field questions on the vehicles. It is debatable whether or not this was an optimal strategy. Spending less on advertising enabled Honda to keep the price of the vehicle low, but heavier advertising might have helped build volume (and thus economies of scale) more quickly.

Conclusion

The introduction of HEVs has been relatively successful so far. In 2002, Honda sold 2,216 Insights and just under 15,000 hybrid Civics, and Toyota sold 20,119 Prius sedans. According to a survey by J.D. Power and Associates, demand for hybrid vehicles was expected to increase to 54,000 in 2003, reaching 500,000 or more by 2008 (Glover 2003). Although these numbers are still very small in comparison to the total new car fleet sold each year, they nevertheless offer tangible evidence of the commercial potential of alternative vehicle technologies. If such evidence helps foster momentum for the production and adoption of HEVs, both Honda and Toyota will be well positioned to lead the next generation of the automobile industry.[8]

8   As well as the material cited in the bibliography, the reader may find the following useful: M. Lieberman and D. Montgomery, 'First Mover Advantages: A Survey', *Strategic Management Journal* 9 (1988): 41-58; E.M. Rogers, *Diffusion of Innovations* (New York: The Free Press, 3rd edn, 1983); M.A. Schilling, 'Technology Success and Failure in Winner-take-all Markets: Testing a Model of Technological Lock Out', *Academy of Management Journal* 45 (2002): 387-98; M.A. Schilling, 'Technological Leapfrogging: Lessons from the US Video Game Console Industry', *California Management Review* 45.3 (2003): 6-32; G. Tellis and P. Golder, 'First to Market, First to Fail? Real Causes of Enduring Market Leadership', *Sloan Management Review*, Winter 1996: 65-75.

The history of electric vehicles

Electric vehicles (EVs) are vehicles that are powered by an electric motor instead of an internal combustion engine. This means that, unlike the conventional gasoline vehicles, the motor is driven by power stored in batteries. Counter to popular belief, EVs have a very long history. In fact, EVs were seen soon after Joseph Henry first introduced the DC-powered motor in 1830.*

The early years (1890–1930)

One of the first EVs, the 1902 Wood's Electric Phaeton, was simply a horseless carriage powered by electricity. Costing about US$2,000, the Phaeton had a range of approximately 18 miles and reached a maximum speed of only 14 mph. Woods would go on to develop a hybrid car that incorporated both an internal combustion engine and an electric motor in 1916.

Electric cars outsold both steam and gasoline powered cars in 1899 and 1900. This success was attributed to the many advantages offered by EVs, such as lack of vibration, smell and noise which were normally associated with gasoline cars, and faster start-up times compared to steam cars. Moreover, the EV's limited range did not pose a serious constraint since most travel at this time was local.

But this success was not long-lived due to some major developments that took place in the early 1900s. The development of better road systems increased the demand for longer-range vehicles. The discovery of crude oil in Texas made gasoline affordable for the average consumer. Furthermore, Henry Ford's mass production of internal combustion engine vehicles brought their prices down to around US$500–1,000 range, making them considerably less expensive than a typical electric vehicle.

The middle years (1930–90)

By around 1935, EVs had all but vanished. It was not until the 1960s that they re-emerged, driven by a growing need for more environmentally friendly cars. At this time, research and development on EVs started up once again. During the 1960s and 1970s, companies such as Battronic, Sebring-Vanguard and the Elcar Corporation developed a number of EVs. These had an average top speed of about 40–45 mph, a range of approximately 50–60 miles and batteries that required recharging. Some were adopted for use as passenger buses or delivery vehicles (e.g. in 1975, the US postal service bought 350 electric jeeps from the American Motor Company to be used in a test programme), but the vehicles failed to penetrate the mass market.*

Recent years (1990 to present)

The 1990s brought about a resurgence in EVs due to several legislative and regulatory events that occurred in the US, such as the 1990 Clean Air Act Amendment, the Energy Policy Act 1992 and regulations issued by the CARB. With the government taking a strong stance on air pollution control, many states passed laws that required reductions in gasoline use and vehicle emissions. In fact, certain states even issued zero-emission vehicle requirements.

Given this pressure, the 'big three' US automobile manufacturers, GM, Ford and Daimler-Chrysler, together with the US Department of Energy and several other companies, became actively involved in EV development through the PNGV. Through this collaboration, several EVs were developed, including the Solectria Geo Metro, which was powered by an alternating-current

* See inventors.about.com, accessed 2 November 2002.

Box 6.2 The history of electric vehicles (continued opposite) motor and lead-acid battery, and the Ford Ecostar utility van, which was powered by an alternating-current motor and sodium sulphur battery.

By the late 1990s, automobile manufacturers such as GM, Honda, Toyota, Nissan and Ford had released a variety of EVs, but they did not catch on with customers. Not only were they very expensive (US$30,000–40,000 on average) but they also required regular recharging. This added inconvenience made consumers shy away from EVs.

Then, in 1997, Toyota and Honda released the world's first HEVs, the Prius and the Insight respectively. These hybrids not only had much lower emissions than solely gasoline powered vehicles but also did not require recharging. Unlike pure EVs, HEVs gradually began to penetrate mainstream consumer markets.

Box 6.2 (from previous page)

References

American Honda Motor Co. Ltd (2001) *An 'Insight'ful First Year,* 6 February 2001.

Anderson, P., and M. Tushman (1990) 'Technological Discontinuities and Dominant Designs: A Cyclical Model of Technological Change', *Administrative Science Quarterly* 35: 604-34.

AP Newswire (2002) 'Toyota, Honda forge ahead in hybrid vehicle development', *AP Newswire,* 13 March 2002.

Automotive Intelligence News (2001) 'Hybrid car sales surge along with gas prices: New Honda Insight ad hits airwaves', *Automotive Intelligence News,* 13 June 2001; www.autointell.com.

Belton, B. (2000) 'The man behind Toyota's green machine', *Business Week Online,* 13 November 2000.

Business Week Online (2000) 'Q&A with Thomas Elliot', *Business Week Online,* 14 August 2000.

Glover, M. (2003) 'Hybrid-powered car sales to soar, report says', *Knight Ridder Tribune Business News,* 6 June 2003.

Guyer, L. (2001) 'The little engines that could, now go whirrr,' *Advertising Age,* 9 April 2001.

Littman, M. (2000) 'Hybrid engine cars do better with hybrid marketing tactics', *Marketing News,* 25 September 2000: 6.

Morrison, D., and L. Eccles (2001) *Electronic Design* (Cleveland).

New York Times (2002a) 'Honda takes up case in US for green energy', *New York Times,* 13 June 2002.

—— (2002b) 'California lawmakers vote to lower auto emissions', *New York Times,* 2 July 2000.

Raeburn, P. (2002) 'Commentary: the Japanese are making the right bet on hybrids,' *Business Week Online,* 14 August 2002.

Reuters (2002a) 'Hybrid cars try merging into the mainstream', 30 May 2002.

—— (2002b) 'Low growth seen for HEVs', 11 September 2002.

—— (2002c) 'Toyota's Prius first to get $2,000 tax deduction OK', 12 August 2002.

—— (2002d) 'US tax credit approved for hybrid Honda vehicles', 10 September 2002.

Welch, D., and L. Armstrong (2000) 'A fast (and lucky) start for Japan's hybrid cars,' *Business Week Online,* 6 July 2000.

7
Cultivating the sustainable corporation

Lise Langeland
Nilfisk-Advance AS, Denmark

This chapter presents, from both a researcher's and a practitioner's point of view, what a sustainable corporation is and how to cultivate sustainability within an organisation.

The increasing depletion of the natural environment and the growing global social imbalance combined with an expected increase in worldwide consumption is likely to present a significant problem in the new century. Yet, according to Richard Welford (1997: 5):

> To date most businesses who have begun to respond to environmental
> issues have done so in quite piecemeal and marginal ways.

The common excuse for not embracing sustainability at corporate level is the complexity of the issues involved and a general tendency to focus on short-term solutions. There is also a widespread misconception that environmental and social issues cause only expense and a related decrease in economic performance. This has resulted in the 'sustainable corporation' being viewed as an abstract and intangible ideal by both researchers and practitioners alike. To the majority of the latter the term even has a tone of naïveté. However, this chapter presents the counter-argument that a sustainable business is a good business. Furthermore, sustainable corporations can prosper and outperform the industry average in their respective market sectors—even when using traditional business measures.

Realistically, corporate sustainability is still years away from becoming an accepted organisational practice (Welford 1997: 6). Some corporations are simply determined not to embrace sustainability. Others have hesitated, addressing sustainability as merely an appendix and refraining from undertaking the necessary substantive organisational changes required. But a precious few serve as an inspiration to others, proving it possible to be both profitable *and* sustainable.

This chapter presents the key findings of conceptual research undertaken by the author while developing a discourse for the 'sustainable corporation'. The sustainable corporation will be presented as an opportunity—an alternative form of organisation—with no contradiction between serving its own interests and the interests of society in general, to the mutual advantage of both.

The basic elements of a sustainable corporation will be illustrated and explained in theory and practice, relying heavily on a case study from an American chain of health foods stores, Whole Foods Market. An examination of generally recognised management tools and philosophies from classical management theory will identify a simple truth—that essentially no company is an island, but is deeply entangled with and dependent on the society to which it belongs, for better or for worse.

The chapter will begin by developing an insight into *what* constitutes a sustainable corporation and then move on to elaborate *how* a sustainable corporation can be developed. The cultivation of a sustainable corporation relies heavily on basic principles from the general theory of organisational development. Finally, conclusions and implications for further research are discussed.

The contents of the sustainable corporation

Sustainability should be seen as an irreducible concept (Welford 1997: 179) and should thus be presented in its irreducibility. The purpose here is to present the essence of corporate sustainability as a soluble 'concentrate'. When fully integrated into an organisation, the 'original concentrate' of sustainability will no longer be identifiable but will have evolved to fit the corporation's situation and needs. Sustainable companies differ from other corporations and no two will be completely alike. Sustainability is defined as a set of core elements, independent of the context and the actualities any corporation faces. Metaphorically this can be described as 'adding sugar to tea' (Langeland 2000: 92), with the sugar representing the core elements of corporate sustainability.

The general definition of sustainability has its roots in the well-known Brundtland definition of sustainable development,[1] which was sharpened with respect to its financial implications by economist Herman Daly in 1996.[2] Sustainability applied to corporations has been interpreted and defined by numerous authors, but I have chosen to focus on a few, broad definitions. Richard Welford defines sustainability as being made up of three closely connected issues: environment, equity and futurity (Welford 1995: 8). From a wide range of interpretations, Thomas Gladwin generates an inclusive definition of sustainability based on five pillars: inclusiveness, connectivity, equity, prudence and security (Gladwin *et al.* 1995: 878). Inspired by these and others,[3] this work will draw on an interpretation of 'sustainability' that incorporates the following three elements:

---

1 'A development which meets the needs of the present without compromising the ability of future generations to meet their own needs' (WCED 1987: 8).
2 'Development without growth beyond environmental carrying capacity' (Daly 1996: 9).
3 Primarily Peattie 1995; Berry and Rondinelli 1998; Stead and Stead 1996.

- Ethical awareness

- Social responsibility

- Environmental consideration

The economic aspects of sustainability are not seen as something separate from this definition but as a necessary condition for sustainable corporate activities. The profitability of the company is seen as the foundation for the sustainable corporation. It is, however, not included as a part of the definition because profitability, in my view, does not indicate sustainability per se. The characteristics of sustainable corporations, as presented in the literature, are summarised in Table 7.1.

Dimension	Characteristic	Presented by:
Societal relations	Social responsibility	Welford 1997
	Environmental considerations	Gladwin *et al.* 1995; Peattie 1995
	Human rights	Stead and Stead 1996
	Philanthropy	Welford 1997; Stead and Stead 1996
Financial time-horizon	Long-term perspective	Gladwin *et al.* 1995; Welford 1997; Peattie 1995
	Holistic perspective (including sustainability)	Gladwin *et al.* 1995; Welford 1997; Peattie 1995
	Thinking in closed loops	Stead and Stead 1996; Peattie 1995
	Eliminating waste	Stead and Stead 1996; Berry and Rondinelli 1998
Management style	Participative	Welford 1997; Peattie 1995
	Visionary	Welford 1997; Gladwin *et al.* 1995; Stead and Stead 1996
	Committed	Welford 1997; Gladwin *et al.* 1995
Organisation	Egalitarian—autonomous	Welford 1997; Peattie 1995
	Decentralised—flat structure	Stead and Stead 1996; Welford 1997; Peattie 1995
	Pluralist	Welford 1997
	Mission of sustainability	Gladwin *et al.* 1995; Starik 1994
Culture	Value-based	Gladwin *et al.* 1995; Stead and Stead 1996
	Corporate ethics	Welford 1997; Peattie 1995
	Trust and mutual respect	Welford 1997; Stead and Stead 1996
	Fair employment	Gladwin *et al.* 1995; Welford 1997; Peattie 1995
	Open communication	Welford 1997; Peattie 1995

TABLE 7.1 Characteristics of sustainable organisations

Source: Langeland 1999a: 225

The concept of corporate sustainability should not be grounded solely on literature from the sustainability side of the theoretical field. Incorporating sustainability as a management concept, in my view, requires inspiration from more traditional management literature. This research on corporate sustainability has also relied on a selection of literature from management thought on visionary and partly normative descriptions of organisations moving beyond the conventional corporate archetypes. I have chosen to focus on some key messages from a small selection of distinguished management thinkers from the 20th century. The selected authors (Andrews 1971; Collins and Porras 1994; McGregor 1960; Peters and Waterman 1982; Sheldon 1923; Taylor 1895; Taylor 1911; Wickens 1995) all examine and prescribe some kind of management ideal, a 'superior organisation'.[4]

Table 7.2 presents an accumulation of some of the significant characteristics of the ideals in management thought, as presented by the selected authors. There are several overlapping areas with each author contributing their own personal perspective on the dimension in question. In summary, Table 7.2 presents characteristics such as social responsibility, ethics and long-term financial perspective as integral parts of the superior organisation. The organisation itself has to be egalitarian, with a flat structure, a culture based on management–worker co-operation and organisational values incorporating a holistic view.

Inspired by literature from both management thought and corporate sustainability:

> A sustainable corporation recognises the connection between and among
> ethical positions, social considerations and environmental concerns, and
> is consciously and continuously seeking to integrate these aspects in its
> value-base from which it permeates all its actions (Langeland 1999b: 2).

It is important to see sustainability as a choice, a conscious and active decision *in favour of* sustainability by the entire corporation. The intentions must be followed by actions (Peters and Waterman 1982: 74) and integrated in the culture of the corporation (Schein 1984: 446).

When accumulating the main points from these seemingly contradictory fields, an interesting conclusion was the similarity in ideals that these theories present (see Langeland 1999a). Even Kenneth R. Andrews, mostly known for defining SWOT analysis (strengths, weaknesses, opportunities, threats), emphasises the importance and benefits of ethical management—to corporations, employees and society in general. He is a strong critic of the general tendency to apply short-term economic measures to foster a corporate culture that is inconsistent with basic ethical principles, and predicts that in the long term financial results will suffer accordingly (Andrews 1971: 10).

The overall definition of a sustainable corporation applied here is described across three dimensions: ethical, social and environmental (Langeland 2000: 35). Table 7.3 presents the core elements of a sustainable corporation, and summarises the research findings. Table 7.3 should not to be seen as a finite, all-encompassing list, but as a presentation of some of the central areas and elements that are of relevance and importance.

4   Author's attempt at a generic term.

Area	Characteristic	Presented by:
Societal relations	Social responsibility	Andrews 1971
	Ethical considerations	Andrews 1971; Wickens 1995; Sheldon 1923
Financial horizon	Long-term perspective	All
	Wider perspective	Wickens 1995; Andrews 1971; Peters and Waterman 1982
	Eliminating waste	Peters and Waterman 1982; Wickens 1995; Taylor 1895
Culture	Strong, based on articulated and embraced values	Peters and Waterman 1982; Collins and Porras 1994
	Respect for the individual	Taylor 1911; Wickens 1995; McGregor 1960
	Responsibility	Andrews 1971; McGregor 1960
	Job enlargement and delegation	McGregor 1960; Wickens 1995; Peters and Waterman 1982
Management style	Participative	Taylor 1911; Sheldon 1923; McGregor 1960
	Visionary leadership	McGregor 1960; Wickens 1995
	Co-operative	Peters and Waterman 1982; Andrews 1971
Organisation	Co-operative	Taylor 1911; McGregor 1960
	Egalitarian	Wickens 1995
	Flat structure	Wickens 1995; Peters and Waterman 1982
	Autonomous workgroups	Wickens 1995; Peters and Waterman 1982
	Dynamic	Peters and Waterman 1982; Collins and Porras 1994

TABLE 7.2 Characteristics of the management ideal

Source: Langeland 2000: 31

Although each point is conceptually comprehensive, this is not a complete list. The future will quite likely bring both new dimensions and extend those presented here. The table's contents are relevant to any corporation moving towards sustainability. Despite the apparent simplicity, each of the core elements is quite extensive and is likely to require rather dramatic changes within the corporation. The dissolution will be individual, but the core elements will remain the same.

Taken to its full extent, corporate sustainability implies a new corporate framework as well as a different role for companies in society (Gladwin *et al.* 1995: 875). It is neither necessary nor expedient for a corporation to undertake every step immediately and simultaneously; but it is important to remember that agreement on the organisation's core values and overall priorities is a prerequisite.

Corporate sustainability can seem both abstract and intangible because of the required change in mind-set at corporate level, as occurred in the Whole Foods Market case, which will be examined in the next section.

T H E S U S T A I N A B L E C O R P O R A T I O N	**Ethical dimension**	• A clear shared sense of the corporation's role in society • A clear shared sense of the corporation's role in the community • A clear shared sense of the corporation's *raison d'être* • An ethical policy • A high degree of ethical code penetration • The practice of a 'corporate conscience' • The practice of assessing the wider consequences of corporate activities and acting on the results
	Social dimension	• A democratic, egalitarian attitude towards employees, based on teamwork and joint responsibilities • A flat organisational structure • A practised human resource policy that emphasises equal rights, ethnic diversity, equal pay for equal work, etc. • The practice of corporate philanthropy through donations and charity • The practice of co-operation with authorities • The practice of co-operation with interest groups • Corporate communication based on dialogue and disclosure • Community relations based on active involvement
	Environmental dimension	• An active and ambitious environmental policy • A constant focus on continuous improvement of environmental performance • The practice of co-operation with environmental authorities • The practice of co-operation with environmental groups • The practice of co-operation with suppliers on their environmental impact • Environmental communication based on openness and dialogue • An in-depth knowledge of the environmental impact of products, e.g. through the use of life-cycle assessments • The continuous removal and substitution of harmful materials and chemicals

TABLE 7.3 Some characteristics and concerns of the sustainable corporation

Source: Langeland 2000: 114

Corporate sustainability in practice

One of the best examples of holistic corporate management is the American chain of quality food supermarkets, Whole Foods Market. A chain of food stores that actively markets and sells a 'happier lifestyle' with delicious, nutritious (mostly organic) foods and a social conscience based on an ethical vision of 'whole foods, whole people, whole planet'.[5] Whole Foods Market was founded on this vision which has been integrated into the company's core values from where it translates into actions every day so that 'It is as natural as breathing', according to Vice President of Governmental and Public Affairs, Margareth Wittenberg.[6]

Whole Foods Market has applied ordinary growth-oriented financial principles to the health food industry with impressive financial results. During the past five years, the company has had an average annual growth in sales of more than 20%, in an industry sector growing just 2–3% annually in peak years. The aggressive growth strategy has resulted in a total of 144 Whole Foods Market stores (as of September 2003). Part of the expansion was achieved through buy-outs and mergers with existing health food and delicatessen stores:[7]

> Throughout our rapid growth, we have remained a uniquely mission-driven company. Our motto—whole foods, whole people, whole planet—emphasises that our vision reaches far beyond just food retailing.[8]

The financial development since the introduction of Whole Foods Market to the stock market[9] is listed in Table 7.4.

	1991	2002	Average annual growth
Sales	US$92.5 million	US$2.69 billion	36%
Net operating profit	US$1.6 million	US$92.7 million	45%
Stores	10	135	27%
Team members	1,102	24,100	32%

TABLE 7.4 Growth of Whole Foods Market since initial public offering in January 1992
Source: Whole Foods Market Annual Stakeholders Report 2000

The vision of Whole Foods Market is measured by a set of core values:[10]

- Selling the highest-quality natural and organic products available

- Satisfying and delighting our customers

---

5 www.wholefoodsmarket.com
6 Personal communication with M. Wittenberg, Austin, Texas, 25 February 1998.
7 Annual Stakeholders Report 1998: 30.
8 Annual Stakeholders Report 2002: 7.
9 NASDAQ: WFMI
10 Annual Stakeholders Report 2002: 2.

- Team member happiness and excellence

- Creating wealth through profits and growth

- Caring about our communities and our environment

Margareth Wittenberg explains: 'These core values reflect what is truly important to Whole Foods Market as an organisation and they are the soul of the company'.[11] By frequently emphasising the importance of these values in all corporate communications, they become self-perpetuating.

The importance of strong, shared core values appear in line with the observations and recommendations presented in the previously mentioned management literature on superior organisations, particularly by Peters and Waterman (1982), Collins and Porras (1994) and Wickens (1995). These authors state the importance of values as the basis for corporate activities and the strength of the resulting culture, but only when the commitment to such values is earned through actions rather than just words. Thus, Collins and Porras (1994: 8) state:

> Core values in a visionary company form a rock-solid foundation and do not drift with the trends and fashions of the day . . . Yet, while keeping their core ideologies tightly fixed, visionary companies display a powerful drive for progress that enables them to change and adapt without compromising their cherished core ideals.

The overall vision also affects the firm's human resources policies. Egalitarian criteria are used to determine salaries and benefits at Whole Foods Market, with a starting entry-level wage approximately 50–60% above legal minimum wage. Annual, anonymous, morale surveys provide the management with valuable insights into how the company is perceived by the customer, as well as how management itself is viewed by all employees. To ensure commitment from the start, every new employee receives two weeks of initial training in organic foods, customer service and the overall corporate vision. Whole Foods Market team member (as employees are called) Jerneene Mapron comments: 'Every team member knows that "customer service" is the most important part of their job.'[12]

The result is high job satisfaction among team members. In a '100 best to work for' survey by *Fortune* magazine, Whole Foods Market ranked 34th among all US companies.[13] Furthermore, the mission statement has helped Whole Foods Market attract motivated employees who are more educated than the average grocery worker (Fischer 1998: 74). In 1998, Whole Foods Market had 170,000 applicants for 14,200 posts (Fischer 1998: 87).

The company's main characteristics are summarised in Table 7.5.

Theory Y (McGregor 1960) attitudes apparently abound in Whole Foods Market. The company's culture is based on trust in people and a belief in the potential of each individual to grow when in the right environment. Team members are given responsibility and are expected to contribute to problem-solving. This is in line with the recommendations of Peters and Waterman (1982) and is a good example of

---

11 Personal communication with M. Wittenberg, Austin, Texas, 25 February 1998.
12 Personal communication with J. Mapron, Washington DC, 25 April 1998.
13 The list was compiled using methodology similar to that used by Anne Fischer (1998).

Area	Characteristics
Business concept	Core values about quality, customer service, team members, welfare, community and environment. Vision on setting the standard, being more than just a food retailer.
Employees	Team members. Trust, respect, and delegation of responsibilities. Profit sharing. Individual adaptation of benefits. Education. Incentive to 'sustainable behaviour'. Knowledge of organic foods and agriculture. Morale surveys. Influence and commitment.
Organisation	Flat. Egalitarian. Democratic.
Community	Active partner. Charity. Volunteer work. 5% days.
Communication	Open, honest, passionate. Inform and educate on organic food and farming. No internal censorship in relation to team members.
Environmental work	Active—both internally and externally. Promotes organic and biodynamic foods. Information (and education) of both team members and customers. Facilitates a healthy lifestyle.
Political work	Works hard to promote (more) organic farming procedures.
Economy	Long-term horizon. Growth- and profit-oriented.
Management	Great commitment to the value base. Respect for the team members and their effort. Informal management style. Open lines of communication.

TABLE 7.5 Characteristics of Whole Foods Market

Source: Langeland 2000: 111

treating people as partners and with dignity and respect. Interestingly, in the case of Whole Foods Market, Theory Y attitudes are combined with a strong mercantile focus and a clear competitive strategy of differentiation—selling a complete shopping 'experience' of quality service and products within a 'fair' financial framework. Thus, customers 'buy' a sense of improved health, contribute in a small way to a better environment and also promote good job opportunities for a large number of people. To many, these benefits justify paying a premium price. On its website, Whole Foods Market declares:

> We are a mission-driven company that aims to set the standards of excellence for food retailers.

The case study of Whole Foods Market proved inspirational for my conceptual work on presenting a discourse for a sustainable corporation. In addition, it illustrates how social, ethical and environmental concerns can be profitably embedded in corporate values.

Cultivating the sustainable corporation

Whole Foods Market was founded on sustainable core values—the vision preceded the company's growth and development. A more typical scenario, however, is the reverse of this process whereby a company decides to move towards greater corporate sustainability.

Generally speaking, the first step is to recognise the need for change. This step is characterised by shifting:

- From **words to action**. 'So, what do we do?' (Welford 1997: 181).

- From **problems to solutions**. Discussing the extent of the problems will not help; 'So, what do we do about it?' (Peters and Waterman 1982: 119).

- From **expense to investment**. Embracing 'softer' areas in a way that helps the corporation think long-term and take potential return on investment into consideration (Andrews 1971: 41-42).

- From a **separate subject to an integrated part** of the company's daily routines, culture and basic values (Schein 1984: 446) rather than a convenient 'satellite' function (Peters and Waterman 1982: 31).

- From **reactive to proactive**. Having the courage to try, and fail, to go beyond market demands and show the way (Welford 1997: 7).

- From **pragmatic to ambitious**. Not settling for 'good enough', but daring to address visions and ideals, having the courage to think big from the beginning (Collins and Porras 1994: 8).

The process towards corporate sustainability must be seen as growing from the inside—as opposed to coming from the outside in—from the top downwards. Sustainability must be seen as a 'green seed' latently present in the organisation but awaiting the opportunity to grow and bloom (Langeland 2000: 94).

This metaphor emphasises two important points. First, that the potential for sustainability is already present in the organisation since many employees instinctively know the 'right' thing to do in most situations (Mauws 1999: 2). Focus should thus be shifted from convincing to cultivating. Reward structures, actions, strategic decisions and management assumptions about employees need to be transformed rather than the employees themselves (McGregor 1960: 42). Second, the process begins internally and is not publicised to the outside world until later on. Communication is internal in the beginning—no proclamation is needed before there is something substantial to tell (Langeland 1998: 21).

Sustainability transformation is a process similar to other organisational development projects that attempt to instil cultural changes in a company. Therefore, the general literature on organisational development and the importance of culture and values has been very inspiring.[14] The model for cultivating a sustainable corporation, developed during this research project, owes much to these authors.

14 Primary sources were Burke 1993, Bendix and Andersen 1995, Morgan 1996, Schein 1984 and Borum 1995.

This model for cultivating a sustainable corporation has three phases (stages), in line with Burke's recommendations for describing the flow of events of an organisational development process (Burke 1994: 80). These are:

- **Stage 1:** creating the vision

- **Stage 2:** choosing the technical solution

- **Stage 3:** realising the investment

During stage 1 a shared vision of the end outcome is created—an image of the company as sustainable. From stage 1, the process moves to stage 2 by 'project-ification'. Stage 2 is the part of the process whereby the vision is executed by way of technical solutions, including plans, tools, resource allocation, tasks, etc. This part of the process has been researched and described extensively; I have therefore chosen to exclude it from this description of the cultivation model.[15] The process moves from stage 2 to stage 3 through the corporation's wish to generate a profit from its new-found sustainability. This 'return on investment' is most likely to be created through increased sales and the application of institutional pressures within the industry. In stage 3 the external realisation is undertaken, mainly through communication to stakeholders and the market in general.

An overview of the cultivation of a sustainable corporation is illustrated in Figure 7.1.

The cultivation model was developed after an extensive, exploratory case study from 1998 to 2000 based on participative observations of the Danish branch of a multinational corporation, here referred to as X-Corp for anonymity (Langeland 2000). In the cultivation model in Figure 7.1, stage 2 is the 'project' part of the process on which, in my experience, most practitioners and consultants prefer to focus. Based on observations of X-Corp, however, I concluded that an important phase preceded the project phase, here referred to as stage 1 'creating the vision' (Langeland 2000: 8). A shared vision of the overall goal is a prerequisite for success at stage 2. This is also in line with the recommendations of Morgan (1996: 143) and Borum (1995: 77), both of whom argue the importance of addressing the cultural blueprint of the organisation before attempting to change it.

Furthermore, experience from X-Corp showed that stage 2 could be extended into a third stage, 'realising the investment' (Langeland 2000: 9). When the implementation of corporate sustainability is only piecemeal, the investment is not realised because the results are rarely demonstrated to external parties. Thus, environmental and social improvements become costs rather than investments. This point will be elaborated later in this chapter.

Like most organisational change processes, corporate sustainability transformation is unlikely to follow a straight and predetermined path (Burke 1994: 147), and the cultivation model takes this into consideration. The process of cultivating the sustainable corporation should not be seen as a prescriptive sequence of events, but rather a description of an essential and typical course of action. Undeniably, this process has a sequence, but it consists of stages rather than steps in line with the

---

15   There are numerous textbooks on environmental management systems: for example, Welford 1995; Starik 1994; Spedding 1996.

Cultivating the sustainable corporation: overview

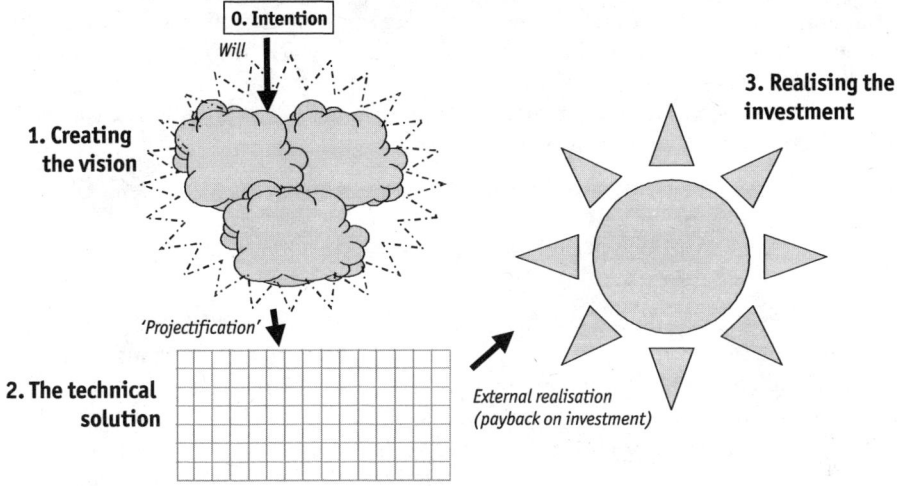

FIGURE 7.1 Overview of the process of cultivating the sustainable corporation

Source: Langeland 2000: 121

unit-by-unit learning process recommended by Beer *et al.* (1990), and the elements can be handled more than once as new information affects the results of other elements. All elements of one stage must be addressed before moving on to the next, but the sequence within each stage will depend on how the corporation decides to face the challenge.

The process begins with 'intention' (stage 0). At this point, the corporation (normally senior management) makes a genuine decision to embrace the concept of sustainability within the organisation. The process is initiated by 'will' in the form of an expression of managerial, financial and organisational support and a willingness to let actions and resources support the declarations of intent. This is inspired both by Welford's emphasis on the importance of real commitment within the organisation (1997: 181) and Burke's statement that unless the need for change is felt none is likely to occur (1994: 142). The X-Corp case showed a similar tendency when one department never made it beyond 'intention' despite many meetings to determine when the process could begin.[16] If top management does not genuinely intend to transform the organisation, the process is unlikely to overcome the obstacles embedded in contemporary corporate life.

There are other initiating factors that might seem to have equal or even more relevance to other researchers, but I have chosen to highlight the importance of the presence of organisational commitment from the start.

The stages of the cultivation process will be described in more detail below.

---

16   X-Corp has three departments, but only two of them went through the transformation process, which was a similar but minimised version of the cultivation model described here.

Stage 1: creating the vision

Stage 1 is the least well-defined stage in the process. It consists of three elements in random order: commitment, values and (organisational) self-examination. The concept leaves room for adding more elements at each stage or enlarging the individual elements.

Collins and Porras found that most companies benefit from articulating both core values and purpose in their core ideology (1994: 78):

> The important step is to get at the deeper, more fundamental reasons for the organisation's existence. An effective way to get at purpose is to pose the question: 'Why not just shut this organisation down, cash out and sell off the assets?'

Figure 7.1 shows a dotted star-like pattern around the three elements, indicating an interaction with the company's stakeholders. The purpose of this interaction is to confront corporate self-perception with the views of the stakeholders to ensure a balance of the internal and external image of the corporation while assessing the environmental demands it faces (Burke 1994: 112). Stage 1 is primarily internal but should not be separated from the surroundings of the corporation (Langeland 2000: 128).

Self-examination starts by analysing what the corporation does and does not do in relation to the demands and needs implicit in sustainability and in the wishes of the stakeholders. Inspired by the first step in Lewin's change model (Lewin 1946), 'unfreeze' self-examination (Borum 1995: 47) can help the organisation realise the extent of the gap between reality and goal. The purpose is to ensure a critical and realistic evaluation of the status quo as the starting point for future development. This is primarily a management task, but it can be relevant to get input from the employees: for example, through the use of anonymous questionnaires or seminars, meetings and the like.

Commitment is necessary to initiate the process and generate sufficient momentum to overcome the obstacles in the turbulent everyday life of modern corporations (Welford 1997: 181). There should be as much enthusiasm, involvement and passion in this initial phase as possible. These emotions should be moderated but never destroyed by self-examination, as the commitment is likely to be a main driver in the organisation. The 'green seed' metaphor also underscores the importance of allowing the necessary space for enthusiasm to spread. The Whole Foods Market case shows the importance of the absence of indifference towards the organisational goals.

The values of the corporation must be addressed in order to anchor the vision in the organisation and, eventually, its culture (Bendix and Andersen 1995: 126). The actual core values of the corporation must be acknowledged by top management through self-examination and then developed to embrace the values of sustainability (Burke 1994: 155). Inspired by Collins and Porras (1994), the process can begin by asking some questions along the lines of: 'What is our *raison d'être*? What should characterise this company a century from now, even if we are punished financially for doing so?' (Collins and Porras 1994: 78). The developed set of values must be a part of the process toward integrating and eventually institutionalising sustainability in the corporation, to the extent that these values become embedded in every corporate action (Collins and Porras 1994: 8).

The process of creating the vision (stage 1) has been undertaken in another case company, ABC,[17] as a preliminary test of the described dynamics and the feasibility of creating a vision from the three elements: commitment, vision and self-examination. The market situation facing ABC was also taken into consideration during this exercise. Following several preparatory interviews, a three-hour workshop was conducted with the management team to undertake the vision creation process and establish a preliminary vision for the company. The session showed that it was possible for the participants to distinguish between the terms 'commitment', 'values' and 'self-examination', and that these distinctions appeared meaningful to the participants. Due to the willingness of the participants openly to discuss ABC's corporate culture and the future of the market, as well as the corporate ideals and current shortcomings from this, the process proved beneficial for both parties.

This opportunity of undertaking the process of determining the *raison d'être* in a company highlighted several important process details. The seminar with ABC started with a circular process of determining the core values and a critical self-examination in relation to status quo. Once an initial agreement on the core values was established, the process moved on to evaluating ABC's commitment to these values and to determining where the commitment lay, still using the element of critical self-examination to generate the forward motion. Finally, the tentative conclusions in relation to the three elements were compared and discussed together, leading to some changes in each.

Figure 7.2 shows a detailed view of the process of cultivating the sustainable corporation.

Once the 'vision' has been created, the corporation is ready to initiate a 'sustainability' project, which brings us to stage 2 (Langeland 2000: 122). As previously mentioned, this is the phase where the corporation decides on the specific goals, objectives, action plans, project team, resources, methodology and so on that it will need to achieve its sustainability vision. This area has already been the subject of comprehensive research and literature, and is therefore not covered in any detail here. Welford (1995) is an excellent source for qualified information on this part of the cultivation process. During stage 2 most of the cost and resources required to cultivate a sustainable corporation orientation are allocated as well as consumed. As previously stated, corporations must see this as an investment rather than a cost. When stage 2 is nearly complete it is time to create a return on investment.

Stage 3: realising the investment

Stage 3 is both an internal and external process, as shown in Figure 7.2 (Langeland 2000: 132). The internal part of stage 3 is mostly related to ensuring that the results

---

17 Name changed for anonymity. ABC is a small entrepreneurial company of approximately 30 employees, operating in a high growth sector and located in Copenhagen, Denmark. The case study was undertaken during the summer of 1999 and consisted of management interviews, a seminar with senior managers, check-up with key employees and a follow-up seminar with top management (Langeland 2000: 130).

Cultivating the sustainable corporation

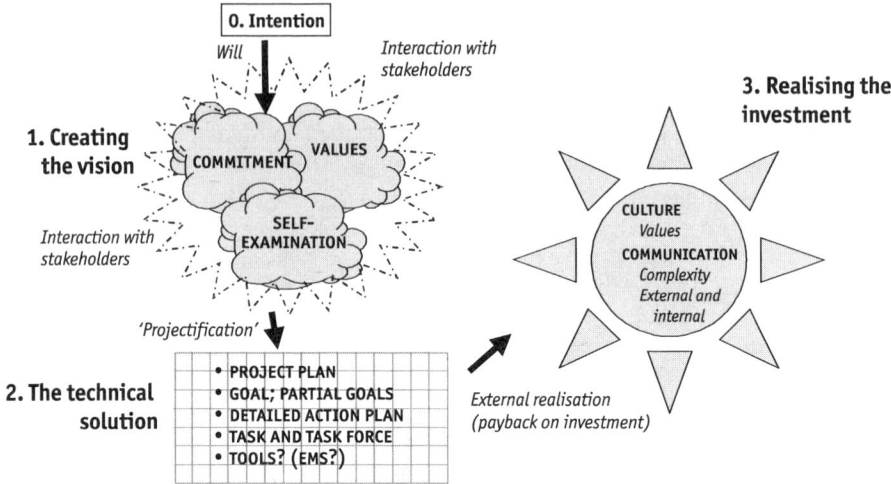

FIGURE 7.2 Detailed view of the cultivation of the sustainable corporation

Source: Langeland 2000: 125

from stages 1 and 2 become integrated into the culture of the organisation. This is to ensure that the whole process is not just a one-off but is fully integrated in the corporation and the actions of the employees (Kotter 1997: 185). Despite the complications involved, changing the culture of an organisation is a necessary part of maintaining the desired change (Morgan 1996: 143).

The external part of stage 3 is mostly concerned with communicating the vision from stage 1 to the outside world, particularly to the organisations' stakeholders. Using the green seed metaphor, the seed of sustainability grew and bloomed through stages 1 and 2, and is now breaking through to the outside world—thus growing even more. When communicating corporate sustainability, the challenge is to keep the complexity and refrain from erasing the nuances of the message, while still making it understandable.[18] There is no shame in profiting from being sustainable—companies must make money to survive. There are, however, many ways of generating a profit, and if stage 3 is not rooted in the values of stage 1 profit is likely to suffer, as will be illustrated later in the next section.

---

18 This (sustainable) communication must be done differently from much of the organisation's ordinary environmental communication, particularly with regards to maintaining the complexity of the communicated subject. It was therefore necessary to build on and develop further the needed theory, which has been published in two articles in *Greener Management International* (Langeland 1998; Langeland 1999c).

The profitability of sustainability

The demands put on management commitment and organisational participation when cultivating a sustainable corporation should not be underestimated. As with other organisational development processes that are likely to require cultural changes within an organisation, it is a complex and resource-consuming challenge (Burke 1994: 160). By generating a profit from becoming a sustainable corporation, the resources consumed are not just expenses but become an investment in the company's future market position.

As previously mentioned, two departments of Danish firm X-Corp undertook a comparable, although minimised, process of cultivating corporate sustainability. In the first department, a wider agenda, ranging from raising environmental and social awareness to sustainability, proved to be a basis for developing an even closer relationship with core customers, in particular, and for providing a better competitive position with regards to environmental demands. In contrast, the second department's overall commitment to the project was much less than in the first,[19] and the manager of department 2 was obviously aiming for an easy solution to a complex problem. There was less emphasis on the consequences and implications of the project in department 2, and the gap between the practised values and what was required by the project was much wider than in department 1 (Langeland 2000: 141). The result of the project in department 2 was improved knowledge among the employees, but little impact on their day-to-day working practices.

However, X-Corp illustrates a competitive advantage that has been left untapped for decades—and is still only used incrementally. Despite obvious positive responses from customers and retailers, the enhanced agenda was never fully embraced and the lack of a created vision (stage 1) seemed to limit the possibilities for realising the investment (stage 3), leaving the potential benefits unachieved. There was never a clear goal nor a 'green' ambition articulated in words and actions. The turbulent environment at X-Corp, no worse or better than many other contemporary corporations, creates a temptation to search for shortcuts and easy solutions.

This underscores a very important point: namely, the importance of stage 1 as a foundation for stage 3. It is very possible and, indeed, tempting to skip stage 1 and go straight to stage 2. But the lack of vision can turn out to be limiting and even paralysing when attempting to realise the investment at stage 3. This is illustrated in Figure 7.3.

In the ABC case, the management team realised the importance of vision creation being the first and necessary stage of the process after having participated in the stage 1 process themselves. Particularly, they recognised the problems resulting from a lack of vision when the company tries to realise the investment and cash in on its efforts.

Corporations survive in the real world by generating profits, and a message of sustainability receives more attention if accompanied by a promise of profit. It can be tempting to claim that corporations should not be moral or green out of altruism,

---

19 Furthermore, the employees in department 1 had begun to feel market pressures (which had not really been the case for employees in department 2), and thus had some personal incentives to participate and commit themselves.

Cultivating the sustainable corporation

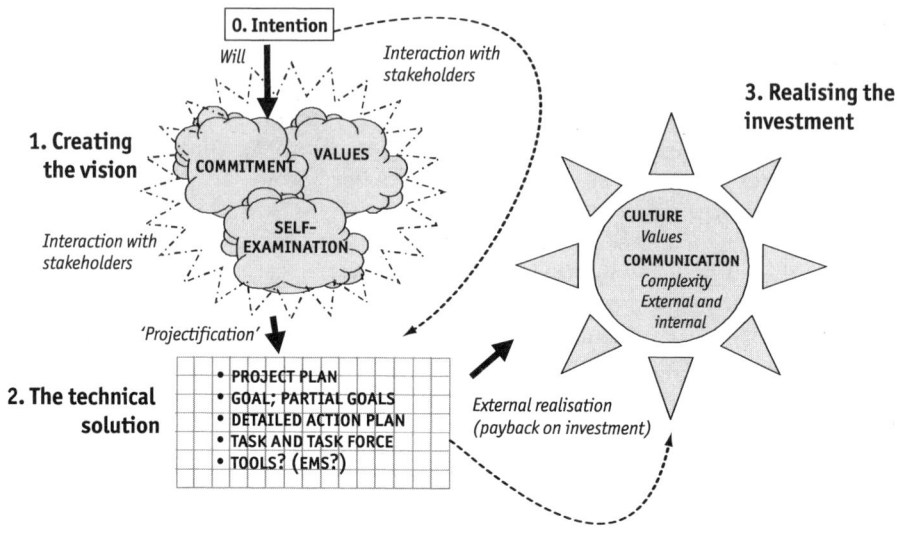

FIGURE 7.3 The limitations of profitability

Source: Langeland 2000: 142

but because it makes good business sense. But an interesting conclusion from both the X-Corp and Whole Foods Market cases indicates the opposite, that if corporate sustainability is not incorporated out of a philanthropic or ethical stance, but primarily from a vision of profits, then the profit seems to be limited. The companies that generate the largest profits through being sustainable, such as Whole Foods Market, seem to adhere to a sustainability code without hesitation. Long-term profitable companies refuse to be limited by an assessment of immediate potential earnings (Andrews 1971: 125). This has also been articulated as 'The Value Paradox', expressed as: 'If you're in it for the money, you won't get any' (Langeland 2000: 143).

Discussion and limitations

While much of the work on corporate sustainability may be common sense, it seems that companies addressing societal concerns are not commonplace. The main point of this chapter is to present sustainability as a feasible alternative for companies and to illustrate how a sustainable corporation can be cultivated. By adopting a proactive approach to sustainability, the business community has the opportunity to participate in setting the agenda for sustainability and to change its activities at its own pace.

There are several possible explanations for the general defensive corporate response, although none of them is a sufficient excuse. Business has to decide whether it is willing to accept the challenge and become a part of the solution. This will require commitment and a change in both mind-set and approach to embracing a wider corporate agenda; it is, however, essential for corporations wishing to claim responsibility for their actions as well as for the future of the planet.

The competitive advantages from turning an enterprise towards sustainability can and should be realised. This chapter questions the myth of ethical and environmental improvements as merely inconveniences and unnecessary expense. But the argument can be strengthened by further research in this field. Specific future challenges for other researchers are:

- **Complete case studies of a full-scale implementation processes**. In my view, the most important next step is to undertake all-encompassing case studies of companies implementing corporate sustainability in order to test the cultivation process as described in this chapter. Such case studies will provide additional valuable information and further insight into the core elements of a sustainable corporation as well as the strengths and limitations of the suggested cultivation process.

- **Sharpening the definitions**. Corporate sustainability, and the process of achieving it, has been presented here, but the definitions still need to be sharpened. Initial applications of the cultivation process (as described above) are likely to bring a clarification on both the content and the cultivation of sustainability. The process of developing the corporate culture to embrace sustainability would especially benefit from further research, as would the development of management tools to support these cultural changes.

- **Quantitative research to verify findings**. The research behind this chapter was conceptual, based on qualitative studies of an exploratory nature. The findings need to be investigated further through quantitative research in order to verify the conclusions and determine if they can be generalised. This should be done primarily by using questionnaires, perhaps supplemented by follow-up interviews, addressed to both corporations who claim some degree of sustainability and those that do not. The questionnaires should seek to compare the values of the participating companies, identify any sustainability processes they may have undertaken and measure their financial results. The overall goal is to provide valuable information on the applicability of corporate sustainability in practice and on how the challenge of sustainability is handled.

- **Measurement of sustainability**. In relation to identifying sustainable corporations and providing management with a more specific guiding tool, methods for measuring sustainability on both 'content' and 'cultivation' indicators should be developed. Content indicators should help identify a given company's extent of sustainability, i.e. to which stage the company has progressed. Cultivation indicators aim at assessing how the move towards sustainability is progressing, i.e. which stage the process is in.

Companies that take no account of societal and environmental considerations, being driven purely by short-term economics, may well prosper. This is, however, not the only feasible way of running a company. This chapter shows that a profitable, realistic alternative exists. In the words of Kenneth Andrews (1971: 238):

> Disagreements about the extent to which ethical behaviour can be prescribed do not obscure the plain fact that, for men of goodwill, ethical leadership is more inspiring than that which is not. Few people have problems in distinguishing the difference.

Put differently, some companies just inspire and generate a good feeling. These are the ones that are inspirational to work for, interesting to talk about, and that one can represent both professionally and in private with a sense of pride. The sustainable corporation is an opportunity, an inspiration for those corporations willing to take a chance and participate in shaping their future as well as that of their industry and society as a whole by challenging the frames and perceptions of a corporation of the 21st century.

References

Andrews, K.R. (1971) *The Concept of Corporate Strategy* (Dow Jones-Irwin Inc.)

Beer, M., R.A. Eisenstat and A. Spector (1990) *Why Change Programs Don't Produce Change*, in D.A. Kolb, D.A. Joyce, S. Osland and I.M. Rubin (eds.), *The Organizational Behavior Reader* (Englewood Cliffs, NJ: Prentice-Hall, 6th edn).

Bendix, J., and O.S. Andersen (1995) *Change Management: Communication, Behaviour and Co-operation* (Copenhagen: Børsen Bøger, in Danish).

Berry, M.A., and D.A. Rondinelli (1998) 'Proactive Corporate Environmental Management: A New Industrial Revolution', *Academy of Management Executive* 12.2: 38-50.

Borum, F. (1995) *Strategies for Organizational Change* (Copenhagen: Copenhagen Business School, in Danish).

Burke, W.W. (1994) *Organizational Development: A Process of Learning and Changing* (Reading, MA: Addison-Wesley, 2nd edn).

Collins, J.C., and J.I. Porras (1994) *Build to Last: Successful Habits of Visionary Companies* (London: Century).

Daly, H.E. (1996) *Beyond Growth: The Economics of Sustainable Development* (Boston, MA: Beacon Press).

Fischer, A. (1998) *The 100 Best Companies to Work for* (New York: Fortune).

Gladwin, T.N., J.J. Kennelly and T.-S. Krause (1995) 'Shifting Paradigms for Sustainable Development: Implications for Management Theory and Research', *Academy of Management Review* 20.4: 874-907.

Kotter, J.P. (1997) *Leading Change* (Copenhagen: Industriens Forlag, in Danish).

Langeland, L. (1998) 'On Communicating the Complexity of a Green Message. Part 1: The Max Havelaar Case', *Greener Management International* 22 (Summer 1998): 96-107.

—— (1999a) 'Superior and Sustainable Organizations: Seeking Integration between the Fields of Corporate Management and Corporate Sustainability', *IABS 1999 Proceedings*: 251-56.

—— (1999b) 'The Sustainable Corporation: A Practical and Economic Option, Illustrated through an American Case Study', *Børsens Ledelseshåndbøger*, August 1999: 1-22 (in Danish).

—— (1999c) 'On Communicating the Complexity of a Green Message. Part 2: The Vigilant Market', *Greener Management International* 25 (Spring 1999): 81-90.

—— (2000) 'The Sustainable Corporation: Exploring the Contents and Cultivation of an Organizational Concept', PhD dissertation, Centre for Technology, Economics and Management, Technical University of Denmark, July 2000.

Lewin, K. (1946) 'Research on Minority Problems', *The Technology Review* 48.3 (January 1946).

Mauws, M.K. (1999) 'Management and Moral Sublimation: A Preliminary Investigation', paper presented at the 10th IABS annual conference, Paris, France, 26 June 1999.

McGregor, D. (1960) *The Human Side of Enterprise* (New York: McGraw-Hill).

Morgan, G. (1996) *Images of Organization* (Thousand Oaks, CA: Sage, 2nd edn).

Peattie, K. (1995) *Environmental Marketing Management: Meeting the Green Challenge* (London: Pitman).

Peters, T.J., and R.H. Waterman Jr (1982) *In Search of Excellence: Lessons from America's Best-Run Companies* (New York: Warner Books).

Schein, E.H. (1984) 'Coming to a New Awareness of Organizational Culture', *Sloan Management Review*, Winter 1984: 3-16.

Sheldon, O. (1923) *The Philosophy of Management* (London: Pitman).

Spedding, L.S. (1996) *Environmental Management for Business* (Chichester, UK: John Wiley).

Starik, M. (1994) *Management and the Natural Environment* (Hinsdale, IL: Dryden Press).

Stead, W.E., and J.G. Stead (1996) *Management for a Small Planet: Strategic Decision Making and the Environment* (Thousand Oaks, CA: Sage Publications, 2nd edn).

Taylor, F.W. (1895) 'A Piece Rate System, Being a Step toward Partial Solution of the Labor Problem', presented at American Society of Mechanical Engineers, June 1895, reprinted in V.E. Sower, J. Motwani and M.J. Savoie (eds.), *Classic Readings in Operations Management* (Hinsdale, IL: Dryden Press).

—— (1911) 'The Gospel of Efficiency: The Principles of Scientific Management', *The American Magazine*, reprinted in V.E. Sower, J. Motwani and M.J. Savoie (eds.), *Classic Readings in Operations Management* (Hinsdale, IL: Dryden Press): 377-423.

WCED (World Commission on Environment and Development) (1987) *Our Common Future* (Oxford, UK: Oxford University Press).

Welford, R. (1995) *Environmental Strategy and Sustainable Development: The Corporate Challenge for the Twenty-first Century* (London: Routledge).

—— (1997) *Hijacking Environmentalism: Corporate Responses to Sustainable Development* (London: Earthscan Publications).

Wickens, P.D. (1995) *The Ascendant Organization: Combining Commitment and Control for Long-term, Sustainable Business Success* (London: Macmillan).

8
Corporate sustainability
INTEGRATING HUMAN AND ECOLOGICAL
SUSTAINABILITY APPROACHES

Andrew Griffiths
University of Queensland, Australia

Dexter Dunphy and Suzanne Benn
University of Technology, Sydney, Australia

It is apparent that current patterns of industrial development are not conducive to the creation of sustainable communities and economies (Senge and Carstedt 2001). The critical situation in which we find ourselves has been brought about by multiple causes. One important contributing factor is the rise of the corporation and the political and economic systems that have supported its evolution into a dominant organisational form. The powerful dynamism of the modern organisation has transformed both nature and society. The central question to be answered in this century is whether the current model of the corporation needs to be modified to contribute to the continuing health of the planet, the survival of humans and other species, the development of a just and humane society and the creation of work that brings dignity and self-fulfilment to those undertaking it (Elkington 1997, 2001; Dunphy *et al.* 2003). In other words, what do sustainable corporations look like and how do we go about building them?

In this chapter, it is argued that building corporate sustainability can lead to sustained long-term performance (Aragon-Correa and Sharma 2003; Russo and Fouts 1997; Sharma and Vredenburg 1998). However, we argue that it requires the integration of two alternate approaches to viewing sustainability—human and ecological (Dunphy *et al.* 2000).

By ecological sustainability we are referring to redesigning organisations to contribute to sustainable economic development and the protection and renewal of the biosphere. Issues relating to ecological sustainability draw on the disciplines of strategic and environmental management (Hart 1997; Starik and Rands 1995; Roome 1992; Hunt and Auster 1990). By human sustainability we are referring to building human capability and skills for sustainable high-level organisational performance, and for community and societal well-being (Dunphy *et al.* 2000). Issues relating to human sustainability draw on research undertaken in the areas of strategic human resource management and change management (Dunphy and Griffiths 1998; Wright and Snell 1998; Lepak and Snell 1999; Huselid 1995).

This chapter outlines a comprehensive sustainability phase model that emerged from a review of the literature on the development of both ecological and human sustainability (Dunphy *et al.* 2003). The framework outlines the developmental phases through which corporations progress toward both human and ecological sustainability. As a tool, the phase model allows meaningful comparisons between organisations, helping to assess current commitment to, and practice of, human and ecological sustainability, and assisting managers in capitalising on the benefits of moving towards more sustainable practices in both areas. Furthermore, it is argued that corporate sustainability is built on the integration of these two alternative approaches to viewing sustainability. Using evidence from case studies, it is suggested that the development of proactive corporate sustainability approaches requires significant investments in the human capital of organisations.

Human and ecological sustainability traditions

There has been a recent surge in work undertaken in both human and ecological sustainability traditions which demonstrates the importance of the development of specific capabilities that enhance an organisation's competitive performance (Egri and Herman 2000; Ramus and Steger 2000; Russo and Fouts 1997; Sharma and Vredenburg 1998; MacDuffie 1995; Huselid 1995). This work has been extended to identify contingent relationships between capabilities and competitiveness, with one suggested avenue of research being the need to examine the impact of human resource capabilities on the development of proactive environmental management practices (Aragon-Correa and Sharma 2003; Wright and Snell 1998).

Various authors have described the historical processes by which corporations have moved towards supporting ecological sustainability (Hunt and Auster 1990; Hoffman 1997; Roome 1992). These studies have identified a range of capabilities and characteristics of ecologically sustainable organisations (ESOs). Leading from the strategic choice literature and based on 'best practice' case studies, models such as Hunt and Auster's (1990) 'five-stage environmental development continuum', Arthur D. Little's (1989) 'state-of-the-art model', Post and Altman's (1992) 'corporate greening model' and Roome's (1992) 'strategic options model' have developed a classification that allows for a systematic comparison between organisations in terms of how sustainable their strategies are and the type of contributions they are making towards sustainability. The underlying assumption of these models suggests that companies have a choice of environmental strategy which classifies them along a continuum according to their degree of proactivity in environmental management (Henriques and Sadorsky 1999; Schaefer and Harvey 1998). Table 8.1 outlines some of the key terms of the major phase models and aligns them with the categories developed later in this chapter.

Roome (1992)	Hunt and Auster (1990)	Dunphy, Griffiths and Benn (2003)	Human sustainability elements added by Dunphy *et al.* (2003)
		Rejection	• Employees a resource to be exploited • Training costs kept to minimum • Organisation does not take responsibility for health/welfare of employees • Does not engage its community or stakeholders
Non-compliance	Beginner	Non-responsive-ness	• Financial and technological factors dominate business strategies • Labour viewed as a cost to be minimised • Industrial relations strategies focus on developing a compliant workforce • Broader issues of community involvement ignored
Compliance	Firefighter	Compliance	• Firm viewed by senior managers as decent employer • Emphasis on compliance with legal standards • HR training strategies and organisation development instigated but not integrated • Community concerns are addressed due to negative publicity, litigation or impact on company bottom line
Compliance plus	Concerned citizen	Efficiency	• Systematic attempt to integrate HR functions to reduce cost/increase efficiency • Focus on training or team development for value adding—i.e. waste reduction, TQM • Community projects undertaken where cost benefit can be demonstrated
Commercial and environmental excellence	Pragmatist	Strategic proactivity	• Workforce skills mix and diversity vital to corporate culture • Intellectual and social capital are used as part of corporate strategy • Corporate competencies developed • Flexible workplace cultures developed • Corporation contributes to community betterment • Actively seeks to engage stakeholders
Leading-edge	Proactivist	Sustaining	• Organisation accepts responsibility for developing and upgrading its own human capital and that of its community • Promotes strong work–life balance • Strong ethical/values corporate position • Pursues general human welfare and engages with stakeholders • Seeks to promote change with other industry–society participants

TQM = total quality management

TABLE 8.1 Phase model characteristics

Source: Adapted from Henriques and Sadorsky 1999

Although the specific names given to the phases in each model differ, they generally share the same characteristics typifying each phase (Post and Altman 1992). Furthermore, the most common environmental management strategy model type utilises stages along a type of continuum or progression (e.g. Hunt and Auster 1990; Arthur D. Little 1989; Roome 1992) rather than distinct categories in which firms can be strictly classified (Hass 1996). There is a great deal of overlap in models such as these, despite differences in the names given to various phases and the different number of phases. Clearly, any generalised phase model is a high level of abstraction from the diversity of corporate life (Kolk and Mauser 2002). Nevertheless, ideal type models of this kind have a long history in the social sciences—without such frameworks it is difficult to compare and contrast individuals, organisations and communities.

Human sustainability perspectives

Studies of historical stages/phases underlying the moves towards human sustainability are rare. However, an increasing body of literature in the management field has emerged over the past 30 years compiling evidence of the importance of people or 'human factors' in transforming and changing organisations (Dunphy and Griffiths 1998). The focus of this research in the management area was to generate organisational structures that contributed to human satisfaction, growth and development while also contributing to the profitability and productivity of enterprises. Management research developed capabilities and knowledge relevant to the effective conduct of the micro and macro elements of organisational change (Mirvis 1988). While early change agents focused on interventions at an individual and/or group level, the focus moved subsequently to the management of large-scale corporate restructuring and to forging links between change management practices and corporate strategy. So, over 30 years, the change movement generated a wealth of information on how to redesign and renew organisational architectures from the individual level to the total corporation (Beer *et al.* 1990).

For instance, the human sustainability traditions have established that, where individual jobs are redesigned to enhance an individual's autonomy in decision-making and are linked to the organisation's central purpose (through skills training, human development and culture change workshops), they would result in greater organisational commitment and employee satisfaction (Kleiner 1995; Mirvis 1988, 1990). Substantial research has shown that, while these initiatives frequently succeeded in enhancing individual skills, if they were not complemented with organisational systems and architectures that rewarded people for using these skills the initiatives would fail to generate sustainable positive outcomes for either individuals or the corporation (Emery 1974; MacDuffie 1995; Huselid 1995; Dunphy and Griffiths 1998).

At the level of the work group or business unit, the human sustainability traditions focused on designing architectures that would both benefit individuals and improve productivity and profitability for the organisation. Team-based organisations were implemented, in which smaller business units were created and, in turn, broken down into semi-autonomous work teams (Walton 1985). These were teams made up of skilled individuals who could take responsibility for planning, scheduling, quality and customer service in the production of goods and services. Such organisational architectures proved to be more effective than their mechanistic counterparts in producing high levels of performance, as well as significantly raising employee work satisfaction. However, they also required significant modification of hierarchical management structures (Lawler 1992).

How these new practices were implemented—through incremental or transformational changes—was a point of debate. Some authors, such as Lawler (1992), argued that levels of participation and involvement were crucial to securing the development of high-performance organisations. Typically this could be achieved through incremental strategies. Others, such as Dunphy and Stace (1990), Stace and Dunphy (2001) and Weick and Quinn (1999), have demonstrated that transformational changes can also provide a means by which organisations achieve sustainable corporate objectives. Despite these differences, the human sustainability tradition has demonstrated the importance of human competencies and capital to sustained competitive performance.

Human resources and environmental management

Our interest in phase models is not to develop historical understanding but rather to better understand the paths corporations must travel to reach a full commitment to corporate sustainability that covers both human and ecological issues (Dunphy et al. 2003).

We argue that the organisational move to ecological sustainability is supported by, and reliant on, 'human sustainability'—development by the organisation of the human capabilities and skills that enable more consistent compliance, the implementation of eco-efficiency measures and forward planning for strategic sustainability. The relationship between the two aspects of sustainability should be recognised as symbiotic rather than artificially divided.

Our approach builds on recent empirical studies that suggest a relationship among human resource policies, practices and the successful implementation of corporate environmental initiatives (Daily and Huang 2001; Dunphy et al. 2000; Dunphy et al. 2003; Egri and Herman 2000; Ramus and Steger 2000; Wilkinson et al. 2001). In particular these studies have found that human resource management—through practices such as values-based management, devolution of authority and skills development has assisted the pursuit of corporate sustainability innovations. For instance, Daily and Huang (2001) found that successful implementation of environmental management system (EMS) programmes in manufacturing organisations was assisted when factors such as training, empowerment, teamwork and rewards were addressed. These results were also backed up by other empirical studies (Ramus and Steger 2000) showing that employees who perceived they were receiving strong supervisory and organisational support and commitment were more likely to implement strategies to address environmental issues in their organisations. The study also demonstrated that 'supervisory support behaviours encouraging environmental innovation, competence building, communication, rewards and recognition and management of goals and responsibilities had a statistically significant impact on employee willingness to promote eco-initiatives' (Ramus and Steger 2000: 623).

Similarly, a study by Egri and Herman (2000) found that non-profit environmental organisations and organisations that had products and services that were environmentally focused had leaders who demonstrated values orientations that reflected a more ecocentric approach. Furthermore, their study found that those businesses with an environmental focus were more likely to be characterised by flat structures, informal arrangements and structures that facilitated empowerment (Egri and Herman 2000: 599). This translates into an important finding—that building human capabilities can enhance the ecological sustainability orientations of organisations.

In line with these earlier studies, it is argued in this chapter that, as corporations move to adopt different sustainability stances, this in turn creates the need to upgrade the human capability requirements of the organisation. In other words, corporations that adopt a low level of compliance or a reactive stance to sustainability appear to require significant investments in human capabilities and organisational systems which can then enable them to develop more proactive stances on sustainability issues. These corporations need to build their human sustainability approaches in order to develop and capitalise on their ecological capabilities.

Scandic Hotels represents an interesting case that highlights the contributions that investments in human capital can have on achieving eco-efficiencies (Nattrass and Altomare 1999). Scandic Hotels introduced The Natural Step (TNS) programme in implementing sustainability practices. This programme was used to instigate a new values approach throughout the organisation and involved all employees and managers being exposed to workshops and the ideas behind TNS. The first efficiency impacts at Scandic were felt almost immediately. Employees identified many 'low-hanging fruit', ripe for picking. For instance, overall soap and shampoo use was reduced by 25 tonnes and waste by 8.5 tonnes annually. This was achieved by the introduction of recyclable soap and shampoo containers and the use of refillable containers (Nattrass and Altomare 1999: 80).

Second, Scandic moved towards efficiency gains through the adoption of value-adding activities. In order to generate value-adding outputs, the company had to first build the capability of its employees. Anticipated efficiency gains were shared with employees by investing in their skills. Emphasis was placed on developing and training employees (enhancing human capital) to identify value-adding opportunities (Dunphy *et al.* 2003). Employees developed and used a range of metrics such as environmental barometers (quarterly benchmarking reports) and an environmental index.

In its first year, average energy consumption in the hotel chain's Nordic hotels was reduced by 7%, water consumption by 4% and unsorted waste by 15%. This resulted in estimated financial benefits of US$800,000 (Nattrass and Altomare 1999: 92). Through investment in such value-adding activities, Scandic built on its cost approach to deliver further efficiency improvements in resource utilisation (Dunphy *et al*. 2003).

Finally, at Scandic, innovation has become another means of gaining further sustainable efficiencies. Renewing and refurnishing are major investment activities in hotels. One major innovation Scandic has developed is the 97% recyclable 'eco-room'. Rooms are designed and built for disassembly and all components that cannot be re-used or recycled are sold. According to Nattrass and Altomare (1999: 97): 'Approximately 2,000 rooms are being refurbished each year with an estimated decrease per year of plastics by 90 tonnes, metals by 15 tonnes and mercury by 50%.'

The Scandic case reinforces two important messages contained in this chapter. First, the move to capture sustainability benefits often starts with an emphasis on meeting compliance and cutting costs. However, to achieve sustainable longer-term gains, the appropriate human systems and cultural values must be built to support value-adding and innovation. Second, corporation efficiency gains need to be shared with employees and a broader set of stakeholders, as well as used to build internal competencies and the reputational capital of the firm (Dunphy *et al*. 2003). In the next section of this chapter, we present the sustainability phase model and outline some of the key ecological and sustainability capabilities associated with each of the phases. The unified approach, combining ecological and human sustainability, is designed to bring about a change in the interpretation of corporate sustainability and to support the activities of change agents in bringing about sustainability in a systematic way.

Corporate sustainability phase model

In this section, we outline the major characteristics of the corporate sustainability phase model. The six phases, ranging from rejection through sustaining, represent a set of ideal types which can be used to help organisations define where they are currently as regards human and ecological sustainability and chart their progress towards a more sustainable position (see Fig. 8.1). At each step of the way, new human capabilities or characteristics of the organisation enable further progression of ecological sustainability. We do not assume that a firm necessarily progresses through the phases step by step on an 'improving' trajectory. On the contrary, an organisation may leapfrog phases or regress by abandoning previously established sustainability practices. Significant shifts are often triggered by changes such as the appointment of a new chief executive, stakeholder pressure, new legislation, economic fluctuations or by the loss of committed enthusiasts.

The characteristics of the phases are outlined below:

1. **Rejection.** Involves an attitude on the part of the organisation's managers that all resources—employees, community infrastructure and the ecological environment—are there to be exploited by the firm for immediate economic gain. The firm disregards any negative impacts of its activities. These firms externalise costs to others. On the human side, employees and subcontractors are exploited. Employees, in particular, are regarded sim-

Ecological sustainability phases

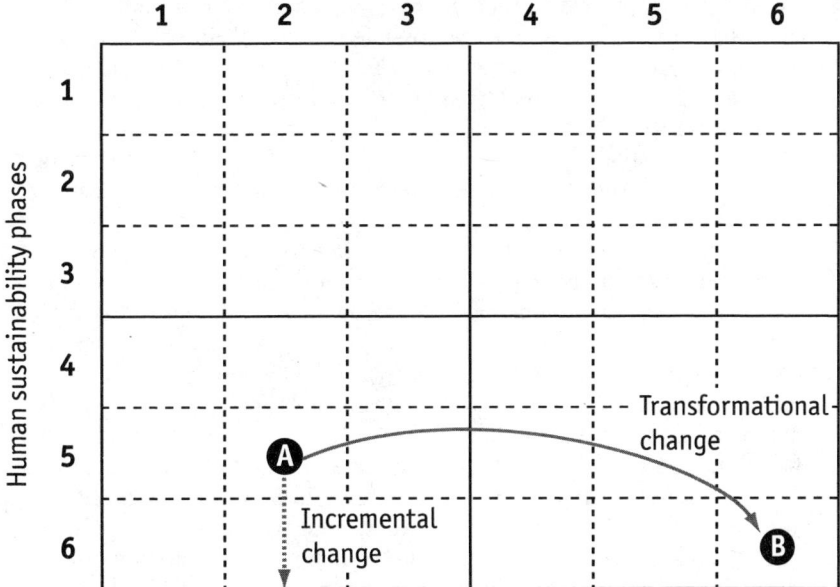

Phases:
  1. Rejection
  2. Non-responsiveness
  3. Compliance
  4. Efficiency
  5. Strategic proactivity
  6. Sustaining

FIGURE 8.1 Sustainability phase model

ply as industrial 'cannon fodder'—there is no commitment to developing them, and health and safety measures are ignored or paid 'lip service'. Community concerns are rejected outright. There is a strong belief that the firm exists simply to maximise profit and any other claims by the community are dismissed as illegitimate. The firm disregards the destructive environmental impacts of its activities and actively opposes any attempts by governments and 'green' activists to place constraints on its activities. The environment is regarded as a free 'good' to be exploited. For instance, Exxon and Mobil are two of several companies, along with several trade associations, that organised against the Kyoto Protocol through the Global Climate Coalition, an organisation formed to co-ordinate business response to the climate change debate (Benn *et al.* 2003).

2. **Non-responsiveness**. Usually results from lack of awareness or ignorance rather than from active opposition to a corporate ethic wider than finan-

cial gain. The firm concentrates on 'business as usual' and ignores issues of sustainability. The firm's human resource strategies, if they exist, are focused mainly on creating and maintaining a compliant workforce. Community issues are ignored where possible and the environmental consequences of the firm's activities are taken for granted and, if negative, disregarded. Environmental risks, costs, opportunities and imperatives are seen as irrelevant. Industrial relations is a major issue with the emphasis on cost of labour. Financial and technological factors exclude broader social concerns and the training agenda focuses on technical and supervisory training.

Increasingly, governments and disaffected communities are imposing tough penalties for non-compliance. Corporations that do not address social and environmental requirements face fines, workers' compensation cases, criminal convictions, payment of clean-up costs and consumer boycotts. The potential for damage liability can make non-compliance a significant business risk, as provided in the examples below.

In the US, the total corporate liability costs for asbestos-related diseases has been estimated at US$30 billion, far more than the product ever earned its manufacturers. In a recent court decision in South Africa, more than 300 workers in an asbestos mine were awarded damages. Claims by the multinational company involved that it could not be held accountable for the actions of subsidiary companies were discounted. A major concern of the workers' lawyers was that, if larger settlements were won, there appeared a strong likelihood that the company would be bankrupted.[1]

In another incident, Esso was found guilty of 11 breaches of the Occupational Health and Safety Act after an explosion and fire at its Australian plant at Longford caused the death of two people and injured many others. Esso was fined US$1 million and is currently facing an additional class action seeking damages of US$650 million (Gregory and Shaw 2001).

3. **Compliance.** Focuses on reducing the risk of sanctions for failing to meet minimum standards as an employer or producer. Changes are primarily reactive to growing legal requirements and community expectations for more sustainable practices. Here, corporate strategies relating to human sustainability focus on policies of legal compliance plus benevolent paternalism with the expectation of employee loyalty in return. The firm is primarily reactive to growing legal requirements and community expectations for more sustainable practices. A recent shift has seen the development of co-regulatory practices. Human resources functions such as industrial relations, training and total quality management (TQM) are instituted but with little integration between them. Only ecological issues that are seen as likely to attract litigation or strong community action are addressed. Firms or industry associations in this phase may take a non-committal position on politicised sustainability issues.

---

1 www.abc.net.au/news, accessed 19 February 2002.

4. **Efficiency.** Reflects the growing awareness on the part of managers in the corporation that there are real advantages to be gained by proactively instituting sustainability practices. In particular, these practices are directed toward reducing costs and increasing operational efficiency. Some organisations capitalise on these cost savings and reinvest them in their employees to achieve sustainable longer-term gains by building the appropriate cultures and human systems that support value-adding and innovation. For example, Scandic, referred to earlier in this chapter, has had considerable success at reducing and eliminating waste and using these cost savings to build its employee skill base (Nattrass and Altomare 1999). The new innovation focus has led to huge cost savings, reduced ecological impacts and enhanced the reputation of the corporation.

   In particular, human resource and environmental policies and practices are used to reduce costs and increase efficiency. Investment in training may involve expense but results in compensating added value through increased quality of products and/or services. Technical and supervisory training is augmented with interpersonal skills training. Teamwork is encouraged for value-adding as well as cost-saving purposes and external stakeholder relations are developed for business benefits. ISO 14000 systems (the international EMS standard) are integrated with TQM and occupational health and safety management systems or other systematic approaches, with the aim of achieving eco-efficiencies. In the name of waste minimisation, sales of by-products are encouraged as are co-operative relationships with other members of the supply chain.

   The case of Placer Dome, a gold mining company, highlights the potential conflict between narrow and broader views of human sustainability. In the 1990s, Placer Dome's human resource policies and strategies had a strong focus on employee development, training, safety and on valuing employee contributions to the company's sustainability efforts. A range of human sustainability initiatives was aimed at developing the capabilities of both employees and local communities affected by mining operations. However, a dramatic decline in the gold price caused a setback in the pursuit of sustainability. The company's decision to 'downsize' led to a substantial reduction in one area of its core capabilities. For instance, at the Marcopper mine site a retrenched employee had to be rehired to undertake negotiations with key stakeholders when it was realised that he was the only one in the company that had developed a strong and trusting relationship with the community stakeholders. This example is an instance of a managerial decision (downsizing), made in the name of efficiency, which can threaten the corporate capabilities required for future competitive advantages (Dunphy *et al.* 2003: 153).

5. **Strategic proactivity.** Appears when sustainability is used to seize emerging opportunities by, for example, improving competitive advantage by positioning the firm as a leader in sustainable business practices. BP has adopted such a strategic approach to sustainability. As one of the world's largest extractive resource-based companies and energy producers, BP has strategically repositioned itself to be seen as moving 'beyond petroleum'.

It has incorporated these goals into its corporate strategies. While BP is in the early stages of the sustainability journey, the company is being positioned as an industry leader (Dunphy *et al.* 2003: 167-68). Proactive environmental strategies are seen as a source of competitive advantage at this stage, with the firm's strategic elite viewing sustainability as providing a potential competitive advantage. The commitment to sustainability is strongly embedded in the quest for maximising longer-term corporate profitability, i.e. it is motivated by intelligent corporate self-interest.

Future corporate performance is seen not simply as a matter of reducing costs and increasing efficiencies but as adding value and maximising speed, flexibility, innovation and responsiveness. Consequently, managers and change agents try to position the organisation as a leader in sustainable business practices—with advanced human resource strategies that help make the organisation an 'employer of choice', with 'corporate citizenship' initiatives that build stakeholder support and with innovative, quality products that are environmentally safe and healthy. Reflecting a growing awareness of the business possibilities associated with sustainable development, the environment industry now encompasses a wide range of products.

Similarly the organisation attempts to develop differentiated stakeholder strategies. This involves designing and implementing various strategies that reflect the needs and interests of different stakeholders (Hirsh and Sheldrake 2001). To achieve this, stakeholder representatives need to be actively involved.

For instance BHP's Carrington silver lead and zinc mine in Queensland has used third-party auditing by the North Queensland Conservation Council as a means of independently monitoring and reporting on the company's sustainable operation of this site. While the council found that BHP performed better than its own targets and legislative requirements, it recommended that the mining operations look further into developing a product life-cycle analysis and seek greater community involvement in risk assessment and revision of mining operations. Third-party scrutiny can be used to push organisations further towards the attainment of strategic sustainability and this can also prove to be of strategic advantage to the firm (BCA 2001).

6. **Sustaining corporation.** Reflects an internalisation of sustainability and actively promotes the emergence of a society that supports the ecological viability of the planet and its species. It contributes to just, equitable and democratic social practices and human fulfilment. There are few organisations that embody this ideal. To date, those most cited include Ben & Jerry's, Patagonia and Interface. And even these have not always been able to maintain the advances they have made. Nevertheless, evidence is emerging of innovative companies implementing sustainability practices in a range of operations. In the process, these companies bring stakeholders into the organisation, build reputational capital, build the capability of the workforce and contribute to ecological and community regeneration. These organisations are building corporate sustainability. The organisa-

tion still pursues the traditional business objective of providing an excellent return to investors, but voluntarily goes beyond this by actively promoting ecological sustainability values and practices in the industry and society generally. Its fundamental commitment is to facilitate the emergence of a society that supports the ecological viability of the planet and its species and contributes to just, equitable social practices and human fulfilment.

The Rabobank group, a large Dutch co-operative bank, is one organisation that has, for many years, demonstrated a collaborative commitment to human and ecological sustainability. The bank was founded as a co-operative in 1888 and has expanded to rank 32nd globally. Rabobank's stated aim is to pursue the goals of 'profit, people and the planet'. Rabobank acts to ensure that it heals the natural environment with care and that its activities support sustainable development. In addition, it is strongly involved in several national and international business forums that exchange information and best practice and which engage in public advocacy for sustainability. In 1999 it launched the RG Sustainable Equity Fund which invests in companies chosen for their ethical approach to social and environmental issues. In the first 11 months 'the fund achieved a return of 59% compared to 45% for its benchmark the Morgan Stanley Capital Index' (Schrama 2001: 77-91). Rabobank regards sustainability as central to its business activities (Benn *et al.* 2003).

Change for sustainability:
incremental and transformational paths

A key issue facing organisations is the implementation of sustainability initiatives. Many organisations prefer to make changes slowly, systematically building on their achievements, while others want to make widespread rapid and quite radical alterations to the way they do business. We have categorised these as 'incremental' and 'transformational' approaches to sustainability.

The corporate sustainability phase model around which this chapter is constructed provides a way of estimating and describing the gap between these two approaches, as well as indicating how to move forward (see Fig. 8.1). For instance, the human sustainability orientations of organisations are identified along the horizontal rows while the ecological sustainability orientations are identified along the vertical columns. Organisations may be at different stages in each of these areas. It is possible for the same organisation to have a highly strategic approach to human sustainability (phase 5) but to be lagging in terms of compliance in the ecological area (phase 2): for example, a mining company that has first-rate human resource policies but which has environmentally destructive operations. The differences between current and envisioned future positions in the matrix define the gap to be bridged. Point A in Figure 8.1, for example, could represent a bank that has systematically built its human resource strategies over a ten-year period in order to attract and retain some of the best talent in the industry. The bank has also been concerned about its contribution to the community and has used its community relations to support its progressive 'concerned and caring' image. This places it in phase 5 (strategic proactivity [HS5]) in the area of human sustainability. It has given little thought, however, to its environmental impact. It uses huge amounts of paper, most of which is not separated for recycling. It constantly updates its computers and peripheral equipment, but commits them by truckloads to landfill. It is discussing developments in the ethical investment fund area, but has not yet launched such a fund or developed an alliance with another financial institution that has. This places it, for ecological sustainability, in phase 2 (non-responsiveness [ES2]). Now, it aspires to be a leader in the introduction of sustainable practices. Clearly it only needs, at the most, incremental change in the human sustainability area, but its transformational change programme needs to centre on ecological sustainability where it has a lot of ground to make up before it reaches its ideal. This transformational change is represented by point B on Figure 8.1.

According to the phase model of corporate sustainability outlined above, the organisations most in need of change are those in the rejection and non-responsive phases. Because expenditure on personal and professional development is kept to a minimum and community concerns are rejected completely, firms in the rejection phase remain ignorant of the benefits of progressing along the sustainability spectrum. In the non-responsive organisation, financial factors so dominate corporate decision-making that often both the human resource and environment factors are taken for granted, usually with the exception of industrial relations issues. Management policy-making of the non-responsive organisation focuses on ensuring that the workforce is easily moulded to the corporate will in order to derive maximum financial return. For organisations such as this, to move to compliance and beyond requires some cultural modification. But, in most instances, this is not the transformational change of the dramatic paradigm shift. This is gradual, planned, continuous and ongoing incremental change. It is often based on TQM, on team building and on the development of new capabilities and values. A risk-free, ongoing position of compliance is not just a matter of changing policies and values— it is assisted by enlisting the commitment of employees and building practical procedures that everyone in the organisation can understand. For instance, Scandic Hotels and Interface transformed their operations incrementally by adopting corporate-wide programmes such as TNS. These programmes became vehicles by which employee capabilities were developed to address sustainability issues. In both cases, the organisations used these initiatives to extend their respective approaches to sustainability to include more strategic issues (Dunphy et al. 2003; Nattrass and Altomare 1999). Typically, incremental changes of this sort involve organisations only moving through or from one phase to another (as outlined in Fig. 8.1).

For other organisations, change along the sustainability phase model will be transformational, requiring a redefinition of the company's core business area, its key manufacturing processes or, perhaps, its human resource policies and community relationships. For example, for the organisation to move from the rejection phase to compliance is a transformative change requiring a major shift in values and a reinventing of the corporate image and culture according to a powerful conception of future need. Generally, the transformational changes would involve organisations leaping through two or more phases as outlined in Figure 8.1.

Transformational change is deep change. It can involve risk and requires new ways of thinking, perhaps surrendering control, often irreversible and discontinuous with the past (Dunphy *et al.* 2003). A key challenge for management is to enable the organisation to make an imaginative leap that is both proactive and flexible. This form of change requires the development of transformational capabilities that support strategic repositioning. These capabilities can enable the organisation to shift to new products and processes that are less environmentally destructive, and are able to give the firm long-lasting high performance. Arguably, this is the sort of organisational change made by Shell in the mid-1990s when it faced international criticism for the proposed sinking of the Brent Spar oil platform and for its apparent support of a repressive political regime in Nigeria. As a result, it made the fundamental decision to integrate social and environmental principles into its business principles. As with other companies faced with the necessity of making such changes, it would have been riskier for Shell *not* to have made this change. While still a fossil fuel firm, Shell has guaranteed to divert a portion of profits to research alternative energy. Shell has moved to a more strategic position on the phase model of sustainability (Dunphy *et al.* 2003).

Lovins *et al.* (1999) have argued that, if firms persist with the win–win business logic of natural capitalism, they can gain long-term competitive advantage. For many organisations, building this perspective into an organisation requires reinvention of organisational norms and the development of innovative capacity. Other organisations may take the transformational path of dematerialisation, where the service flow is maintained or increased, while reducing physical resource input (Sutton 2003). A firm that has made such a strategic transformation will have the capability and learning capacity to recognise and develop the skills and organisational culture necessary to innovate in line with the new business standards set by ecological modernisation (Hoffman 1997; Mol and Sonnenfeld 2000).

Hewlett-Packard's environmental strategies and solutions programme, for instance, showed that sustainability can offer companies a strategic competitive advantage (Preston 2001). The firm based the programme on the premise that the planet is a closed system which will eventually face limits, placing the firm in a new social and economic situation. In other words, the firm strategically scoped the challenges of a new business environment, developing strategies that would transform potential environmental liabilities such as climate change, resource exhaustion and the energy crisis into competitive advantage (Preston 2001: 29).

Transformative change at Fuji Xerox

The highly successful Fuji Xerox Eco-Manufacturing Centre at Zetland in Sydney serves as a case study to demonstrate that a very positive relationship between human and ecological sustainability can generate transformative change (Benn *et al.* 2003). The concept of 'eco-manufacturing' involves detailed analysis of why things fail and produces remanufactured products with improvements intended to eliminate future failures. Remanufacturing goes beyond efficiency measures to the more strategic aim of supplying local operators with high-quality locally reprocessed parts. The firm has positioned itself as a market leader in this technology. The transformational aspect of the change is that the firm now has the potential to transfer remanufacturing skills developed with printers and photocopiers to other industry sectors.

Eco-manufacturing takes used components and tests, re-engineers and reassembles them into 'new' products while ensuring that the production process and the final products have no adverse environmental effects. To produce a quality re-engineered product, and to meet the new and higher environmental safety standards required of an eco-manufacturing process, means going beyond mere replication. It requires complex technological challenges to be addressed. For example, the materials of the components may have changed during their first use due to heat, vibration or some other physical effect of the operational processes within the equipment.

Fuji Xerox managers describe the work of the Eco-Manufacturing Centre as re-engineering and redesigning a product or product component and developing it to as good as, or even better than, new. This process involves scientifically examining the causes of failure while looking for opportunities to extend the life of the product and improve its performance more generally. These processes also have environmental benefits by reducing demand for raw materials, energy and waste to landfill. Another major benefit to the business is the acquisition of data about problems that develop in its products over time. That data was previously lost as used defective products were simply sent straight to landfill. Part of the new remanufacturing/re-engineering process involves analysing the defects in the components that have been returned. This analysis provides information that can be used to improve component design and thereby leads to better remanufactured products. There are therefore multiple benefits from remanufacturing including: decreased costs due to recycling over the year 2001–02 were approximately AUS$22.5 million; improved design for increased reliability and enhanced performance; and savings from import substitution and new export earnings.

Not only are parts renewed or recycled, but the technical processes involved in achieving this have been developed to eliminate environmentally damaging emissions, pollution and waste. For example:

- All solvents have been eliminated from the cleaning of parts and components.

- Frozen carbon dioxide (dry ice) is used under high pressure to clean components, a process that creates no liquid wastes or pollutants.

- Environmentally 'neutral' bicarbonate of soda is used under high pressure to remove the old coating from the fuser rollers used in photocopiers. The spent bicarbonate of soda is then re-used as an industrial water softener.

- A carbon by-product of waste toner (57,000 kg a year.) is extracted and can be used as a combustion agent in steel making.

- Reduction in energy use through the implementation of a range of initiatives and monthly tracking to evaluate improvement.

- All unusable metal parts are sent to Sims Metal to be recycled.

- In collaboration with Collex Waste Management, carrying out ongoing research and development into ways of reducing all packaging waste through re-use of a range of packaging materials, including plastics.

The Eco-Manufacturing Centre has clearly reached beyond the efficiency phase in these measures. Cultural and human resource factors at the Zetland plant have enabled this strategic perspective. A key success factor has been a small group of skilled, innovative and committed managers willing to listen to staff, customers and other stakeholders. Staff are assigned to teams, each team being responsible for quality, engineering and production capacity around products or product groups, for example, print cartridges or lasers. The product-based team structure promotes multi-skilling, enhances communication around problem identification and problem-solving, builds deep expertise and accumulates experience, and ensures that improved quality is constantly built into the work process. Managers at Fuji Xerox see this structure as the leading cause of the high level of innovation in the plant. It has also led to a close working relationship between the engineers and the production workers, with joint ownership of production targets and product quality.

The plant is systematically building the human capabilities of its staff. Staff members are offered a range of developmental opportunities and most have had training in various aspects of 'people management'. Employees are also well remunerated. Staff turnover has been low over the last eight years, a period of growth for the company. In 2000, 37 staff were employed on contract work and, of these, 28 stayed on to become permanent employees. Clearly, Fuji Xerox is seen as an employer of choice. The shift towards a more enabling and committed culture at Fuji Xerox Eco-Manufacturing Centre has been significant.

The organisational changes at Fuji Xerox illustrate the links between an organisational culture of innovation and one designed to deliver sustainability. Practices geared to enhance human sustainability and social capital within the organisation (such as empowerment, teamwork and continuous learning), underpin the capacity to innovate and escape from rigid models of operation and production.

Arguably, implementing practices that support human sustainability create an organisational culture that also facilitates product differentiation (Orssatto 2000). A number of companies have been successful in employing a strategy of environmental product differentiation. While Reinhardt (1999) argues that the success factors of such a strategy include consumers who are prepared to pay more and a product sufficiently differentiated for long enough for a profit to be made, Reinhardt also acknowledges that the benefits must be able to communicated readily. Communication systems are a feature of the human sustainability of the organisation.

In other words, innovation, business concept redesign and human sustainability can be readily linked in a dynamic relationship aimed at delivering long-term business advantage. Importantly, such qualities enable the corporation to be more responsive to the external drivers of change. That is, it can readily translate social and moral issues into market issues and can exploit the potentially huge market that ecological sustainability, in particular, represents. But, more than that, such an organisation can more critically reflect on the possibilities of new relationships among nature, society and technology that will mark a new, more sustainable age (Hajer 1995).

Conclusion

In this chapter, we have argued that the development of a more proactive position on corporate sustainability issues requires significant investments in human capabilities—the human sustainability approaches of organisations. Our research indicates that firms that progress toward ecological sustainability are also investing in the development of human capital. For instance, the sustainability initiatives pursued at Scandic Hotels and Fuji Xerox were dependent on the development of the internal human capital of these organisations. Because their employees are viewed as a long-term investment, the companies have been prepared to put resources into their environmental training and into the time allocated for environmental projects. Some of the key internal human sustainability elements are:

- Adopt a strategic perspective to workplace development
- Build the corporate knowledge and skill base (intellectual and social capital) of employees—develop human potential
- Foster productive diversity in the workplace (health and safety, gender equity, participative decision-making, work–life balance)
- Develop the capability for continuing corporate reshaping and renewal, including visionary change leadership
- Create communities of practice to diffuse knowledge and skills
- Provide relevant expertise in the best way to organise work for high performance and satisfaction
- Represent employees' concerns to management, while simultaneously giving employees an increased role in organisational decision-making

Furthermore, these cases illustrated that the development of these internal human sustainability orientations complemented the development of external human sustainability approaches. For instance, the attainment of ongoing eco-efficiencies in both organisations was reliant on the development of good stakeholder relations. In some cases, this meant the ability to influence supply chain relationships to drive further environmental improvements in dematerialisation of products and services. In other cases it meant opening up the organisation to third-party scrutiny and evaluation. Some of the key external human sustainability elements are:

- Reinterpret strategy around a wider range of stakeholders and develop co-operative strategies with them (responsiveness)
- Add rather than subtract value for all relevant stakeholders

- Build a culture of workplace learning and commitment to a 'generative society' through a declared and enacted value base

- Initiate and sustain an ongoing dialogue with stakeholders to define key elements of social responsibility—set priorities (accountability)

- Define social goals, develop action plans to reach these goals, monitor and disclose performance against key performance indicators (transparency)

- Seek genuine feedback on performance from stakeholders—welcome and learn from criticism

- Win, by responsible informed action, the support of all stakeholders for the organisation's continued existence and growth

A corporate sustainability phase model was also developed in this chapter that demonstrated the links between human and ecological sustainability issues as organisations adopted different sustainability stances. The phase model represents an ideal model type and an organisation would only seek to approximate it. The model comes with a set of indicators that allow managers and others to chart where the organisation is on the path, assess what actions are needed to capitalise, in a business sense, on the current phase and to plan the next logical move forward (for example, in anticipating increased compliance standards or identifying strategic opportunities). A particular strength of the model is the balance it provides in emphasising both the human and ecological bases of a comprehensive approach to sustainability.

Finally, some key issues involved in moving organisations between different sustainability phases were outlined, whether through the adoption of incremental or transformation change approaches. We have argued that the implementation of change for sustainability will become an increasingly important issue facing organisations now and in the future. Further research needs to be undertaken. Some of the key issues for the future include:

- How effective are different types of change strategies at creating and maintaining a sustainability focus within organisations? For instance, what are the limits of technical versus values-driven change approaches in achieving sustainability outcomes for organisations?

- What are the specific types of human capabilities in each of the phases that lead to the development of proactive environmental management practices? And what are the specific human capabilities required for shifting organisations between phases?

- How do organisations, once they have achieved strategic sustainability, maintain their sustainability orientation?

- How do large-scale organisations transform corporate cultures to embrace proactive corporate sustainability approaches?

- What is the role of external stakeholders in driving or assisting corporations to achieve sustainability outcomes?

- How do organisations shift between incremental and transformational change approaches?

- What role do senior managers play in pursuing either transformational or incremental change approaches?

The phase model presented in this chapter is not without its limitations. First, the ideal types were developed from an examination of a diverse range of case studies. More detailed empirical investigation is required to further test and refine the model, and the characteristics of each of the phases of corporate sustainability. Second, the model does not directly link external drivers/motivators for sustainability to decisions made by senior managers to pursue proactive corporate environmental approaches. Despite these limitations, the phase model presented in this chapter does allow managers to assess the sustainability orientation of their organisation/business unit and devise strategies to move towards a desired sustainability stance. The model presents a comprehensive case for integrating human and ecological sustainability approaches and is an initial platform to further develop an understanding of the change processes involved in shifting organisations to corporate sustainability.

References

Aragon-Correa, A., and S. Sharma (2003) 'A Contingent Resource-Based View of Proactive Corporate Environmental Strategy', *Academy of Management Review* 28.1: 71-88.

Arthur D. Little (1989) *State-of-the-Art Environmental Health and Safety Management Programs: How Do You Compare?* (Cambridge, MA: Arthur D. Little Inc.).

Beer, M., R.A. Eisenstat and A. Spector (1990) 'Why Change Programs Don't Produce Change', *Harvard Business Review* 68.6 (November/December 1990): 158-66.

Benn, S., D. Dunphy and A. Griffiths (2003) *Organizational Change for Corporate Sustainability* (TELA Discussion Paper; Canberra: Australian Conservation Foundation).

BCA (Business Council of Australia) (2001) *Towards Sustainable Development: How Leading Australian and Global Corporations are Contributing to Sustainable Development* (Melbourne: BCA).

Daily, B., and S. Huang (2001) 'Achieving Sustainability through Attention to Human Resource Factors in Environmental Management', *International Journal of Operations and Production Management* 21.12: 1,539-52.

Dunphy, D., and A. Griffiths (1998) *The Sustainable Corporation: Organisational Renewal in Australia* (Sydney: Allen & Unwin).

—— and D. Stace (1990) *Under New Management: Australian Organisations in Transition* (Sydney: McGraw-Hill).

——, J. Benveniste, A. Griffiths and P. Sutton (2000) *Corporate Sustainability* (Sydney: Allen & Unwin).

——, A. Griffiths and S. Benn (2003) *Organisational Change for Corporate Sustainability* (London: Routledge).

Egri, C., and S. Herman (2000) 'Leadership in the North American Environmental Sector: Values, Leadership Styles and Contexts of Environmental Leaders and their Organizations', *Academy of Management Journal* 43.4: 571-604.

Elkington, J. (1997) *Cannibals with Forks* (Oxford, UK: Capstone).

—— (2001) *The Chrysalis Economy* (Oxford, UK: Capstone).

Emery, F. (1974) *Futures We're In* (Canberra: Centre for Continuing Education, Australian National University).

Hajer, M. (1995) *The Politics of Environmental Discourse* (Oxford: Clarendon Press).

Hart, S. (1997) 'Beyond Greening', *Harvard Business Review*, January/February 1997: 66-76.

Hass, J.L. (1996) 'Environmental Management Typologies: An Evaluation, Operationalisation and Empirical Development', *Business Strategy and the Environment* 5: 58-68.

Henriques, I., and P. Sadorsky (1999) 'The Relationship between Environmental Commitment and Managerial Perceptions of Stakeholder Importance', *Academy of Management Review* 42.1: 87-99.

Hirsh, B., and P. Sheldrake (2000) *Inclusive Leadership* (Melbourne: Information Australia).

Hoffman, A. (1997) *From Heresy to Dogma* (San Francisco: New Lexington Press).

Hunt, C., and E. Auster (1990) 'Proactive Environmental Management: Avoiding the Toxic Trap', *Sloan Management Review* 31.2: 7-18.

Huselid, M. (1995) 'The Impact of Human Resource Management Practices on Turnover, Productivity and Corporate Financial Performance', *Academy of Management Journal* 38: 635-72.

Kleiner, A. (1995) *The Age of Heretics* (New York: Doubleday).

Kolk, A., and A. Mauser (2002) 'The Evolution of Environmental Management: From Stage Model to Performance Evaluation', *Business, Strategy and the Environment* 11: 14-31.

Lawler, E. (1992) *The Ultimate Advantage: Creating High Involvement Organizations* (San Francisco: Jossey-Bass).

Lepak, D., and S. Snell (1999) 'The Human Resource Architecture: Toward a Theory of Human Capital Allocation and Development', *Academy of Management Review* 24.1: 31-48.

Lovins, A., L.H. Lovins and P. Hawken (1999) 'A Road Map for Natural Capitalism', *Harvard Business Review*, May/June 1999: 145-58.

MacDuffie, J. (1995) 'Human Resource Bundles and Manufacturing Performance: Organizational Logic and Flexible Production Systems in the World Auto Industry', *Industrial and Labor Relations Review* 48: 197-221.

Mirvis, P. (1988) 'Organization Development Part 1: An Evolutionary Perspective', *Research in Organizational Change and Development* 2: 1-57.

—— (1990) 'Organization Development Part 2: A Revolutionary Perspective', *Research in Organizational Change and Development* 4: 1-66.

Mol, A., and D. Sonnenfeld (2000) 'Ecological Modernisation around the World: An Introduction', *Environmental Politics* 9.1: 3-16.

Nattrass, B., and M. Altomare (1999) *The Natural Step for Business* (Gabriola Island, Canada: New Society Publishers).

Orssatto, R. (2000) 'The Ecological Competence of Organisations: Competing for Sustainability', paper presented at the *16th EGOS Colloquium*, Helsinki, Finland, 1–4 July 2000.

Post, J.E., and B.W. Altman (1992) 'Models of Corporate Greening: How Corporate Social Policy and Organisational Learning Inform Leading-edge Environmental Management', *Research in Corporate Social Performance* 13: 3-29.

Preston, L. (2001) 'Sustainability at Hewlett-Packard: From Theory to Practice', *California Management Review* 43.3: 26-38.

Ramus, C., and U. Steger (2000) 'The Roles of Supervisory Support Behaviours and Environmental Policy in Employee Eco-initiatives at Leading-edge European Companies', *Academy of Management Journal* 43.4: 605-26.

Reinhardt, F. (1999) 'Bringing the Forest Down to Earth', *Harvard Business Review*, July/August 1999: 149-57.

Roome, N. (1992) 'Developing Environmental Management Strategies', *Business Strategy and the Environment* 1: 11-24.

Russo, M., and P. Fouts (1997) 'A Resource-Based Perspective on Corporate Environmental Performance and Profitability', *Academy of Management Journal* 40.3: 534-59.

Schaefer, A., and B. Harvey (1998) 'Stage Models of Corporate Greening', *Business Strategy and the Environment* 7: 109-23.

Schrama, G. (2001) 'Sustainability Banking at Rabobank', in K. Green, P. Groenewegen and P. Hofman (eds.), *Ahead of the Curve: Cases of Innovation in Environmental Management* (Dordrecht, Netherlands: Kluwer Academic Publishers).

Senge, P., and S. Carstedt (2001) 'Innovating Our Way to the Next Industrial Revolution', *Sloan Management Review* 42.2 (Winter 2001): 24-38.

Sharma, S., and H. Vredenburg (1998) 'Proactive Corporate Environmental Strategy and the Development of Competitively Valuable Organisational Capabilities', *Strategic Management Journal* 19: 729-53.

Stace, D., and D. Dunphy (2001) *Beyond the Boundaries: Leading and Recreating the Successful Enterprise* (Sydney: McGraw-Hill).

Starik, M., and G. Rands (1995) 'Weaving an Integrated Web: Multilevel and Multisystem Perspectives of Ecologically Sustainable Organisations', *Academy of Management Review* 20.4: 908-35.

Sutton, P. (2003) 'Innovating to an Ecologically Sustainable Economy in 30 Years or Less', www.green-innovations.asn.au, accessed 15 March 2003.

Walton, R. (1985) 'From Control to Commitment in the Workplace', *Harvard Business Review* 63.2 (March/April 1985): 72-84.

Weick, K., and R. Quinn (1999) 'Organizational Change and Development', *Annual Review of Psychology* 50: 361-86.

Wilkinson, A., M. Hill and P. Gollan (2001) 'The Sustainability Debate', *International Journal of Operations and Production Management* 21.12: 1,492-502.

Wright, P., and S. Snell (1998) 'Toward a Unifying Framework for Exploring Fit and Flexibility in Strategic Human Resource Management', *Academy of Management Review* 23.4: 756-72.

9
Business ecology
THE FUTURE OF GREEN BUSINESS?

Amy K. Townsend
Sustainable Development International Corporation, USA

Corporate environmentalism has grown tremendously in the US over the past decade. One Arthur D. Little study in 1995 suggested that, of 187 companies surveyed, only 4% seriously considered the environment in their business practices (Finnegan 1999: 54). However, by 1997, one Standard & Poor's 500 survey indicated that 97% of large manufacturing firms had a written, formalised environmental policy while 79% of service companies had such policies (Frankel 1998: 51). That same study reported that 97% of S&P 500 companies also performed environmental audits (Frankel 1998: 51), although many of the audits were conducted to ensure compliance with government regulations (Frankel 1998: 199). Furthermore, 80% of *Fortune* 500 companies had created environmental charters, and most multinational firms, responding to stakeholder pressures, had designed environmental strategies (Maxwell *et al.* 1997). By 1998, one poll by *Industry Week* reported that 90% of 287 companies were considering environmental management in their business strategies (Finnegan 1999: 54). By the end of the decade, a myriad of concepts—such as natural capital (Hawken *et al.* 1999), product life-cycles (Allenby 1999) and technical nutrients (McDonough and Braungart 2002)—had begun to affect the ways in which green business was considered. Many corporate sustainability best practices—including life-cycle analysis (Winsemius and Guntram 2002; DeSimone and Popoff 2000), design for disassembly (DeSimone and Popoff 2000), and product take-back programmes (Allenby 1999; DeSimone and Popoff 2000)— were introduced as businesses, academicians and organisations worked to find solutions for the environmental damage created by non-sustainable businesses.

This growth of interest in green business seems to have emerged from the confluence of several factors, including the publication of Rachel Carson's *Silent Spring* (1962) and pollution-related crises, such as that associated with the Love Canal in the US. New environmental laws were enacted in the US in the 1970s and 1980s, including the Clean Air Act, Clean Water Act and the Superfund Amendments and Reauthorisation Act (SARA) Title III, which required companies to report their releases of particular chemicals annually. Terrible environmental accidents, such as Union Carbide's 1984 Bhopal disaster and the *Exxon Valdez* oil spill (Buchholz 1998), brought worldwide attention to the widespread and severe environmental harm that businesses could cause.

A growing number of companies recognised the need to address environmental concerns affecting multiple stakeholders, including the stakeholder upon which all others rely—the environment (Callenbach *et al.* 1993). In 1992, nations from around the world came together to hold the Earth Summit, which DeSimone and Popoff (2000) have cited as a major impetus for corporate greening. Other factors, however, also played a role, including the growing demand for greener products. A 1990 survey reported that environmental concerns had led 71% of survey participants to change product brands and that 27% of respondents had boycotted a company because of its negative environmental record (Callenbach *et al.* 1993). Additionally, some businesses, such as Dow and 3M, successfully implemented resource efficiency programmes that have resulted in significant economic and ecological benefits (DeSimone and Popoff 2000), and other companies have followed suit (Rowledge *et al.* 1999). Since the creation of 3M's Pollution Prevention Pays programme in 1975, the company has saved over US$750 million and reduced its discharges by nearly 4 billion gallons for waste-water, 474,000 tonnes for solid waste and sludge, and over 250,000 tonnes for air and water pollutants combined (DeSimone and Popoff 2000: 2).

More recently, a number of companies from several industries have sought to become more environmentally friendly. For example, IKEA, the Swedish furniture manufacturer, requires its retail outlets to recycle, re-use or produce energy using their waste.[1] IKEA in Singapore recycles about 75% of its waste. Meanwhile, clothing designer Giorgio Armani has embraced hemp as a source of fibre for some Armani garments. He has suggested that he was drawn to hemp because of its environmental benefits; it can be grown without pesticides or synthetic fertilisers, and the result is a strong yarn that requires little processing (Boodro 2002). Carpet manufacturer Collins & Aikman recycles used carpets, incorporating their fibres into the manufacture of new carpet.

Although many businesses have improved their respective environmental performances with regard to reducing pollution and increasing resource efficiency (DeSimone and Popoff 2000; Romm 1999), today's best practices do not result in green companies (Stead and Stead 1996; Rowledge *et al.* 1999). Instead, even those companies that are committed to improving their environmental performances, including Patagonia and Interface, have suggested that they have not achieved ecological sustainability (Rowledge *et al.* 1999). There are several reasons for this.

First, the focus of greening business typically is on reducing a company's environmental harm through a number of strategies (Hart 1995). Although reducing environmental harm is important, it is not the same as preventing harm, and only the latter is ecologically sustainable. Companies interested in being ecologically sustainable over time will need to rebuild depleted ecosystem resources and renew the health and vitality of degraded ecological systems.

Second, firms tend to rely on what I refer to as 'reduction and replacement' strategies. Thus, they seek to reduce resource use, waste and pollution via improve-

1   www.ikea.com.sg/about_ikea/environment.asp, accessed 14 July 2005.

ments in resource efficiency (DeSimone and Popoff 2000) and by replacing harmful substances with less harmful ones. Although such strategies may help a company reduce its adverse environmental effects, they do not enable it to maintain or enhance ecosystem health.

Third, greening efforts rarely include the entire company. Instead, they tend to focus on developing more efficient production processes (DeSimone and Popoff 2000), greener facilities (Rocky Mountain Institute 1998) and the like. This chapter suggests that companies that wish to be truly green need to include all business elements, which are categorised here as their missions, employees, operations, facilities and sites, and products and services.

Fourth, few of the approaches used for greening business are based on an understanding of how ecological systems work. Those that do incorporate ecological principles, such as The Natural Step, tend to offer generic greening approaches rather than strategies tailored to meet the needs of specific ecological systems.

Fifth, the focus of corporate sustainability typically has been on the integration of the environment into every business system (Allenby 1999; Winsemius and Guntram 2002). In order to become green, however, businesses will need to reverse that goal, instead seeking to intentionally integrate their business systems with ecological systems for mutual benefit.

Sixth, many best practices, such as benchmarking and eco-audits, are largely if not exclusively quantitative. As a result, they do not account for such qualitative issues as social equity, the rights of future generations and other species, and quality of life.

Seventh, green business best practice tends to focus on a single (human) scale in space and time. However, ecosystems simultaneously operate on multiple scales both within and across ecosystems, and those scales are connected through ecological relationships (Turner *et al.* 2001; Capra 1996).

Eighth, best practices typically emerge from only one or a few disciplines. Yet sustainability requires an approach that is both multidisciplinary and transdisciplinary (Berkes and Folke 1998).

In order for businesses to become ecologically sustainable, this chapter asserts that they will need to implement the practice of **business ecology**. Still in their infancy, the business ecology concept and high-level process presented herein are provided in an attempt to help businesses to change their fundamental relationships with nature. A business–ecological relationship would be characterised not by resource depletion and ecological degradation but by a company's full engagement with ecosystems in ways that benefit both nature and the firm. Thus, the ultimate goal of business ecology is the renewal and ongoing health of the world's ecosystems and human enterprise.

Purpose and rationale

This chapter emerged from a study that sought to develop a new approach to green business. Clearly, the world's ecosystems cannot forever sustain current business practices, which have already inflicted considerable damage (Hart 1995). Some companies, responding to the growing body of stakeholders calling for businesses to be ecologically accountable, are turning to green business best practices in order to reduce their environmental impacts. Yet some literature has suggested that today's best practices have not resulted in ecologically sustainable companies (Stead and Stead 1996; Rowledge *et al.* 1999).

The study was undertaken to determine both why current best practices do not result in green companies and what approaches might lead to the desired result of business–ecological sustainability. It culminated in a conceptual framework that elucidates how businesses might partner with ecosystems for mutual benefit.

Although it is unclear if business–ecological sustainability is possible—whether through business ecology or by other means—this study assumed that it is. Several ethnographic (Berkes and Folke 1998; Shepard 1998) and historical (King 1995) studies have indicated that there have been numerous examples of sustainable human enterprise within certain cultural, societal and economic contexts. Principles have been extrapolated from some of these studies in order to identify the qualities associated with sustainable patterns of human–ecological behaviour (Folke *et al.* 1998; Berkes and Folke 2002). This chapter suggests that business might become sustainable if reconsidered and restructured at its most fundamental levels.

Of course, businesses alone cannot ensure global ecological sustainability. They exist in a larger context of economies, politics and cultures (Starik and Rands 1995); however, addressing all of the changes that might be required for a successful implementation of business ecology was beyond the scope of this study.

Key terms

There are several terms that deserve some clarification. **Business ecology** refers to the full ecological synchronisation and integration of a business with the sites that it inhabits, uses and affects. In business ecology, companies would seek to integrate themselves fully into ecosystems rather than merely working to integrate environmental considerations into their strategies and activities. The ultimate goal of business ecology is business–ecological sustainability. **Sites** refer to the specific areas that a company inhabits through its facilities, uses for resources and affects ecologically. These three site types are referred to as primary, secondary and tertiary sites, respectively. An **ecosystem** is a community made up of different species that interact with each other and with their abiotic and biotic environments. In an ecological context, **sustainability** is a quality in which something—for example, an idea, design, product, entity (e.g. a business), behaviour or event—can be carried out over time without reducing ecosystem function. I use this word interchangeably with 'green', 'environmentally friendly' and 'eco-friendly'. **Green business** refers to: the academic field that studies the greening of business; the practice of working with businesses to help them become more environmentally friendly; or an ecologically sustainable business. Within this chapter, this term is context-sensitive.

Chapter outline

The remainder of this chapter examines the need for green business. It discusses some of the environmental problems that are associated with business activities. Then it expresses the need for businesses to embrace ecological renewal if sustainability is to be possible. It divides the firm into five elements to be greened. It then provides a conceptual framework and high-level process for business ecology. It suggests that, with further development, business ecology might enable companies to become ecologically sustainable.

Why green businesses are needed

The movement toward greener business is important for many reasons. It offers numerous benefits, such as cost savings resulting from eco-efficiency, enhanced company image, improved relationships with local communities, access to new green markets and superior competitive advantage, among others (Shrivastava 1995). Companies also can profit from improved productivity (Rocky Mountain Institute 1998) and the ability to pre-empt regulations (Shrivastava 1995). However, one of the most important reasons for companies to become greener is to stop the resource depletion and degradation of ecosystems upon which we all depend for our resources, health and lives (Hart 1995; Stead and Stead 1996). This section discusses two ways in which companies harm the environment—resource overuse and pollution.

Depleting ecological resources

Natural resources worldwide provide the materials used for all economic activity (Gladwin *et al.* 1995), fuelling domestic, international, and global economies through manufacture, trade, and consumption. Thus, everything that businesses use comes from nature (Stead and Stead 1996; Schumacher 1973). This includes: trees for building materials, fuel and charcoal; human labour; water for production processes and products such as foods and beverages; petroleum for fuel and the manufacture of plastics; soils for agricultural production; metals and minerals for industrial production; and a host of other resources. Even 'man-made' products, such as nylon and formaldehyde, have their origins in natural materials (Schumacher 1973).

These materials are more than just resource stockpiles. They have functional roles in the Earth's systems, of which climate regulation, soil production and water circulation are just a few (Daily 1997). Yet resources are extracted at alarming rates. In 2000, natural resource extraction contributed nearly US$10 trillion to the US GDP (2002 US dollars) (US Census Bureau 2002: 541). This came from several sectors, including agriculture, forestry, fishing, timber-related production, and minerals and metals. Together, agriculture, forestry and fishing accounted for US$135.8 billion of the US GDP in 2000 (US Census Bureau 2002: 541).

Much of this natural resource extraction was carried out by businesses. Although businesses continue to benefit financially from such extraction, their effective extraction techniques reduce the resources available for current and future generations of humans and other species. Resource overuse and resulting ecosystem degradation also place at risk the long-term survival of the very companies that depend on those materials as they undergo significant cost fluctuations and increases (Allenby 1999).

Pollution

Resource extraction is not the only way by which firms cause environmental harm. They also harm ecosystems through pollution, habitat fragmentation, the introduction of non-native species and other means. For example, businesses in the US emit over 5.5 billion pounds of toxic chemicals every year.[2] Although the US Environmental Protection Agency (EPA) monitors business releases of particular chemicals under its Toxics Release Inventory (TRI), it only requires companies to report the release of 643 of the 72,000 chemicals used commercially (White 1999). Of those chemicals that are reported, many cause cancer, damage the vital organs, harm the respiratory tract, cause development problems in unborn children, and so on.

Pollution imposes costs on business and government as well as on the health of humans and other species that are affected by it both now and in the future. Every year, the US government pays more than US$600 million to collect environmental data (Heinz Centre 2002: 3) while the annual cost for environmental clean-up is about US$500 million (Wade 1992).

A call for ecological renewal

When businesses degrade ecosystems, they reduce the viability of the Earth's systems to function properly. By changing the ozone layer, climate regulation and biogeochemical cycling, they threaten to shift Earth's systems into increasing states of instability while placing the survivability of humans and other species at risk. As a result, businesses often unwittingly carry out activities that change ecological systems in irreversible and irreparable ways (Adam 1998).

These problems are due, in part, to traditional business management practices and economic theory. Hart (1995) has explained that management theory historically has not recognised the constraints inherent in businesses' ecological contexts. In the past, management theory has virtually ignored nature, focusing instead on economic, political, technological and social contexts. Thus, as ecological problems continue to increase, current views of management theory have proven to be deficient (Hart 1995). Similarly, Shrivastava (1995) has explained that neither organisational nor management theory has addressed the need to redesign busi-

2 'About Scorecard: What's New', Environmental Defense Fund, www.scorecard.org/about/txt/new.html, accessed 22 October 2003.

ness for the sake of ecological sustainability. Meanwhile, Costanza (1991) has discussed some of the deficiencies inherent in economic theory, while Curtis (2003) has developed an alternative economic theory for ecological sustainability.

Companies that are interested in helping the environment, surviving over time and avoiding the liability issues that are inherent in compromising ecospheric functions will need to undertake the ambitious goal of rebuilding the world's resources and repairing damaged ecological systems to the fullest extent possible. Although several firms have expressed the desire to become ecologically sustainable (Rowledge *et al.* 1999), only a few have recognised the necessity of ecological renewal.

The remainder of this chapter focuses on two topics. First, it explores the five elements of a firm and suggests that companies must green all of them in order to become ecologically sustainable. Then, it proposes a 12-step process for business–ecological sustainability.

The five elements

The process of greening any company is necessarily broad in scope. For simplicity's sake, this study divides the company into five parts—its mission, employees, operations, products and services, and facilities and sites. This study refers to these as the company's five **elements**.

Although the growing body of environmental management literature offers case studies and best practice guidance for enhanced environmental performance, much of it focuses on greening only one or two business elements to the exclusion of the others. For example, some literature has highlighted firms that have made their products and services greener largely through reduction and replacement strategies (Rowledge *et al.* 1999; DeSimone and Popoff 2000). Other literature has addressed the need for solid leadership (North 1992; Chinander 2001) and organisational changes (Hutchinson 1995). Although each of these approaches is important, only when the entire firm is the focus of greening can it ever hope to become truly ecologically sustainable.

While the green business literature espouses a fairly limited set of best practices, there are several additional fields that have developed best practices that can contribute to business greening. These include industrial ecology, green architecture, green landscape design, ecological economics and systems science (see Fig. 9.1).

Each of these fields can contribute significantly to greening businesses; however, their practices have not been integrated sufficiently to result in business–ecological sustainability. Moreover, as this chapter will discuss, other areas of expertise also need to be incorporated into green business practice if firms hope to become ecologically sustainable.

The remainder of this section further explores the five business elements using as illustrations examples from the outdoor clothing company Patagonia. Although Patagonia is not a green company, it has made significant improvements in each of the five elements.

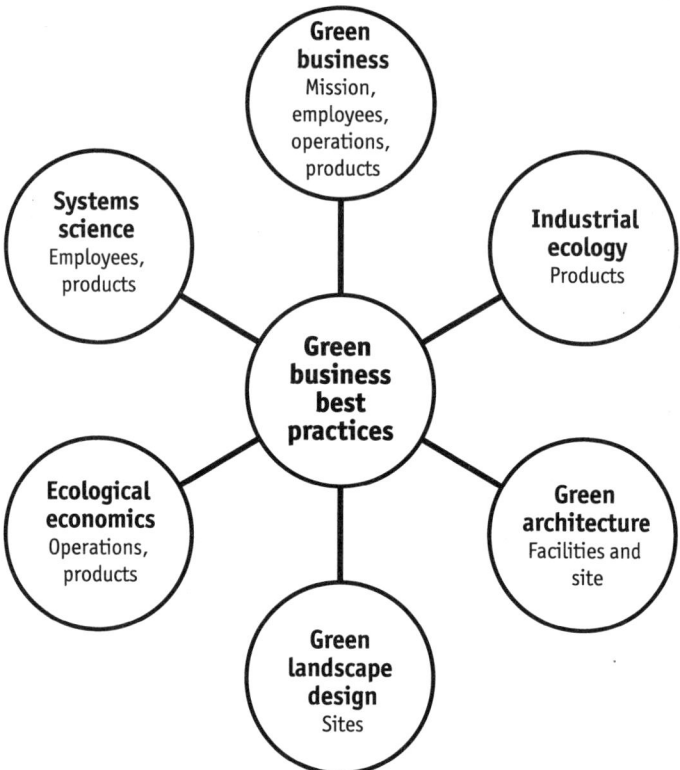

FIGURE 9.1 Some source fields of green business best practices

Mission

A 'green mission' is a key element for any company that wants to become eco-logically sustainable. A company cannot be green if its inherent purpose is not sustainable. Generally, the mission statement provides the company's purpose and helps to set the organisational direction and values (Hutchinson 1995).

Environmental health is an inherent part of Patagonia's mission statement: 'Patagonia exists as a business to inspire and implement solutions to the environmental crisis' (Patagonia 1998: 29).

Employees

The success of any company's mission depends on its employees—particularly senior management. Therefore, any firm committed to sustainability will need to ensure that each of its employees is capable (i.e. skilled and empowered) of carrying out its green mission and strategies.

The need to green employees has been addressed in the green business literature. For instance, North (1992) has suggested that employees must exhibit a combination of skill and commitment to carry out sustainable business practices. DeSimone and Popoff (2000) have stated that greening also requires staff to be personally involved in company greening. Callenbach *et al.* (1993) have asserted that employees must be inspired, empowered and environmentally aware for greening to be successful. Furthermore, Corraliza and Berenguer (2000) have examined the need to align employees' personal values with those of the company and for companies to give consistent signals that support staff in carrying out their greening activities.

Due, in part, to the company's primary activity—manufacturing technical outdoor-wear—and to its mission, Patagonia hires only employees that are involved in the outdoors. The company actively fosters a great deal of environmental appreciation and awareness. For example, Patagonia pays its employees to work up to two months for environmental organisations and encourages environmental activism in the development of new skills among staff (Rowledge *et al.* 1999).

Operations

Operations can include a wide variety of company activities, such as accounting, business travel, employee commuting, food service, company fleets, hiring, investing, lobbying, marketing, printing and graphics, procurement, public relations and recycling. There are ways in which to improve the environmental performance of each of these activities. For example, a firm might practise socially responsible investing, ensure that its company fleet runs on renewable fuels, such as 100% biofuel, seek to procure greener office supplies and lobby for effective environmental regulations.

Patagonia has undertaken several activities to green its operations. Every department within the company is required to carry out company-wide environmental goals. These include educating customers about specific environmental issues, such as the need to protect salmon or buy organic rather than conventionally grown cotton. They also include: educating suppliers about the company's environmental criteria; purchasing greener supplies; increasing resource efficiency; reducing waste; and using accounting methods that incorporate environmental costs that typically are externalised (Rowledge *et al.* 1999). Through its tithing programme, the company also donates either 1% of its sales revenue or 10% of its pre-tax profits, whichever is greater, to grass-roots environmental organisations. Between 1985 and 1998, Patagonia gave over US$13 million to such organisations (Patagonia 1998: 25).

Facilities and site(s)

One of the ways in which a company can signal its environmental commitment is by ensuring that its facilities and sites are green (Rocky Mountain Institute 1998). 'Facilities' refer to any building structure, including warehouses, hotels, hospitals, office buildings and manufacturing facilities. In order to green its facilities, a company needs to analyse each life-cycle stage of its facilities from design and construction to renovation, operations and maintenance, and deconstruction. Typically, companies that seek to green their facilities focus on improvements in energy efficiency and the health of their buildings. The discipline of green architecture has developed best practices that can be used to make facilities greener.

Sites generally refer to the areas in which the company's facilities are located, with their greening sometimes falling under the purview of green landscape design. However, this study used a broader definition. 'Sites' were defined as those locations that the company inhabits through its facilities, uses for resources and affects through its activities. These are the company's primary, secondary and tertiary sites, respectively.[3]

Both primary and secondary sites are typically defined by boundaries of land use or ownership. Some tertiary sites can be far more difficult, if not impossible, to identify as they can be distant in space and/or time, making their perception a challenge. The global climate is one example of a firm's tertiary site when it emits carbon dioxide into the atmosphere. A frog's reproductive system is another example of a tertiary site when the dioxins emitted by a pulp and paper mill's operations cause genetic mutation.

A site is defined not merely by its geographic location on a map but also by the matrix of relationships among biotic and abiotic ecological components that exist on multiple spatial and temporal scales within and across that location. In any given site, there are no absolute lines delineating the site from its larger ecological context. Instead, species and other biotic and abiotic site constituents might exist within the site's conceptually constructed boundaries or move beyond them at various times. Sites can vary in size, from a microscopic soil community to a small plot that falls within an ecosystem to a large landscape that encompasses one or more ecosystems. They also span numerous temporal scales from the present moment to decades, centuries and millennia (Adam 1998). As a result, environmental impacts that occur through time or in different locations might be difficult or impossible to perceive or track.

By this definition, sites are highly significant because they provide both the ecological contexts and focal areas of ecological accountability for all business activities.

Patagonia's Customer Service Centre in Nevada was designed to use green features, such as photovoltaic panels, a closed-loop heating system, less-toxic construction materials and carpeting, and bathroom countertops made of 100% recycled products. The company was California's first to commit to 100% wind energy for its California-based facilities. Due to efficiency measures, the centre will require 20% less energy each year, a saving that will fund the company's transition to renewable energy (Rowledge *et al.* 1999: 108). Additionally, an organic garden on site is cared for by the employees. Water that runs off the roof and the parking lot is used for irrigation. Detailed information regarding the firm's secondary and tertiary sites is not available.

---

3 The use of the terms 'primary', 'secondary' and 'tertiary' does not indicate a ranking of site importance.

Products and services

Firms also will need to ensure that their products and services are compatible with the goal of sustainability and that they are environmentally benign—or even beneficial—throughout their life-cycles. For example, some companies might discover that their products or services are inherently incompatible with sustainability (Winsemius and Guntram 2002). If they are, the company might choose to discontinue them for both ecological and ethical reasons.

Additionally, products and services will need to be benign throughout their life-cycles. The **product** life-cycle spans from the time that a product is conceived and designed through the extraction of materials used to make the product and its manufacture, use, re-use and disposal. Industrial ecology best practices have contributed to the life-cycle development of greener products. For **services**, the life-cycle includes the entire development process of the service—from its planning and organisation to its use and discontinuation.

Patagonia began to study the environmental effects of its products more than a decade ago by researching the fibres used in the company's clothing. The company was surprised to learn that cotton, the 'natural' fibre, is the most pesticide-intensive crop in the US when grown using conventional farming methods. Seeking greener alternatives, the company discovered the benefits of organic cotton and committed to using it exclusively. Then, it sought to educate its employees, suppliers and customers about the benefits of organic cotton. It also encouraged Adidas, Nike and Levi's to commit to buy at least some organically grown cotton in order to provide a stable market for the cotton farmers. The companies complied, committing to buy 3% of their cotton from organic growers (Rowledge *et al.* 1999).

Patagonia also has undertaken other steps to green its products. For example, to reduce the waste that resulted during the manufacturing process, the company started an infant clothing line named Seedling. This clothing is made by piecing together scraps of fabric that otherwise would have been thrown away. Currently, the company is looking for other ways to reduce waste.

Business ecology

Thus far, this chapter has explored some of the ways in which businesses harm ecosystems. It has explained that, despite the significant strides made in greening businesses over the past decade, even the greenest firms are not ecologically sustainable (Stead and Stead 1996). There are several reasons for this, including the fact that companies tend not to green in their entirety. This chapter has suggested that a company can be divided into five elements—mission, employees, operations, facilities and sites, and products and services. Each of these elements needs to be greened before a company can be considered ecologically sustainable. This chapter also has proposed that, in order to be green, companies will need to maintain and/or renew the ecosystem integrity of their primary, secondary and tertiary sites.

This section suggests that, in order for businesses to become ecologically sustainable, they will need to take an entirely different approach, referred to here as

business ecology. As used here, business ecology is a concept, a high-level process and a new field that holds great promise for informing business–ecological relationships.

Definition

The concept of business ecology is not new. In fact, it has met two uses, indicating everything from tightly operating networks of business[4] to businesses with enhanced environmental performances (Abe *et al.* 1998). The former definition uses **ecology** more as a metaphor for business systems; the latter has not been well defined and is devoid of an ecologically based approach.

The study from which this chapter emerged defined business ecology as 'the complete ecological synchronisation and integration of a business with the sites that it inhabits, uses and affects' (Townsend 2004: 89). This definition has several implications that require some articulation. These are summarised below.

The definition stresses a *complete* integration of businesses with their sites, meaning that a company that wishes to be sustainable will include all five business elements in its greening strategies and activities. This will be a fundamental change for most businesses, which often focus on greening only parts of one or two elements rather than all of them.

The definition also indicates that a business would *integrate with its sites* and not the other way around. This is the reverse of that suggested by the strategic environmental management literature which proposes that in order to become ecologically sustainable businesses must integrate environmental concerns into all company strategies (Buchholz 1998; Winsemius and Guntram 2002; Stead and Stead 1996). By integrating with their sites, businesses acknowledge their fundamental material and functional dependence on, and responsibility to, their sites.

This definition also asserts that companies need to be accountable to their sites. Although the study encouraged companies to be fully accountable to their primary, secondary and tertiary sites, it also recognised that such accountability is impossible because firms can never know all of their current environmental impacts or the future repercussions of those impacts. Nonetheless, full (or nearly full) ecological accountability remains a key component of business ecology and one that should be achieved to the greatest extent possible.

The above definition of business ecology indicates that the criteria and priorities for a company's integration with its sites will be derived from the specific characteristics of those sites. This differs from most current green business best practices which tend to be based not on specific ecological contexts but on generalised sets of principles, priorities, activities and desired outcomes. Ultimately, the success of any given approach will be determined by the sites themselves. Each individual site will provide the decisive context in which green business methodologies will result in either ecological renewal or continued degradation.

Although it is beyond the scope of this chapter to address economies, it is important to note that, as businesses begin to make this shift toward integrating with

---

4   'The New Intel', section 'Digital Rebar', paragraph 1, www.businessweek.com/2000/00_11/b367200i.htm, accessed 7 August 2002.

particular sites rather than merely industries and economies, the world's economies would do well to respond by removing the economic barriers to sustainability and being ecologically responsive themselves (Starik and Rands 1995). Additionally, consumer behaviour will need to shift to become sustainable (Shrivastava 1995).

The transdisciplinary nature of business ecology

In order to carry out business ecology as defined above, the study delineates a high-level business ecology process founded on concepts from 12 fields (see Fig. 9.2).

As mentioned earlier, the current green business best practices that touch on one or more of the five business elements are informed by some of these fields; however, practitioners from these fields have not worked together sufficiently to share knowledge and develop more integrated approaches to business–ecological sustainability. As a result, today's best practices are incomplete. Moreover, they are not broad enough in scope to result in businesses that are ecologically sustainable.

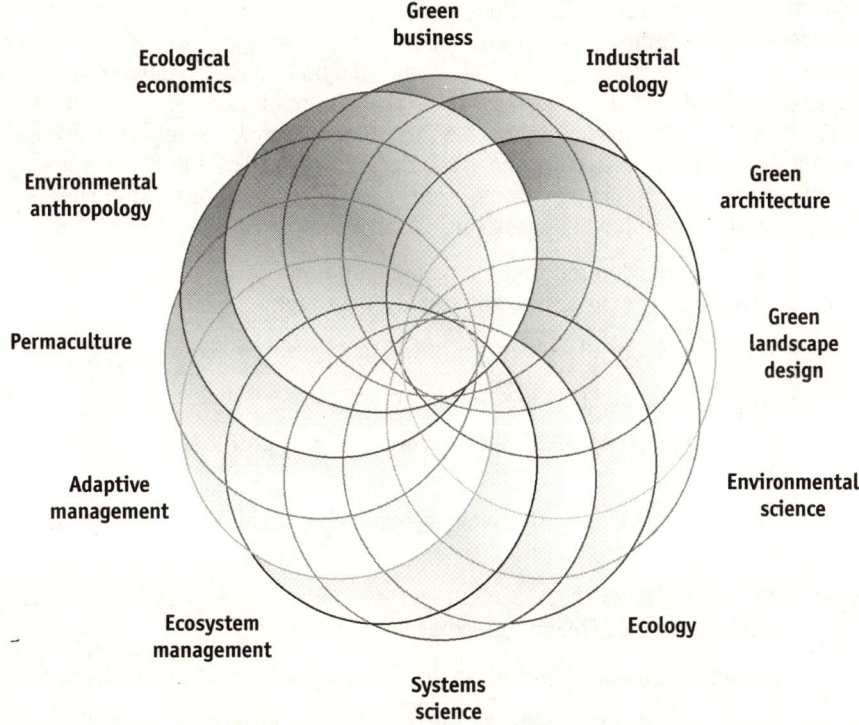

FIGURE 9.2 The business ecology universe

Two types of information are missing from much of today's green business literature. The first is a holistic approach to understanding ecosystems. Disciplines that discuss those issues include ecology (particularly with the spatial and temporal considerations offered by the sub-discipline of landscape ecology) and environmental sciences (e.g. geology, hydrology and soil science).

The second type of missing information explores how human business systems might merge with ecological systems in ways that benefit both.[5] The latter type of information has been virtually ignored in the move to green businesses—perhaps because its application might not be readily apparent. The disciplines that contribute this information include environmental anthropology, permaculture, adaptive management and ecosystem management.

A high-level process for business ecology

A few authors have called for a transdisciplinary approach to sustainability (Gladwin *et al.* 1995; Frankel 1998). As developed thus far, business ecology is both multidisciplinary and transdisciplinary in nature. It requires a broad array of expertise in business, human and environmental issues while requiring that experts from each of those fields move beyond their traditional boundaries to develop a holistic approach to sustainability that is greater than the sum of all fields represented.

The business ecology process described here emerged from blending the strengths of multiple sets of sustainability and green business principles. Fifty principles were identified as important for business–ecological sustainability, and these are grouped under the following 12 organising meta-principles:

- **Commitment.** Commit to the ongoing adoption, use and improvement of business ecology principles and practices throughout a company.

- **Alignment.** Align all elements of the firm to business ecology.

- **Scope.** Identify the primary, secondary and tertiary sites.

- **Ecological knowledge.** Develop general and site-specific ecological knowledge on multiple spatial and temporal scales.

- **Ecological niche.** Identify an ecological niche, or role, for the business in its sites.

- **Integrative design.** Create an integrative, appropriately scaled design for mutually beneficial business–ecological relationships.

- **Habitation.** Engage with the sites by inhabiting the company's niches.

- **Feedback.** Develop, use and refine site-specific, business–ecological feedback mechanisms. Monitor general business and ecological trends on multiple spatial and temporal scales.

---

5   Although disciplines such as green architecture, green landscape design and ecological economics recognise the human–environment interface, they were not designed to green companies as such.

- **Adaptation**. Adapt to and with specific ecological contexts through time as they respond to change on different scales.

- **Networks**. Create linkages up and down the value chain; also, network outward with local landholders working to regenerate sites.

- **Accountability**. Acknowledge and practise complete responsibility to all stakeholders.

- **Transparency**. Operate with openness and honesty regarding company activities and potential and real impacts on stakeholders.

These 12 meta-principles, shown in Figure 9.3, serve as the basis for business ecology practice.

Each of these 12 steps would be practised continuously in the context of the company's five elements. The remainder of this section discusses each of these steps in brief.

Commitment

This first meta-principle acknowledges the role of commitment in business ecology. It suggests that, just as a firm must be committed to any sustainability endeavour (North 1992; Hart 1995; DeSimone and Popoff 2000), so it must be to business ecology, which is a means to achieving sustainability. Callenbach *et al.* (1995) have stated that such long-term commitment to sustainability is needed, in part, because transitioning to sustainability can take years to occur. Because business ecology represents a significant conceptual and practical shift for both new and existing companies, it is likely that such a transition will take time to implement. Without such commitment, sustainability efforts will fail (Winsemius and Guntram 2002).

Alignment

Alignment refers to the company's need to align all of its elements—including its vision, values, goals and organisational structure—to business ecology. Many authors have discussed the need for alignment, which Senge (1990) has noted is a vital part of any company's success. Hutchinson (1995), Stead and Stead (1995) and Dobers and Wolff (1995) have addressed the importance of aligning a company's values in order to achieve sustainability by, for example, transitioning from valuing growth to valuing sustainability (Callenbach *et al.* 1993). Companies also will need to reassess their organisational structures in order to determine if they will adequately support the company's business ecology practice. Furthermore, some authors (Winsemius and Guntram 2002; Hutchinson 1995) have suggested that sustainability might require firms to become less hierarchical and more decentralised to enhance the companies' capacities for learning and response.

Scope

If a company is to become ecologically sustainable with respect to its primary, secondary and tertiary sites, it will need to identify them. Brussard *et al.* (1998)

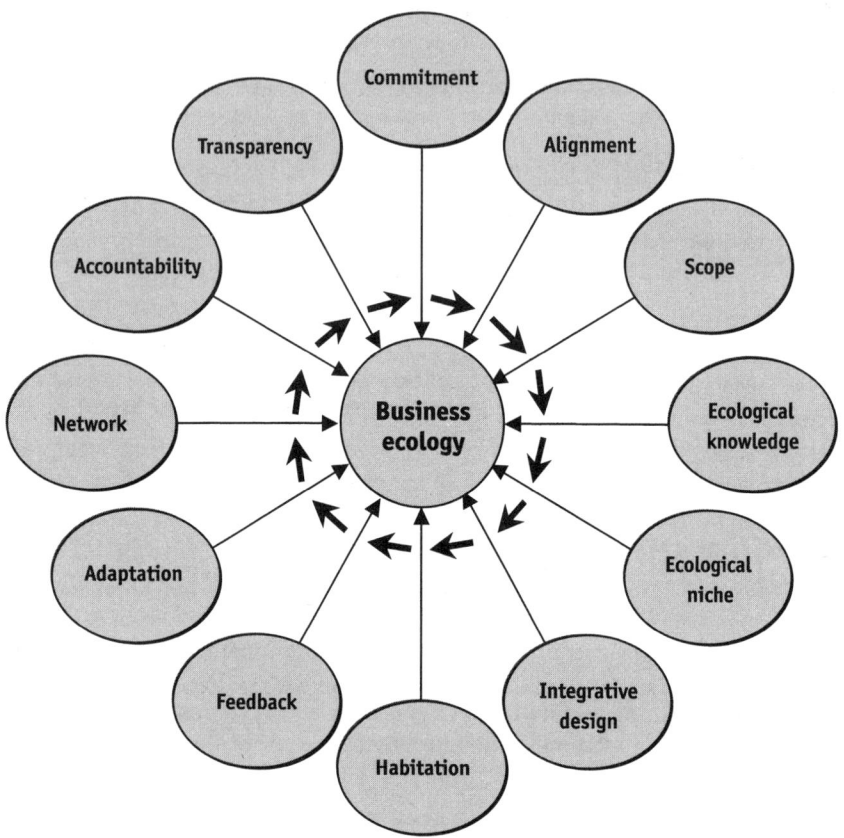

FIGURE 9.3 The 12 steps of business ecology

have discussed the need to define and delineate any ecosystem that will be managed.[6] Although recognising primary and secondary sites is fairly simple, as mentioned previously, identifying all tertiary sites is impossible because a company can never know all of the ways in which it has affected Earth's systems. Such impacts occur on multiple scales of space and time, from the microscopic to the macroscopic and in the present as well as decades, centuries and millennia from now. Regardless, it is important for the company to be diligent in identifying its sites to the best of its abilities—especially those that it is harming the most.

6   A fundamental difference exists between the intention of Brussard and business ecology, as business ecology seeks to manage not an ecosystem but the firm's part in its *relationships* with its sites.

Ecological knowledge

Once the sites have been identified and their boundaries delineated, companies will need to develop specific ecological knowledge about each of these sites. North (1995) has explored the need for companies to become more environmentally knowledgeable. Folke *et al.* (1998: 418) have suggested that one of the characteristics of sustainable social–ecological systems is the 'general accumulation and transmission of ecological knowledge'. However, Dobers and Wolff (1995) have suggested that most organisations are ecologically incompetent and have emphasised the need for organisational learning on the subject. Both general (e.g. hydrological cycles) and site-specific (e.g. species, soils) ecological knowledge will be required as companies seek to learn about their sites in order to establish fruitful partnerships with them. This includes gathering information on ecosystem composition, structure and processes (Brussard *et al.* 1998). Composition refers to the material aspects of the site while structure deals with the way in which the site is organised, including both horizontal and vertical perspectives. Meanwhile, processes refer to the relationships within and across the ecosystem. Lyle (1999), Bell (1999), Mollison (1988) and Ndubisi (2002) have discussed ways by which to learn about particular sites.

Ecological niche

Once a company has learned about the ecology of its specific sites, it will need to identify an ecological niche[7] that it can inhabit. An ecological niche refers to the way of life or functional role that a species plays within an ecosystem (Miller 2002). Although companies are not species, the humans that run them are and so can develop functional roles in ecosystems under the conceptual umbrella of business. Currently, firms develop niches in a human-designed marketplace and view ecological systems as providing both opportunities (resources) and constraints (limits to using those resources). This step suggests that companies will need to consider their ecological contexts *before* considering their economic ones in order to identify the ecological constraints and opportunities afforded by the system.

Integrative design

Once the company has identified its ecological niche for a particular site, it will need to create a design for inhabiting that niche. Integrative design is closely aligned with Van der Ryn and Cowan's (1996) ecological design, which is specific to the field of architecture. It is also similar to Benyus's (1997: 2) biomimicry, 'the conscious emulation of life's genius', which can be applied to any number of fields, such as building and product design. Integrative design details the steps that the company will take in order to make the transition from its current ecological relationships with its sites to relationships defined by business–ecological sustainability. For companies that are preparing to occupy a niche in a site that is new to

---

7　The development of a business ecological niche differs from businessman Peter Drucker's 'ecological niche strategy', which uses an ecological metaphor to refer to a company's need to define its unique place in the business world (Drucker 1993).

them,[8] this strategy will detail how they will integrate into their sites in as benign a way as possible.

Habitation

During this stage, the company inhabits its niche to increasingly renew its sites. Renewal refers to restoring the normal dynamics of ecosystems, which David (1997) refers to as 'hemeorhetic stability'. It does not mean restoring the site to an earlier state prior to disturbance; nor does it mean restoring its homeostatic equilibrium. Thus, the company's main goal cannot be focused on trying to stabilise either the site or a particular resource within the site. Instead, it will be to ensure that its sites are allowed to be dynamic and ever-changing so that ecological resilience and integrity may be maintained or restored and evolutionary opportunities maximised.

Feedback

After a company has inhabited its ecological niche, it will need to monitor feedback continuously so that it can respond in ways that will move it closer to sustainability. Feedback refers to the ways in which a site (i.e. its components, structures and processes) responds either to the company's presence and activities or to ecosystem changes that occur due to internal or external pressures. It occurs on a number of spatial and temporal scales (Townend 2002). Therefore, it is important to monitor multiple scales (David 1997; Kay et al. 1999). Although it can be difficult to track feedback that is temporally or spatially distant,[9] the use of feedback mechanisms is required if organisations are to learn and adapt their behaviours (Castilla 2000). Berkes and Folke have suggested the need to develop 'appropriate feedback mechanisms' to make the connection between human activities and ecological consequences (Berkes and Folke 1998: 19).

Adaptation

During this step, the company will work to continuously adapt to and with its primary, secondary and tertiary sites. It will need to use the information that it has gained by monitoring those sites as well as methods of adaptive management that

8   Companies establishing new primary, secondary or tertiary sites will find that their greatest business–ecological opportunities are in degraded areas. Thus, they would do well to avoid those that are ecologically fragile or 'pristine'. There are many degraded sites that need to be renewed, and sites that are fragile or pristine should remain undisturbed if possible. With regard to pristine sites, it is unclear whether business ecology, a new process, can benefit such sites. Additionally, pristine areas can serve as models to inform businesses and others about what healthy sites in that area contain, how they are structured and how they function. With regard to fragile sites, the activities of a business might do irreparable harm no matter how well intended. Nevertheless, a business can help to safeguard the health of either of these sites by choosing a site in a nearby area that has been degraded through such means as land fragmentation, pollution, soil loss and resource over-extraction, and work to renew it.
9   For a detailed discussion of the temporal and spatial complexities of environmental problems, you may wish to refer to social theorist Barbara Adam's book *Timescapes of Modernity* (1998).

are inherently co-evolutionary (Berkes and Folke 1998). Adaptive management involves mutual feedback between the business and the site and focuses on the organisation's ability to learn and change (Berkes and Folke 1998). Adaptation has long been a key factor in building and maintaining sustainable human–ecological systems (Berkes and Folke 1998) and promises to be equally important in the development and maintenance of business–ecological systems. Like adaptive management, the adaptation that will be required in business ecology is likely to have a strong experimental component as businesses learn what works and what does not, and change their relationships with their sites accordingly.

Network

Networking refers to the need for companies to establish greening leverage in order to help strengthen ecosystem health and secure resources for the future. It consists of two parts. First, companies will help to green the value chain, including suppliers, retailers and consumers. Second, companies can work with local landowners and users to develop ever-increasing areas of renewed land—rebuilding soils, establishing wildlife corridors, re-establishing native species, restoring the health of watersheds and reducing land fragmentation—thereby protecting ecosystem resilience and the survival of individuals and species while securing the future of companies dependent on healthy ecosystems for their own survival. Jennings and Zandenbergen (1995) have repeated ecologists' sentiments that, while individual companies might contribute to ecological sustainability, they are most effective when they focus on improving specific ecosystem areas and when they develop regional networks of organisations that work together to make a positive difference. Such networks are important because they can lead to the renewal not just of individual sites but also of entire ecosystems and landscapes.

Accountability

Accountability refers to the company's need to be environmentally accountable to all its stakeholders, including present and future generations of all species. It calls for companies to prevent harm (e.g. eliminate waste) and recognises the need to renew sites that they have degraded. Both the Coalition for Environmentally Responsible Economies (CERES)[10] and McDonough and Braungart (2002) have expressed this need for environmental restoration. As Jennings and Zandenbergen (1998: 1,023) have explained: 'Organisations must be made accountable for where and in what they invest.'

Transparency

Transparency calls for firms' full honesty and disclosure with regard to their potential and real environmental impacts. Both CERES and the Business Council for Sustainable Development[11] have recognised the need to increase firms' trans-

10 'The CERES Principles', www.ceres.org/coalitionandcompanies/principles.php, accessed 14 July 2005.
11 'The Business Charter for Sustainable Development: 16 Principles', www.iccwbo.org/home/environment_and_energy/charter.asp, accessed 7 August 2001.

parency by involving and communicating openly with stakeholders regarding company activities. One important way in which companies are communicating with stakeholders is through the creation of corporate environmental reports. Many companies, such as Chiquita and Interface, update such reports annually to share information regarding company environmental performance goals, progress and areas for improvement.

Examples

Because business ecology is new, there are no examples of business–ecological success. However, two companies are using many of the steps discussed above to renew ecosystems. They are the Regenesis Group (for-profit) and the Land Institute (non-profit). Each is discussed below.

Regenesis

The Regenesis Group is a for-profit business based in Santa Fe, New Mexico, that specialises in ecologically regenerative real estate development. According to Ben Haggard, one of the company's principals, 'regenerative development starts from the belief that we can achieve continuous improvement of living conditions on Earth for human and natural communities by developing in harmony with nature' (Haggard 2002). This is accomplished when the company synchronises its work with the unique qualities of every site. This, Haggard has suggested, 'requires close attention to the uniqueness of a site, using the particularities of a given place as parameters for determining the kind of engineering and design solutions that are appropriate and possible in that place' (Haggard 2002).

Regenesis seeks to:

- Understand how each site's ecological processes work and have been altered or disrupted over time

- Work with the local community to engage it in development and regenerative activities

- Design with the site to ensure that its health is supported and improved

- Co-evolve with the local ecological and human communities in ways that benefit both sites and clients.

It does this, in part, by studying the site's environmental history, ecological (including human) patterns and other factors in order to understand what has happened there over time. Then, it works with clients to best meet their needs and those of the site in a way that maximises the site's evolutionary potential.

Regenesis's Tim Murphy has explained that there is no recipe to regenerative work.[12] Instead, sites articulate themselves through patterns and relationships, making regenerative opportunities apparent. As a result, Murphy sees himself as a 'matchmaker' between the site and the client. He does this by engaging the client

---

12   Personal communication with T. Murphy, Santa Fe, New Mexico, 16 October 2001.

with the site and articulating the patterns of the place (e.g. flow dynamics), thereby helping to provide a common language through which they can work toward regenerative design.

Currently, Regenesis is partnering with others to develop a new town in Arizona called Willow Springs. Located between Tucson and Phoenix, this town is being developed with goals of social, ecological and economic regeneration. Although water rights are typically an issue in the dry south-west, Regenesis, by learning the land and its processes, has identified ways to make Willow Springs a place in which the region's water resources are increased (Haggard 2002). Based, in part, on permaculture techniques, the company will accomplish this by enabling the land to capture and hold water by cycling it through the ecosystem again and again. As a result, this desert town will be self-sustaining with regard to water and help to rebuild the groundwater resource as well.

The Land Institute

Located in Salina, Kansas, the Land Institute is a non-profit organisation that was founded in 1977 'to develop an agriculture that will save soil from being lost or poisoned while promoting a community life at once prosperous and enduring'.[13]

The institute sits on 370 acres of healthy, biologically diverse farmland modelled on the native prairie ecosystem. With a PhD in genetics, the institute's co-founder Wes Jackson believes that the till-based agricultural model that has been used around the world since farming began about 10,000 years ago is not ecologically sustainable. According to Jackson, this method of farming has resulted in wide-spread ecosystem degradation. He employs an alternative method of farming, modelled after nature, which enhances biological diversity while satisfying human needs.

While most farming is based on the idea of planting annuals, harvesting them seasonally and then tilling the soil and replanting, the Land Institute harvests foods without digging up plants or breaking up the soil. It plants domesticated wild perennials which have adapted naturally to local conditions. The institute also grows major grain crops as perennials. Planting perennials that stay in place over time means that the plants' root systems are able to develop, keeping soils in place and retaining moisture. The organisation also plants mixtures of crops rather than monocultures, including both warm-weather and cool-weather varieties. This mixed planting helps to prevent losses due to agricultural pests.

The Land Institute is working to change conventional farming practices so that farmers can work to rebuild ecosystems *through* farming while meeting human needs.

13   www.landinstitute.org/vnews/display.v/ART/2000/08/10/37a747b43

Conclusions

In 1990, Edgar Woolard, a former chief executive of DuPont, stated that environmental thinkers will imagine the 21st century's green lifestyles and economies, but it will be up to industry to bring those lifestyles and economies to fruition (Winsemius and Guntram 2002). However, in order for that to occur, businesses will need to move beyond today's green business best practices, instead embracing an ecologically based concept and process such as business ecology.

Business ecology is predicated on the understanding that, in order for business to be ecologically sustainable, it must learn about, integrate with and adapt to the ecosystems of which it is a part and upon which it is fully dependent. Although today's focus on resource efficiency signals significant strides in business greening, business ecology recognises that, in order for business to be ecologically sustainable, companies will have to fundamentally change their roles in the world—a need already recognised by Shrivastava (1995) and others.

Companies will need to shift their focus to ecological renewal by developing business–ecological relationships that produce yields for businesses while allowing natural systems to renew themselves rather than becoming depleted. Businesses also will need to understand that the ecological opportunities and constraints afforded by the world's ecosystems allow for 'enough': they do not allow for the ideal of maximising profits through unlimited growth. Eventually, unlimited growth is likely to lead to reduced profits as ecosystems are increasingly degraded and resources become harder to procure.

Business ecology holds great promise as an ecologically based practice as well as a multifaceted field that can bring businesses into the ecological fold. However, this will be possible only through the development of site-specific greening methods that focus on all five business elements. Only by moving away from generic green templates and toward methods based on specific ecological contexts, such as the business ecology approach discussed in this chapter, will sustainable business be possible. Ultimately, companies will need to become beneficial, functioning partners with the rest of nature.

If ecological integrity is to be maintained or revitalised through time, businesses—as a proxy for human needs and desires—must intentionally become co-creators with nature as they mindfully integrate every element of their existence into ecological systems. The successful practice of business ecology will require both companies and those who depend on them to change their expectations and behaviours if both humans and other species are to survive through time with a broad array of evolutionary choices intact.

Implications

This study has far-reaching implications for environmental health, businesses, the world's economies, consumption, sustainability and governance. First, if businesses become environmentally knowledgeable and beneficial, their relationships with the biosphere will be changed forever. Ecosystems could begin to renew themselves, regaining health and resilience.

Second, business ecology will require companies to undergo fundamental reflection and change in every respect. Although some companies recognise that they will have to make considerable changes, the level of change needed is debatable. DeSimone and Popoff (2000: 244) have written that 'companies that cannot adapt may go out of business' and have suggested the need for a 'new contract' among business, government and society. Under this contract, companies would commit to sustainability, vowing 'to achieve radical rather than incremental environmental improvement over the long term, to work to reduce global inequalities and to be responsible employers and community members' (DeSimone and Popoff 2000: 244). Only by committing to such radical change can businesses hope to achieve sustainability. Sustainability will require firms to integrate beneficially with ecosystems; otherwise, even companies with improved environmental performances will continue to deplete ecological systems to the detriment of the world's economies and its human and non-human communities.

Yet SC Johnson, a US-based multinational firm that makes household products, has indicated that this transition to sustainability might take years (Rowledge *et al.* 1999: 166). 'Ask anyone at SC Johnson and they will readily acknowledge that they are not now sustainable, that they do not have a comprehensive sustainability programme, that it is very possible they may be many years away from sustainability being a core driving force in their major business strategies.' This statement begs answers to two questions: 'Can we wait years for SC Johnson and other firms that are sincerely committed to become ecologically sustainable?' and: 'Are their products and services valuable enough that they are worth the trade-off in lost ecosystem services and later attempts at and costs of ecological repair?'

In other words, can we afford the economic and ecological costs of allowing businesses to conduct business as usual or even a greener version of business as usual? What are the alternatives?

Third, the success of business ecology will require some significant changes in business, economies, regulation and other areas. For example, if companies are to partner with, and be accountable to, their primary, secondary and tertiary sites, the world's economies need to reflect environmental costs in the prices of products and services as accurately as possible. Otherwise, those companies committed to environmental health by maintaining or rebuilding natural capital could incur the greatest costs while others that do ecological harm are not held financially accountable, putting greener companies at a disadvantage.

Fourth, the world's citizens and their governments have important roles to play in determining which companies succeed and the extent to which companies are afforded the power to interfere with ecosystem services in order to capitalise on some product or service. As customers learn more about companies' effects on the environment and, as a result, their own health, they can choose to support those companies that are working to implement business ecology practice and stop supporting non-sustainable firms. Current movements to reduce resource consumption via voluntary simplicity and self-reliance decrease the demand for companies' products and services for environmental and other reasons.

Fifth, this and future studies could result in changed rules around the provision and maintenance of corporate charters. In order to gain a corporate charter, companies might need to prove that their activities will do at least as much good as harm. As long as a company provides benefits to humans and ecosystems, it might be allowed to exist; however, if it does more harm than good, it might lose its charter, signifying a loss of public trust. Although such measures of 'more good than harm' might be difficult to assess, from an ecological perspective most of today's firms would not pass that test.

Sixth, business ecology might inform other disciplines, contributing as much to them as they have contributed to it. For example, it can benefit considerably from adaptive management, environmental anthropology, ecological economics and others. Perhaps business ecology can contribute another testing ground for all of these fields, one that challenges the theories and approaches of each, helping to hone them and enabling them to make significant contributions to global ecological health at a crucial crossroads in Earth's existence.

Limitations

This study was limited with regard to expertise, the paucity of business–ecological models, scope and the lack of a transition strategy. First, although sustainability is inherently multidisciplinary and transdisciplinary, the author's expertise is limited to a few fields only. Thus, the concept of and approach to business ecology that are stated here offer a limited viewpoint that can be greatly enriched by others who choose to contribute to the development of this field.

Second, the development of the business ecology approach is limited by the lack of business–ecological models. Although the Regenesis Group and the Land Institute serve as strong models with regard to how organisations develop renewing relationships with sites, extrapolating directly from these land-based models to current companies that represent a variety of industries is a big leap. For now, the burden remains on today's companies to cross the gap that exists between their own practices and those suggested by companies such as the Regenesis Group and the Land Institute. Furthermore, while excellent research has been conducted into sustainable human–ecological organisations in order to identify the patterns of behaviour that have led to and maintained such sustainability (Berkes and Folke 1998), again, extrapolating from these studies to modern businesses is challenging. This is a gap that adaptive managers, environmental anthropologists, businesses and others must work together to fill.

Third, the primary focus of this author's contribution to business ecology has been on creating ecological sustainability by changing the business–environment relationship. This is important because of the severe ecological challenges that the world faces. However, this conception of business ecology to date has paid little attention to the issues of cultural and social sustainability. This exclusion does not reflect a belief that these issues are inconsequential. Rather, it simply indicates the author's assumption that ecological health is necessary for healthy cultures and societies to exist.

Fourth, Tickner and Raffensperger (1998: 75) have stated that a sustainable business strategy requires a 'road map to the future, which can direct investments, technology, and process and product development'. Such a 'road map' or transition strategy has yet to be developed for business ecology, and its creation may well prove difficult. Because companies are under increasing economic and regulatory pressures, it is highly likely that the transition to business ecology will be a great challenge for many companies.

References

Abe, J., P. Dempsey and D. Bassett (1998) *Business Ecology: Giving Your Organization the Natural Edge* (Boston, MA: Butterworth-Heinemann).

Adam, B. (1998) *Timescapes of Modernity: The Environment and Invisible Hazards* (New York: Routledge).

Allenby, B.R. (1999) *Industrial Ecology: Policy Framework and Implementation* (Upper Saddle River, NJ: Prentice Hall).

Bell, S. (1999) *Landscape: Pattern, Perception and Process* (New York: Spon).

Benyus, J.M. (1997) *Biomimicry* (New York: Quill Books).

Berkes, F., and C. Folke (1998) 'Linking Social and Ecological Mechanisms for Resilience and Sustainability', in F. Berkes and C. Folke (eds.), *Linking Social and Ecological Systems: Management Practices and Social Mechanisms for Building Resilience* (New York: Cambridge University Press).

Boodro, M. (2002) 'Armani Leads the Way', *Organic Style*, March/April 2002: 72-81.

Brussard, P.F., J.M. Reed and C.R. Tracy (1998) 'Ecosystem Management: What is it Really?', *Landscape and Urban Planning* 40: 9-20.

Buchholz, R.A. (1998) *Principles of Environmental Management: The Greening of Business* (Upper Saddle River, NJ: Prentice Hall).

Callenbach, E., F. Capra, L. Goldman, R. Lutz and S. Marburg (1993) *Eco-Management: The Elmwood Guide to Ecological Auditing and Sustainable Business* (San Francisco: Berrett-Koehler).

Capra, F. (1996) *The Web of Life* (New York: Anchor Books).

Carson, R. (1962) *Silent Spring* (New York: Houghton Mifflin).

Castilla, J.C. (2000) 'Roles of Experimental Marine Ecology in Coastal Management and Conservation', *Journal of Experimental Marine Biology and Ecology* 250: 3-21.

Chinander, K.R. (2001) 'Aligning Accountability and Awareness for Environmental Performance in Operations', *Production and Operations Management* 10.3: 276-91.

Corraliza, J.A., and J. Berenguer (2000) 'Environmental Values, Beliefs and Actions: A Situational Approach', *Environment and Behavior* 32.6: 832-48.

Costanza, R. (1991) *Ecological Economics* (New York: Columbia University Press).

Curtis, F. (2003) 'Eco-localism and Sustainability', *Ecological Economics* 46: 83-102.

Daily, G. (ed.) (1997) *Nature's Services: Societal Dependence on Natural Ecosystems* (Washington, DC: Island Press).

David, C.A. (1997) 'Managing the Invisible', in M. Boyce and A. Haney (eds.), *Ecosystem Management: Applications for Sustainable Forest and Wildlife Resources* (New Haven, CT: Yale University Press): 94-129.

DeSimone, L.D., and F. Popoff (2000) *Eco-efficiency: The Business Link to Sustainable Development* (Cambridge, MA: The MIT Press).

Dobers, P., and R. Wolff (1995) 'Managing Ecological Competence: Empirical Evidence and Theoretical Challenges', *Greener Management International* 11 (July 1995): 32-48.

Drucker. P. (1993) *Innovation and Entrepreneurship* (New York: HarperBusiness).

Finnegan, L. (1999) 'Sustainable Development: Business without Footprints', *Occupational Hazards* 61.5 (May 1999): 54-56.

Folke, C., F. Berkes and J. Colding (1998) 'Ecological Practices and Social Mechanisms for Building Resilience and Sustainability', in F. Berkes and C. Folke (eds.), *Linking Social and Ecological Systems: Management Practices and Social Mechanisms for Building Resilience* (New York: Cambridge University Press).

Frankel, C. (1998) *In Earth's Company: Business, Environment and the Challenge of Sustainability* (Gabriola Island, Canada: New Society Publishers).

Gladwin, T.N., J.J. Kennelly and T-S. Krause (1995) 'Shifting Paradigms for Sustainable Development: Implications for Management Theory and Research', *Academy of Management Journal* 20.4 (October 1995): 874-907.

Haggard, B. (2002) 'Green to the Power of Three', *Environmental Design and Construction*, www.edcmag.com/CDA/ArticleInformation/coverstory/BNPCoverStoryItem/0,4118,75525,00.html, accessed 11 August 2002.

Hart, S.L. (199) 'A Natural-Resource-Based View of the Firm', *Academy of Management Review* 20.4: 986-1,014.

Hawken, P., A. Lovins and L.H. Lovins (1999) *Natural Capitalism: Creating the Next Industrial Revolution* (New York: Little, Brown).

Heinz Centre (2002) *The State of the Nation's Ecosystems: Measuring the Lands, Waters and Living Resources of the United States* (Cambridge, UK: Cambridge University Press).

Hutchinson, C. (1995) *Vitality and Renewal: A Manager's Guide for the 21st Century* (London: Adamantine Press).

Jennings, D.P., and P.A. Zandenbergen (1995) 'Ecologically Sustainable Organizations: An Institutional Approach', *Academy of Management Journal* 20.4: 1,015-52.

Kay, J.J., H.A. Regier, M. Boyle and G. Francis (1999) 'An Ecosystem Approach for Sustainability: Addressing the Challenge of Complexity', *Futures* 31: 721-42.

King, A. (1995) 'Avoiding Ecological Surprise: Lessons from Long-standing Communities', *Academy of Management Review* 20.4 (October 1995): 961-85.

Lyle, J.T. (1999) *Design for Human Ecosystems: Landscape, Land Use and Natural Resources* (Washington, DC: Island Press).

Maxwell, J., S. Rothenberg, F. Briscoe and A. Marcus (1997) 'Green Schemes: Corporate Environmental Strategies and their Implementation', *California Management Review* 39.3 (Spring 1997): 118-20.

McDonough, W., and M. Braungart (2002) *Cradle to Cradle: Remaking the Way We Make Things* (New York: North Point Press).

Miller, G.T., Jr (2002) *Living in the Environment* (Belmont, CA: Wadsworth Group).

Mollison, B. (1988) *Permaculture: A Designer's Manual* (Tyalgum, Australia: Tagari Publications).

Ndubisi, F. (2002) *Ecological Planning: A Historical and Comparative Synthesis* (Baltimore, MD: The Johns Hopkins University Press).

North, K. (1992) *Environmental Business Management* (Geneva: International Labour Office).

Patagonia (1998) 'Defining Quality: A Brief Description of How We Got Here', www.patagonia.com/pdf/defining_quality.pdf.

Rocky Mountain Institute (1998) *Green Development: Integrating Ecology and Real Estate* (New York: John Wiley).

Romm, J.J. (1999) *Cool Companies: How the Best Businesses Boost Profits and Productivity by Cutting Greenhouse Gas Emissions* (Washington, DC: Island Press).

Rowledge, L., R.S. Barton and K.S. Brady (1999) *Mapping the Journey: Case Studies in Strategy and Action toward Sustainable Development* (Sheffield, UK: Greenleaf Publishing).

Schumacher, E.F. (1973) *Small is Beautiful: Economics As If People Mattered* (Point Roberts, WA: Hartley & Marks Publishers).

Shepard, P. (1998) *Coming Home to the Pleistocene* (Washington, DC: Island Press).

Shrivastava, P. (1995) 'Ecocentric Management for a Risk Society', *Academy of Management Review* 20.1: 118-37.

Senge, P.M. (1990) *The Fifth Discipline: The Art and Practice of the Learning Organization* (New York: Doubleday).

Starik, M., and G. Rands (1995) 'Weaving an Integrated Web: Multilevel and Multisystem Perspectives of Ecologically Sustainable Organizations', *Academy of Management Review* 20.4: 908-35.

Stead, W.E., and J.G. Stead (1996) *Management for a Small Planet* (Thousand Oaks, CA: Sage).

Tickner, J.A., and C. Raffensperger (1998) 'The Precautionary Principle: A Framework for Sustainable Business Decision-making', *Corporate Environmental Strategy* 5.4 (Summer 1988): 75-82.

Townend, I.H. (2002) 'Marine Science for Strategic Planning and Management: The Requirement for Estuaries', *Marine Policy* 26.3: 209-19.

Townsend, A.K. (2004) 'An Assessment and Critique of Green Business Best Practices', PhD dissertation, Antioch University.

Turner, M.G., R.H. Gardner and R.V. O'Neill (2001) *Landscape Ecology in Theory and Practice: Pattern and Process* (New York: Springer Verlag).

US Census Bureau (2002) *Statistical Abstract of the United States 2002: The National Data Book* (Washington, DC: US Census Bureau, 122nd edn).

Van der Ryn, S., and S. Cowan (1996) *Ecological Design* (Washington, DC: Island Press).

Wade, B. (1992) 'Losses mount as owners seek allies in battle to clean up', *Corporate Cashflow* 13.2: 20-22.

White, A.L. (1999) 'Sustainability and the Accountable Corporation: Society's Rising Expectations of Business', *Environment* 41.8: 30-43.

Winsemius, P., and U. Guntram (2002) *A Thousand Shades of Green: Sustainable Strategies for Competitive Advantage* (Sterling, VA: Earthscan Publications).

Biographies

Roger Ballentine is the President of Green Strategies Inc., where he advises and represents businesses, associations, government agencies and non-profit entities on domestic and international public policy issues and business strategies, focusing on energy and environmental matters. Roger is also a senior fellow at the Progressive Policy Institute in Washington, DC. He previously served as senior advisor to the Kerry–Edwards campaign on energy and environmental matters. Roger served Bill Clinton as chairman of the White House Climate Change Task Force and Deputy Assistant to the President for Environmental Initiatives; prior to that he was Special Assistant to the President for Legislative Affairs.

roger@greenstrategies.com

Dr **Suzanne Benn** is a biochemist and social scientist with research interests and international publications in collaboration for environmental sustainability and corporate sustainability. She is a Senior Lecturer at the University of Technology, Sydney.

Suzanne.benn@uts.edu.au

Robert G. Boutilier PhD is an associate at the Centre for Sustainable Community Development, Simon Fraser University, Vancouver, Canada. His current research examines the role of stakeholder relationships in building social capital, with particular emphasis on the role of corporations in strengthening communities in developing countries.

boutilier@sfu.ca

Rick Bunch is executive director of Bainbridge Graduate Institute (BGI), which offers a groundbreaking MBA in Sustainable Business. BGI's innovative curriculum preserves the rigour of a traditional MBA programme, while infusing corporate ethics, environmental sustainability and social responsibility throughout every course. From 1996 to 2003, Bunch was director of business education at World Resources Institute in Washington, DC. Previously, he was executive director of the Washington Public Interest Research Group (WashPIRG), a grass-roots environmental and consumer protection organisation based in Seattle. Bunch holds an MBA and environmental management certificate from the University of Washington and a BA in political science from Yale University.

Rick.Bunch@BGIedu.org

Professor **Dexter Dunphy** is Distinguished Professor at the University of Technology, Sydney. He is widely published in the areas of corporate sustainability, the management of organisational change and human resource management.

dexter.dunphy@uts.edu.au

Christopher P. Durney is a Senior Vice President at ICF Consulting, working in the Enterprise Solutions group. His areas of interest include leadership development, business process improvement and programme evaluation. Chris conducted the programme evaluation of the US Environmental Protection Agency's involvement in South Florida that provides background for the chapter in this volume. Chris holds a BA in philosophy from Providence College, an MBA from Marymount University and a PhD in management science from the George Washington University.

cdurney@icfconsulting.com

Carolyn Egri is a Professor of Management and Organisation Studies in the Faculty of Business at Simon Fraser University. Her research and teaching interests include corporate environmental and social responsibility, leadership and organisation change, and international management. She has significant experience in executive leadership development in Asia, Europe and North America. Carolyn has been a director of the Organisational Behaviour Teaching Society and the Vancouver Folk Music Festival Society, as well as Chair of the Organisations and the Natural Environment Interest Group of the Academy of Management. She received her PhD in Organisational Behaviour from the University of British Columbia.

egri@sfu.ca

J. Glenn Eugster is Assistant Regional Director for Partnerships at the National Park Service (NPS), National Capital Region in Washington, DC. He has worked for 29 years locally, regionally, nationally and internationally, with NPS and the US Environmental Protection Agency. His work emphasises watershed stewardship, wetlands protection, heritage conservation, sustainable development and fundraising. He was educated in landscape architecture and ecological planning at the Universities of Georgia and Pennsylvania.

Glenn_Eugster@nps.gov

Deborah Rigling Gallagher received a BS in Chemical Engineering from Northwestern University, a master's in Public Policy from Harvard University and a PhD in Public Policy Analysis from the University of North Carolina at Chapel Hill. Her 20-year career spans private-sector environmental management and public policy. Her current research focuses on the relationships between organisational behaviour, business strategy, public-sector institutions and the environment.

deb.gallagher@duke.edu

Dr **Andrew Griffiths** is a Senior Lecturer at the University of Queensland Business School. He directs and undertakes research on the corporate sustainability programme in the business school.

a.griffiths@business.uq.edu.au

James Johng works for Tishman Speyer Properties. He holds a MBA from the Stern School Business at New York University.

jjohng@tishmanspeyer.com

Yong-Joo Kang is an Associate at PricewaterhouseCoopers. He received a MBA at New York University's Stern School of Business and a MS in Engineering Economics at Stanford University.

yong-joo.kang@us.pwc.com

Lise Langeland received her PhD from the Technical University of Denmark in 2000. In 1997 and 1998 she was a visiting scholar at George Washington University, Washington, DC. Her research, publications and teaching are primarily on corporate sustainability, organisational development, environmental communication and social responsibility. Lise Langeland has worked as a freelance consultant and is currently employed as Marketing Manager with Nilfisk-Advance AS, Copenhagen, Denmark.
llangeland@nilfisk-advance.dk

Melissa A. Schilling is an Associate Professor of management and organisational behaviour at New York University's Stern School of Business. Her research focuses on technological innovation and knowledge creation.
mschilli@stern.nyu.edu

Sanjay Sharma is a Professor of Strategy and Sustainability at Wilfrid Laurier University, Canada. He is the past chair of the Organisations and the Natural Environment interest group at the Academy of Management. His research focuses on processes via which organisations can develop capabilities to generate innovations in products, processes and business models for sustainable corporate strategies, especially those involving disruptive business models for markets at the base of the global economic pyramid.
ssharma@wlu.ca

Peter Stanwick is an Associate Professor in the Department of Management at Auburn University in Auburn, Alabama. He received his undergraduate degree from the University of Western Ontario, his Master of Business Administration degree from the University of Washington, and his doctoral degree from the Florida State University. At Auburn University he teaches strategic management at undergraduate and graduate levels and organisational theory at the doctoral level. His research focuses on environmental issues, corporate governance and ethics as they relate to business.
pstanwik@business.auburn.edu

Sarah Stanwick is an Associate Professor in the School of Accountancy at Auburn University in Auburn, Alabama. She received her undergraduate degree from the University of North Carolina at Greensboro, her Master of Accountancy degree from the University of North Carolina at Chapel Hill, and her doctoral degree from the Florida State University. At Auburn University she teaches financial and cost accounting. Her research explores social issues, including corporate governance and environmental issues, and their relationship to accounting. She is a Certified Public Accountant.
stanwsd@auburn.edu

Mark Starik is a Professor of Strategic Management and Public Policy at the George Washington University (USA) School of Business and the Director of its Environmental and Social Sustainability Initiative. His research, teaching, consulting and service experiences include global strategic sustainability management and policy, and sustainable entrepreneurship. He is a co-founder of the Academy of Management Organisations and the Natural Environment (ONE) interest group and Co-Editor of the journal *Organization and Environment*. Mark received his PhD from the University of Georgia (USA) in Strategic Management and his master's in Natural Resources Policy and Administration from the University of Wisconsin-Madison (USA).
starik@gwu.edu

Jane Sul is an Equity Research Analyst at Samsung Securities. She received a MBA at New York University's Stern School of Business.

Masayuki Takanashi is a Vice President at Sumitomo Mitsui Banking Corporation. Currently, his main job is to revive the bank by decreasing the amount of non-performing loans the bank has on its books.

Takanashi_Masayuki@ay.smbc.co.jp

Amy Townsend PhD is President of Sustainable Development International Corporation and an Adjunct Associate professor at James Madison University. She conducts research, writes and consults on organisational sustainability.

akt@smartoffice.com

John W. Wilson is a senior analyst in the Office of Water, US Environmental Protection Agency (EPA). He is interested in developing innovative approaches to community-led efforts to promote sustainability. John led EPA's 'South Florida initiative', which supported the state and local effort known as Eastward Ho! He is currently Senior Programme Analyst in the Office of Water's Assessment and Watershed Protection Division. He has a BA in Japanese studies and botany and a master's in public administration from the Kennedy School.

Wilson.John@epamail.epa.gov

Abbreviations

BTU	British Thermal Unit
CARB	California Air Resources Board
CAS	complex adaptive system
Cd	coefficient of drag
CERES	Coalition for Environmentally Responsible Economies
CO_2	carbon dioxide
DDT	dichlorodiphenyltrichloroethane
DOE	US Department of Energy
DOJ	US Department of Justice
DOT	US Department of Transportation
ECHO	Enforcement and Compliance History Online (US EPA)
EHS	environmental health and safety
EMAS	EU Eco-Management and Audit Scheme
EMS	environmental management system
EMT	ecological modernisation theory
EPA	US Environmental Protection Agency
ESO	ecologically sustainable organisation
EV	electric vehicle
FEMA	US Federal Emergency Management Administration
GDP	gross domestic product
GIN	Greening of Industry Network
GM	General Motors
HEV	hybrid electric vehicle
HPA	heritage protection plan (US EPA)
HUD	US Department of Housing and Urban Development
ICCR	Interfaith Center for Corporate Responsibility
IMA	integrated motor assist
IRRC	Investor Responsibility Research Center
IRS	US Internal Revenue Service
ISO	International Organisation for Standardisation
KET	Kappa Energy Technologies
MML	Misima Mines Limited
MNC	multinational corporation
MNE	multinational enterprise
MSWG	Multi-State Working Group
NAEP	National Association of Environmental Professionals (USA)
NASA	US National Aeronautical and Space Agency
NDEMS	National Database on Environmantal Management Systems

NEP	new environmental paradigm
NGO	non-governmental organisation
NLEV	national low-emission vehicle
NPDES	National Pollutant Discharge Elimination System
ONE	Organisations and the Natural Environment
OSHA	Occupational Safety and Health Administration
PDI	Placer Dome Inc.
PNGV	Partnership for a New Generation of Vehicles
R&D	research and development
SARA	US Superfund Amendments and Reauthorisation Act
SME	small or medium-sized enterprise
SWOT	strengths, weaknesses, opportunities, threats
TNS	The Natural Step
TQM	total quality management
TRI	Toxics Release Inventory
TTR	through-the-road
ULEV	ultra-low emissions vehicle
USABC	US Advanced Battery Consortium
USDA	US Department of Agriculture
VOC	volatile organic compound
WCED	World Commission on Environment and Development
WVS	World Values Survey

Index